W9-BMP-003

6 STEPS
TO SONGWRITING
SUCCESS

The Comprehensive Guide to Writing and Marketing Hit Songs

REVISED & EXPANDED EDITION

6 STEPS

TO SONGWRITING SUCCESS

The Comprehensive Guide to
Writing and Marketing Hit Songs

REVISED & EXPANDED EDITION

JASON BLUME

BILLBOARD BOOKS
An imprint of Watson-Guptill Publications
New York

Executive Editor: Bob Nirkind
Editor: Meryl Greenblatt
Production Manager: Ellen Greene
Cover design: Cooley Design Lab
Interior design: Cheryl Viker

First published in 2004 by Billboard Books
an imprint of Watson-Guptill Publications
a division of VNU Business Media, Inc.
770 Broadway, New York, NY 10003
www.wgpub.com

Library of Congress Cataloging-in-Publication Data
The CIP data for this title may be obtained from the Library of Congress
Library of Congress Card Number: 2003116047

ISBN: 0-8230-8412-4

Printed in the United States

First printing, 2004

2 3 4 5 6 7 8 9 / 10 09 08 07 06 05

*This book is dedicated to my songwriting students,
who continue to teach me every day. Your willingness to learn,
to rewrite, and to follow your dreams despite the inevitable
disappointments keeps me doing the same. I also dedicate this book
to every person who told me, "You'll never make it—
the chances are a million to one." I thank you for strengthening
my resolve to become the best writer I can be.*

Acknowledgments

There are several individuals without whom this book could never have been written. I'd like to express my heartfelt gratitude to my Executive Editor, Bob Nirkind, and my Editor, Meryl Greenblatt, whose talents and contributions made it possible for me to write the book I always wanted to write. I'm deeply grateful to my literary agent, Rita Rosenkranz, for her expertise and belief in this project. I could never find sufficient words to thank Neil Rice for making everything behind the scenes work so smoothly and for his inestimable contribution to my work and my life.

Thank you to all of my teachers and to Keith Urban, Paige Levy, Janis Ian, Melissa Manchester, Brendan Okrent, Barbara Rothstein, Gloria Sklerov, Harlan Howard, Karen Taylor-Good, Carol Elliott, Buddy Mondlock, Sherrill Blackman, Barbara Cloyd, Greg Barnhill, Tom Luteran, Regie Hamm, Paul Rolnick, Steve Seskin, Alan Brewer, Steve Bloch, Herb Tassin, David Friedman, Wade Kirby, Roger Sovine, Mike Sistad, Wayne Perry, Justin Wilde, Craig Wiseman, Gary Baker, Mark Mason, Bryan Cumming, David Roth, Lee Groitzsch, Janice Cook, Virginia Rice, Jim Cooper, Phil Goldberg, Bart Herbison and staff at NSAI, Wayne Tester, Robert K. Oermann, Tommy LiPuma, Jeff Fenster, Judy Phelps, Allan Rich, Ira Greenfield, Thom Schuyler, Billy Steinberg, Aaron Meza, Franne Golde, Frank Liddell, Teri Muench and Steve Diamond, Marty Wheeler, Judy Stakee, Kathleen Carey, Debbie Zavitson, Jeff Carlton, Jeff Little at Borman Entertainment, Sandy Carothers and Phyllis Austin of Bull's Creek Music, John Van Meter, Steve Weaver, Rick Chudacoff, Steve Gibson, and all of the talented song-writers and music industry professionals who contributed so generously to this book—and especially to Jane Snyder.

I owe a special debt to Michael Hollandsworth, who believed in my talents and taught me how to be a songwriter, and to Britney Spears, Collin Raye, the Backstreet Boys, Leslie Mills, Chris Pelcer, Sherry Kondor, Jesse McCartney, Don and Gayle Goodman, Adam Sandler, Liz Rose, A.J. Masters, Lis Lewis, Stephanie Cox, John and Robin Berry, David Gray, Eric Beall, and all of the others who've contributed so much to my career.

Thank you: Gordon Pogoda (for the musical notation and the wonderful quote); Bryan Cumming for the charts—and for being such a wonderful, talented friend; Amy Smith Heinz for pitching my songs; Mark Mason, Deanna Bruton, Michelle Andrade-Wright, Gabrielle Hoffman, Julie Jarett, and the staff at BMI; Michael Laskow, Michael Lederer, Doug Minninck, and the staff at Taxi; and Penny Nichols at SummerSongs for giving me the opportunity to do the thing I love the most—teach developing songwriters.

I'd also like to acknowledge Camilla Kleindienst of Banner/Planet Happy Publishing and Dave Olsen and Hope Chirino of Warner Bros. Publications for their patience and cooperation (beyond the call of duty) in helping me to secure permissions to reprint the lyrics contained in this book.

Thank you to Debbie Chessor for your valiant effort to make me look like I'm nineteen in the photo. And a very special thank you to Claire Ulanoff; Wayne Moore; Ruth Rosen; Renee Lopez; Marvin Werlin; Andrea Horstman; Mark Werlin; Coreen Davis; Maris, Mark, Jamie, and Adam Goldberg; Alana Amadeo; Todd and Laura Serinsky; Leslie Brenner; Hal Holzer; Carol Elliott; Katy Garvey, for your continued love and support—and to my first collaborator and biggest supporter, Maureen Custer, who listened to my struggles and encouraged me more than she'll ever know. And to Opie, Duncan, and Coin (the cats) who sat on my lap, my desk, and my computer, providing unsolicited editorial advice.

And a final heartfelt thank you—to the source from which all creativity flows.

Contents

Introduction

Since the first publication of *6 Steps to Songwriting Success: The Comprehensive Guide to Writing and Marketing Hit Songs* in 1999, dramatic changes have taken place in the music industry. The manufactured, synthesizer-driven teen pop that ruled the charts from the mid- to late 1990s has been replaced by more guitar-oriented, alternative rock and pop, while hip-hop has crossed over from the urban charts to dominate the Top 40 airwaves and increase its hold on listeners. In addition, solo singer-songwriters are back in vogue again, and country music has experienced a marked shift from slick pop-influenced sounds to more organic, traditional-sounding songs, artists, and production. As Sonny and Cher sang, "The Beat Goes On," and soon many of today's superstars and their songs will be relegated to bargain bins and oldies stations as a new generation of artists and music assumes prominence.

Changes in the business of music have been even more dramatic. The advent of MP3s, digital downloading, and hard drive recording technology; the demise of cassettes as the primary format for pitching songs; and the consolidation and closure of numerous record labels and music publishers have altered the landscape for songwriters and recording artists at every stage of their career development. Most notably, the rampant downloading of "shared" songs via the Internet has led to tremendous losses within the music business, and the issues of how to compensate songwriters and recording artists for downloaded music and how record labels can survive in the current marketplace remain in flux. The good news is that, despite it all, there are still outlets for truly great songs with exceptional melodies and lyrics that touch listeners—and I believe there always will be.

The primary focus in this book's first edition was on learning to write and market the sorts of songs recorded by artists who typically do not create their own material. This outlet has shrunk considerably. Today's songwriters need to be increasingly aware of the necessity of finding an inside track, cowriting with artists and producers, and writing songs that can fill slots artists and producers are unable to fill. They also need to understand that there are fewer opportunities for writers who only write songs, as opposed to those who wear the hat of artist or producer as well. This updated and expanded edition focuses on both of these issues, as well as on how to thrive in today's challenging marketplace, where I suggest alternative avenues to generating income from our songs.

Since writing *6 Steps*, I've taught more than a hundred workshops, and I've listened to the concerns and feedback of thousands of songwriters. Much of the first edition has been rewritten to address their questions and the issues that are important to them. Addressed too are the unique considerations of artists who are writing songs for themselves, or for their own self-contained bands, to perform and record.

New topics in this edition include using songs to define artistic identity, using technology to capture your best vocal performance, writing turnarounds, saving key words, writing lyrics to an existing melody, using fresh rhythms, incorporating modulations, using samples, writing jingles, placing songs in commercials and with music libraries, and avoiding plagiarism. Also covered are MP3s and digital technology, and what to do if you write only melody or only lyrics.

In addition, ten new exercises have been added, as have song examples from today's hottest artists and songwriters, and advice from some of the industry's most respected artists, writers, and behind-the-scenes decision makers. Finally, information for writers in the Christian market, especially regarding Church Copyright License Royalties, has been expanded, and the Appendix has been completely updated to provide the most comprehensive listing of songwriters' resources in print.

Those who have read the first edition of this book or *Inside Songwriting*—my second book—or who have attended my workshops, know that success did not come easily or quickly for me. I've felt the frustration and pain of working at a day job I hated, while knowing in my heart that I was meant to be writing songs and enjoying success. Along the way I've lived in a cockroach and mouse-infested room, have shared a bathroom with the junkies and hookers who lived down the hall, and have even eaten cat food to survive.

When I took my first songwriting workshop in 1979, I had no idea that songs were supposed to have any particular structure, or that the title was supposed to be in the song. Ten weeks and ten songs later, I left with the basic tools that allowed me to begin crafting songs that had verses and choruses, rhymes, repetition, hooks, and memorable melodies. I was on my way! From then on I took every class and workshop I could find, and my life revolved around one thing—writing songs.

At one class, the critique of my song was nothing less than brutal. The instructors concurred that my song, the best I'd ever written to this point, was a shining example of everything that amateurs do wrong; they proclaimed that it would "never, never, never" be played on the radio. That night, as I lay awake replaying every negative comment, I realized that the teachers were right. It was like a lightning bolt when it hit me: I had been writing from my heart, with no consideration of the commercial market.

Through the pain came the realization that there really were differences between my songs and those that were hits on the radio, and that the problem was not that I wasn't lucky or lacked the right connections. Until that moment, my writing had been a means of self-expression—a catharsis I had hoped would also, by pure coincidence, be something to which millions of others could relate. Until that night, there had been no consideration, or even awareness, of the listener; when I wrote, it was solely to please myself. I just assumed that if my songs meant so much to me, they would have meaning to others as well. But somehow, something that had been said that night broke through the wall. It was suddenly clear that while the inspiration that came from my heart was crucial, it was only one part of the equation.

Since that night I've realized three things:

1. There are specific elements that are consistently found in the melodies, lyrics, and structures of hit songs.

2. These elements can be learned and incorporated into my songs.

3. The fact that I was writing songs at that point in my development that were not up to professional standards did not mean I was incapable of writing hit songs in the future.

At first, I couldn't imagine ever mastering the techniques that contributed to so many songs becoming hits, and I couldn't conceive of employing those principles without sacrificing the soul of my songs. But I was wrong.

As a songwriting teacher for Broadcast Music International (BMI) and the Nashville Songwriters Association International (NSAI), I've analyzed hundreds of hit songs in a variety of musical styles to try to understand why these songs became so successful—and why others had not. I've examined structures, chord progressions, melodies, lyrics, rhythms, rhymes, titles, concepts, and more. After years of study I've concluded that there are no rules in songwriting. But while there are no magic formulas that guarantee hits, there are tools, techniques, and principles that can help us to express ourselves through our songs so that we can communicate what we feel in such a way that our listeners feel it, too. I've also concluded that with lots of practice, these tools, techniques, and principles can be assimilated to such a degree that you won't even have to think about them—so that the spark of inspiration that starts deep in your heart can express itself in a way that can indeed touch millions of listeners.

What are the common denominators? What are the factors that separate the good songs from hit songs, and the merely talented writers from the successful ones? The 6 steps to songwriting success are:

1. Developing successful song structures
2. Writing effective lyrics
3. Composing memorable melodies
4. Producing successful demos
5. Taking care of business
6. Developing persistence and realistic expectations

Since I began teaching, I've seen my students "graduate" to publishing songs, writing hit songs, winning major competitions, and signing staff-writing deals. Since the first edition of this book I've also received countless letters from readers telling me how using the prescribed tools and techniques has helped them to craft the songs they'd always hoped to write—so I know that these tools work.

Thankfully, there are brave, creative writers who stretch the boundaries. It would get awfully boring if every song incorporated each of the techniques outlined in this book. No doubt there are exceptions to every tool and suggested technique discussed here, and some songs become hits simply on the strength of the artist or the production. But since the vast majority of hit songs incorporate many of the tools and techniques presented in this book, you'll have a much better chance of achieving your goals if these tools and techniques are learned before you make the conscious choice to deviate from them.

The tools and techniques addressed in this book apply to most mainstream genres of music. However, as you'll learn, there do tend to be differences between the kinds of songs that are typically recorded by artists who do not exclusively write their own material and those that are successful for performing songwriters—artists who write or cowrite their own material. I've written this revised and expanded edition of 6 Steps to Songwriting Success to benefit writers in both of these categories.

A last word: After countless meetings marketing my own songs to publishers, record label executives, and producers, as well as critiquing songs written by aspiring writers, I've become more sensitive than ever to the importance of presenting our listeners with songs that are not just "perfectly crafted," but also include lyrics and melodies that are fresh, unique, and truly exceptional. It's my hope that after reading the lessons and completing the exercises presented throughout this book, you'll be inspired to risk pushing the creative envelope and infusing your writing with the spark that is uniquely you. It's my wish that you'll follow your dreams and enjoy the journey!

Developing Successful Song Structures

Learn the techniques and structures so well that when the great idea or inspiration comes, your technical ability doesn't hinder your creativity. Learn and practice the basics so they become second nature. Then when you are ready to create something new or the inspiration hits you, the building blocks will already be in place. We all like to think that there are shortcuts to life and sometimes they do work for a while, but I feel it is better to learn the trade so that you can understand the tricks of the trade.

MIKE SISTAD (Nashville Director of Member Relations, ASCAP)

CHAPTER 1

Identifying the Most Successful Song Structures—and Why They Work

Songwriting seems to start with an introspective base as a stage. From there, serious songwriters need to step outside of themselves to develop their craft. Ideally, somewhere down the road the two meet again to combine resources in more well-crafted unique songs.

BRENDAN OKRENT (Los Angeles Senior Director of Repertory, ASCAP)

I recently had an opportunity to consult with a writer who explained to me that after more than twenty years of dabbling in songwriting as a hobby, he had decided to invest his life savings, more than twenty thousand dollars, to record professional demos of ten of his songs. He was meeting with me with the hope that I would be so impressed by his songs that I would steer him toward the success he hoped for.

When the CD began to play I was instantly impressed: the production was pristine; the demo singers sounded as good as hit artists; and the musicianship was top-notch. But as I listened it became painfully clear that these songs had no discernible structure. None of the sections repeated, the titles were not necessarily included within the songs, and while the overall effect was quite pleasant, each one was more like a musical stream of consciousness than an actual song. If this writer were a jazz instrumentalist or a new age artist writing for his own album, it's likely that this approach would have worked fine. But his plan was to pitch these songs to publishers with the hope of getting his work recorded by major pop recording artists who do not write all their own material.

I got a sick feeling in my stomach as I listened to song after song, noting that each one meandered without the benefit of any structure or form. The wonderful melodic phrases and interesting lyrics showed me that this writer was clearly talented, but I knew that his chance of finding the success he sought with these songs was negligible.

No one is born with the knowledge of how popular songs are typically structured; this information has to be acquired. I wrote my first song, "Eternal August," at age twelve by strumming the three chords I'd taught myself on my father's mandolin and singing whatever I felt. If any sections repeated or if the title appeared in the song, it was by pure chance. It never crossed my mind that the songs I loved and sang along with had been constructed using only a handful of specific structures that incorporated verses, choruses, and bridges in specific orders. Although I'd heard those structures at least a thousand times, like most listeners, I was never aware of them.

At the first workshop I ever attended I quickly discovered that my rambling, free-flowing style of songwriting was not likely to get my songs on the radio. This made me angry because I didn't want to change the way I wrote—I just wanted millions of listeners to love my songs "as is." I felt that employing song structures and formulas was analogous to selling out and was the antithesis of creative expression.

I didn't want to place constraints on my music, and deep down, I didn't believe that I could learn the formulas even if I'd wanted to. But in time, I came to recognize that:

- There are a limited number of song structures commonly heard in hit songs. These structures can be easily learned and used effectively.

- It is possible to take an idea that starts in my heart and communicate it within the confines of one of these structures—without compromising the integrity, the meaning, or the essence of the song.

My first teachers explained that songwriting is an art that is based upon successful communication. Crafting songs that incorporate one of the most popular structures is analogous to using proper grammar and punctuation to better communicate our ideas when we speak or write. Using song structures does not alter the message or the essence of our songs; rather, it helps us deliver our melodic and lyrical ideas to listeners, enabling them to more readily feel those feelings that we hope to evoke.

With very few exceptions, the vast majority of hit songs that are written by "outside" writers (writers who are neither the artist, the producer, nor otherwise involved in the recording project) employ one of the following four basic structures or a variation on one of them:

1. Verse - Chorus - Verse - Chorus
2. Verse - Chorus - Verse - Chorus - Bridge - Chorus
3. Verse - Chorus - Verse - Chorus - Verse - Chorus
4. Verse - Verse - Bridge - Verse

Writers who are performing songwriters—those who are writing material primarily for themselves or for their own band—also tend to use these structures the majority of the time, but they do have more latitude to explore variations than those writers who are writing for outside acts.

> *I've known tremendously successful songwriters who are embarrassed that they write "commercial songs" rather than "artistic songs." People get confused; is it okay to be commercial? Should I be an "artiste"? I say "hooey" to all that! If it makes you feel—be it tapping your toe or busting out in tears—it's worthy. Our job is to communicate, period.*

All great songwriting is the marriage of art and craft—whether the writer knows it or not. When I first started writing and recording, I was too young to have much craft; my talent led me in the right directions. But I noticed over the years that I'd write ten songs, and one would be good; the rest would just be practice. Coming to Nashville in 1986 put me on the trail of my craft, and I'm so grateful for it. Your craft is what gets you through when you're tired, when you're trying to make a deadline, when you're stuck.

JANIS IAN (Nine-time Grammy nominee, with more than fifteen
Platinum albums worldwide and hits including "Jesse," "At Seventeen,"
and "Stars," recorded by over twenty-five other artists)

Learning song structures is not the most exciting, creative, or interesting part of the songwriting process, but it is important. Whether we're conscious of it or not, we've been trained by years of listening to the radio to expect one of the forms I've listed, or something close.

IDENTIFYING THE COMPONENTS OF A SONG

"Radio-friendly" songs are typically built by combining the following elements:

- Verses
- Pre-Choruses
- Choruses
- Bridges

Each of these components has a specific function within the song. Let's examine them individually before attempting to put them together into a complete song.

The Verse

The primary function of the verse is to provide the exposition—the information that will lead to the song's hook or title. The verse is the place where the listener is introduced to the characters. It tells the story and sets the emotional tone. The verse lyric—its words—contains the plot, the details, and the action.

Each verse of a song typically has the same melody—or music—and new lyrics. The first line of the first verse should have approximately the same number of syllables as the first line of the second and (if applicable) third verses. The emphases should also be in the same places. This applies to all lines of the verses. Although there is some room for variation, a drastic difference in the length of corresponding lines in various verses will make it impossible to sing the same melody for each verse.

Although there are no hard and fast rules in songwriting, just guidelines, most often, each verse is four or eight lines long, expressed in either eight or sixteen musical bars. (Readers who require additional understanding of musical bars or measures would likely benefit from a study of basic music theory.) It is unusual for a popular song to contain an odd number of lines of lyrics, or bars of music, in its verses, choruses, or bridge, but there are many successful exceptions.

In songs that include choruses, the song title usually does not appear in any of the verses. However, there are exceptions. For example, in traditional country songs each verse may end with the title, which is then repeated at the beginning of the chorus.

The Pre-Chorus

Within a verse there may be a "pre-chorus"—a two- or four-line section, immediately preceding the chorus. The pre-chorus is sometimes referred to as the lift, channel, climb, set-up, or B-section. Including a pre-chorus is optional. However, if one verse includes a pre-chorus, all verses typically include a pre-chorus.

The pre-chorus will have a different melody and rhythm from the other sections of the song and is typically four bars long. Although some successful songs have included pre-choruses that are eight bars, it would be quite rare to have this section exceed eight. This building block is crafted to connect and propel the listener, both melodically and lyrically, into the chorus.

All pre-choruses in a song have the same melody. It is acceptable for each verse's pre-chorus to repeat the same lyric—or each pre-chorus may introduce a new lyric. The lyric that follows contains a pre-chorus that reiterates the same lyric each time.

COMPLICATED

VERSE 1
Chill out—Whatcha yelling for
Lay back—It's all been done before
And if you could only let it be
You will see

I like you the way you are
When we're driving in your car
And you're talking to me one on one
But you become

PRE-CHORUS
Somebody else 'round anyone else
You're watching your back—like you can't relax
You're trying to be cool
You look a fool to me (Tell me)

CHORUS
Why'd you have to go and make things so COMPLICATED
See the way you're acting like you're somebody else gets me frustrated
Life's like this—You fall and you crawl and you take what you get
And you turn it into honesty—promise me I'm never gonna find you fake it—no, no no

VERSE 2
You come over unannounced
Dressed up like you're something else
Where you are ain't where it's at
You see you're making me

Laugh out when you strike your pose
Take off all your preppy clothes
You know you're not fooling anyone
When you become

PRE-CHORUS
Somebody else 'round anyone else
You're watching your back—like you can't relax
You're trying to be cool
You look a fool to me (Tell me)

(REPEAT CHORUS)

VERSE 3
Chill out—Whatcha yelling for
Lay back—It's all been done before
And if you could only let it be
You will see

PRE-CHORUS
Somebody else 'round anyone else
You're watching your back—like you can't relax
You're trying to be cool
You look a fool to me (Tell me)

(REPEAT CHORUS TWICE)

WRITTEN BY Avril Lavigne and The Matrix:
Lauren Christy, Scott Spock, and Graham Edwards;
RECORDED BY Avril Lavigne.

The Chorus

*The chorus to me is the gist of the song; that's where the idea is delivered.
I make sure the chorus is as good as it can be. If I don't get the chorus right,
it's no use in me writing the song.*

TOBY KEITH (BMI Country Songwriter of the Year;
CMA and ACM Male Vocalist of the Year)

Melodically, the chorus is the catchy, repetitious part of a song that you sing along with. Lyrically, the chorus' job is to summarize the idea and emotion of the song in a general way and to hammer home its title. Ideally, the chorus lyric is constructed so that it sounds natural to have it repeated following each verse (and the bridge, if the song includes a bridge). The chorus should be easy to remember and is not the place to introduce new, detailed information; this belongs in the verses.

Lyrically, the chorus is typically four or eight lines long, which most often translates to eight, twelve, or sixteen musical bars. However, like everything else in songwriting, this is not a precise science and there have been many hit songs with choruses of different lengths.

Most important, the chorus has the same melody and almost always has the same lyrics each time it is repeated. Having all choruses within a song be the same, both lyrically and melodically, helps your listeners remember the chorus and sing along. However, if you feel strongly that changing some, or all, of the lyrics in various choruses will improve your song, then make that creative decision with the awareness that it is rarely done.

Note that in the successful exception that follows, in addition to having different lyrics for each chorus, each pre-chorus also has a different lyric.

I'M ALREADY THERE

VERSE 1
He called her on the road
From a lonely cold hotel room
Just to hear her say "I love you" one more time
And when he heard the sound
Of the kids laughing in the background
He had to wipe away a tear from his eye

PRE-CHORUS 1
A little voice came on the phone
And said, "Daddy, when you coming home?"
He said the first thing that came to his mind

CHORUS 1
I'M ALREADY THERE
Take a look around
I'm the sunshine in your hair
I'm the shadow on the ground
I'm the whisper in the wind
I'm your imaginary friend
And I know I'm in your prayers
I'M ALREADY THERE

VERSE 2
She got back on the phone
Said "I really miss you darling"
Don't worry about the kids they'll be alright
Wish I was in your arms
Lying right there beside you
But I know that I'll be in your dreams tonight

PRE-CHORUS 2
And I'll gently kiss your lips
Touch you with my fingertips
So turn out the light and close your eyes

CHORUS 2
I'M ALREADY THERE
Don't make a sound
I'm the beating in your heart
I'm the moonlight shining down
I'm the whisper in the wind
And I'll be there till the end
Can you feel the love that we share
Oh, I'M ALREADY THERE

BRIDGE
We may be a thousand miles apart
But I'll be with you wherever you are

CHORUS 3
I'M ALREADY THERE
Take a look around
I'm the sunshine in your hair
I'm the shadow on the ground
I'm the whisper in the wind
And I'll be there till the end

Can you feel the love that we share
Oh, I'M ALREADY THERE
I'M ALREADY THERE

Written by *Gary Baker, Frank J. Myers, and Richie McDonald;*
Recorded by *Lonestar.*

The title almost always appears at least once in the chorus. Among the rare exceptions to this are Kenny Rogers' "The Gambler" (written by Don Schlitz) and the self-penned Goo Goo Dolls' "Iris," Ashanti's "Foolish," and Train's "Drops of Jupiter." Vanessa Carlton's Grammy-nominated song, "A Thousand Miles," was initially titled "Interlude." According to Ron Fair, producer of the single, as well as head of A&M Records, "She was adamant about it being called 'Interlude,' and I finally had to say, 'Look, I'm the president of the label, we're not calling it "Interlude."' When you're trying to launch a career, people need a handle to pick things up from, and the word 'Interlude' is never in the song."

The vast majority of songs that do not include the title in the chorus are songs that are written or cowritten by the artist. There are no rules as to where the title of a song should appear within the chorus. For example, the song title can appear in the first line of the chorus and nowhere else within the chorus:

SHE'S NOT THE CHEATIN' KIND

Chorus
SHE'S NOT THE CHEATIN' KIND
She's been cheated one too many times
She's never fooled around
He's still lyin'—She's through cryin'
She's not foolin' now

Written by *Ronnie Dunn;*
Recorded by *Brooks & Dunn.*

The song title can also appear in both the first and second lines of the chorus:

ONE OF US

Chorus
What if God was ONE OF US
Just a slob like ONE OF US
Just a stranger on a bus
Trying to find his way home

Written by *Eric Bazilian;* Recorded by *Joan Osborne.*

The song title can also appear as the first and last lines of the chorus as in the example that follows. This technique, sometimes referred to as "book-ending," can be very effective, but only if the lyric is crafted to logically lead the listener back to the title.

BREATHE

Chorus
I can feel you BREATHE
It's washing over me
Suddenly I'm melting into you
There's nothing left to prove
Baby all we need is just to be
Caught up in the touch
The slow and steady rush
Baby, isn't that the way that love's supposed to be
I can feel you BREATHE—Just BREATHE

Written by *Holly Lamar and Stephanie Bentley;*
Recorded by *Faith Hill.*

In some instances, the song title begins the chorus, is repeated one or more times within the chorus, and ends the chorus. This technique can add a powerful emotional punch, especially if the last line of the chorus brings the listener back to the title from a new angle or perspective.

CHANGE MY MIND

Chorus
CHANGE MY MIND
Say you couldn't live without me
Say you're crazy about me
With a look—With a touch
CHANGE MY MIND
I'm looking in your eyes
For the love we left behind
It's not too late to CHANGE MY MIND

Written by *Jason Blume and A.J. Masters;*
Recorded by *artists including John Berry and the Oak Ridge Boys.*

The song title might even be the only lyric in the chorus, except for the last line. When using this form, the last line should tie the chorus together and provide an emotional "payoff."

HIT ME WITH YOUR BEST SHOT

CHORUS
HIT ME WITH YOUR BEST SHOT
(Come on and) HIT ME WITH YOUR BEST SHOT
HIT ME WITH YOUR BEST SHOT
Fire away

WRITTEN BY *Eddie Schwartz;* RECORDED BY *Pat Benatar.*

Another option is for the song title to be saved until the last line of the chorus. To be effective, the lines of melody and lyric that precede the last line of the chorus need to be exceptionally catchy in order to sustain the listeners' attention all the way through the verse and chorus before giving them the title:

STUCK

CHORUS
I can't take it—What am I waiting for?
My heart's still breaking—I miss you even more
And I can't fake it—The way I could before

I hate you—But I love you
I can't stop thinking of you—It's true
I'm STUCK on you

WRITTEN BY *Kevin Kadish and Stacie Orrico;* RECORDED BY *Stacie Orrico.*

A last option is for the chorus to simply repeat the title lyric and contain no words other than the title. While this is a very unusual structure, Dolly Parton's "I Will Always Love You," employing this form, has been a huge hit four times (twice for Dolly Parton as a solo artist; once with duet partner Vince Gill; and once on Whitney Houston's mega-selling soundtrack album *The Bodyguard*). Another successful example of this structure is Tim McGraw's "Grown Men Don't Cry" (written by Steve Seskin and Tom Douglas).

You may have heard a chorus described as the "refrain." In the era of Cole Porter and Irving Berlin the terms chorus and refrain were used interchangeably. However, refrain is no longer used in the vocabulary of contemporary songwriters and publishers.

The Bridge

The bridge serves as a departure, or a release, from the rest of the song. It usually consists of two or four lines of lyric and four or eight musical bars. Occasionally, the bridge might be instrumental, but this is not often the case. There are also instances of successful songs that repeat a pre-chorus between the second and third choruses, essentially using it in place of a bridge.

The bridge's job is to add contrast, a new perspective, or additional information; to take the song to the next level; and to lead the listener back to the chorus and title from a new angle. This allows the title to "pay off" one last time. If that's not enough of a challenge, the bridge needs to accomplish all of this while still managing to sound consistent with the rest of the song.

When using a structure that includes verses and choruses, the bridge typically occurs in only one place—between the second and third choruses (Verse - Chorus - Verse - Chorus - Bridge - Chorus). When using the "A - A - B - A" song form discussed later in this chapter, the bridge will be between the second and third verses (Verse - Verse - Bridge - Verse). Ideally, the bridge will add a new dimension to the song, both lyrically and melodically. Note that outside the US the bridge is sometimes referred to as "the middle eight," although it is not literally in the middle of the song and might not necessarily contain eight bars.

The title does not typically appear in the bridge, although there are many successful exceptions to this. Tools that can help differentiate your bridge lyrically from the rest of the song include:

- Revealing an added element to the story—a payoff—that ties it all together.
- Switching from specific, detailed imagery to general or philosophical statements (or vice versa).
- Alternating the time frame (i.e., looking back on the past, if the rest of the song is in present tense, or vice versa; or imagining what the future might hold).
- Disclosing a surprise (if applicable).

Musically, effective bridges may add an element of contrast by:

- Introducing one or more chords that have not previously been used in the song.
- Employing a melody and rhythm that are different from those heard in other sections of the song.
- Using notes that are either higher or lower than those used in the other sections.

The most effective bridges provide seamless, melodic, and lyrical "bridges" that connect back into the verse or chorus that follow them. The bridge is the last new section of your song to be introduced. It's your final chance to make the listener love your song—so make it powerful.

In songs that employ one of the Verse - Chorus structures, including a bridge is entirely optional. Factors that will help you decide whether your song might benefit from a bridge include whether there is additional information you want to convey, and the song's length. Most popular songs are between three and four minutes long. If your song is only two minutes long, it may be time to cross that bridge. However, if your song is already three-and-a-half minutes long without a bridge, adding one may make it too long if you are hoping to have it played on mainstream radio.

BUILDING A SUCCESSFUL SONG

Now that you know all of the pieces of a successful song, it's time to learn how to put them all together. In order to create the kinds of songs listeners expect to hear on mainstream radio (pop, adult contemporary, urban, and country), you will want to join verses, pre-choruses, choruses, and bridges in specific ways. Note that these structures may not apply to dance, folk, heavy metal, alternative rock, blues, or rap music.

Verse - Chorus - Verse - Chorus

This structure begins with a first verse that tells the story, introduces the characters, and lets the listener know how the singer feels about the situation. The first verse leads the listener, both lyrically and melodically, into the first chorus. It typically does not include the title, but is crafted to guide the listener to the song's title. The verses may, or may not, include a pre-chorus.

In this structure the first chorus follows the first verse. The chorus includes the song title at least once and summarizes the idea of the song in a general way. The second verse follows the first chorus. Lyrically, it continues the story, provides the listener with additional information, and leads back to the chorus. Melodically, it is identical (or almost identical) to the first verse. The second chorus follows the second verse and is almost always identical to the first chorus.

An example of this structure, often referred to as "A - B - A - B" (A = Verse, B = Chorus) follows.

THESE DAYS

VERSE 1
Hey Baby, is that you—Wow your hair got so long
Yeah, yeah I love it—I really do
"Norma Jean," ain't that the song we'd sing in the car drivin' downtown
Top down makin' the rounds checkin' out the bands on Doheny Avenue
Yeah, life throws you curves but you learned to swerve
Me, I swung and I missed and next thing ya know I'm reminiscing
Dreamin' old dreams—wishin' old wishes
Like you'll be back again

CHORUS
I wake up in teardrops that fall down like rain
I put on that old song we danced to and then
I head off to my job guess not much has changed
Punch the clock, head for home
Check the phone, just in case
Go to bed and dream of you
That's what I'm doing
THESE DAYS

VERSE 2

Hey someone told me after college you ran off to Vegas
Married a rodeo cowboy, Wow that ain't the girl I knew
Me, I've been a few places—mostly here and there once or twice
Still sortin' out life but I'm doin' alright—Yeah, it's good to see you too
Well, hey girl you're late and those planes they don't wait
But if you ever come back around this sleepy ol' town
Promise me you'll stop in to see an old friend
And until then

(REPEAT CHORUS)

WRITTEN BY Danny Wells, Steve Robson, and Jeffrey Steele;
RECORDED BY Rascal Flatts.

Other examples of this structure that you may want to check out include "You Oughta Know" (Alanis Morissette), "You're Still the One" (Shania Twain), and "Change the World" (Eric Clapton).

Verse - Chorus - Verse - Chorus - Bridge - Chorus

This structure is the most popular song form in current use. It has a first verse, first chorus, second verse, and second chorus that follow the guidelines described in the previous example. However, a two- or four-line bridge, which is a musical and lyrical departure (as described previously in this section) follows the second chorus. After the bridge there is a third chorus, which is almost always identical, melodically and lyrically, to the previous choruses.

This structure is often designated as "A - B - A - B - C - B" (A = Verse, B = Chorus, C = Bridge). An example of the A - B - A - B - C - B structure follows.

BECAUSE YOU LOVED ME

VERSE 1

For all those times you stood by me
For all the truth that you made me see
For all the joy you brought to my life
For all the wrong that you made right
For every dream you made come true
For all the love I found in you
I'll be forever thankful Baby
You're the one who held me up
Never let me fall
You're the one who saw me through—through it all

CHORUS
You were my strength when I was weak
You were my voice when I couldn't speak
You were my eyes when I couldn't see
You saw the best there was in me
Lifted me up when I couldn't reach
You gave me faith 'cause you believed
I'm everything I am
BECAUSE YOU LOVED ME

VERSE 2
You gave me wings and made me fly
You touched my hand I could touch the sky
I lost my faith, you gave it back to me
You said no star was out of reach
You stood by me and I stood tall
I had your love I had it all
I'm grateful for each day you gave me
Maybe I don't know that much
But I know this much is true
I was blessed because I was loved by you

(REPEAT CHORUS)

BRIDGE
You were always there for me
The tender wind that carried me
A light in the dark shining your love into my life
You've been my inspiration
Through the lies you were the truth
My world is a better place because of you

(REPEAT CHORUS)

WRITTEN BY *Diane Warren;* RECORDED BY *Celine Dion.*

Other examples of this structure include "I'm With You" (Avril Lavigne), "Don't Speak" (No Doubt), and "Sometimes When We Touch" (Dan Hill).

Verse - Chorus - Verse - Chorus - Verse - Chorus

In this structure there are three verses, each followed by a chorus. Each verse may or may not include a pre-chorus. Lyrically, every verse contains new information and develops the story further, but will have the same melody. All of the choruses will typically be identical to each other.

Only a small percentage of successful songs employ this structure. This is most likely because the verse is not intended to be the most memorable part of the song and unless it is exceptionally well crafted you run the risk of boring the listener. However, this structure does work especially well in "story" songs, songs that have a great deal of information to impart lyrically in order to tell their story. This structure also tends to work well in songs in which each verse consists of a little scene, or self-contained story. Songs that contain three separate vignettes that each relate back to the same chorus can be exceptionally powerful, as illustrated by the lyric to the following Grammy-nominated song, which employs this so-called "A - B - A - B - A - B" (A = Verse, B = Chorus) form.

HOW CAN I HELP YOU SAY GOODBYE

VERSE 1
Through the back window of our fifty-nine wagon
I watched my best friend Jamie slippin' further away
I kept on wavin' till I couldn't see her
And through my tears I asked again why we couldn't stay

PRE-CHORUS
Mama whispered softly time will ease your pain
Life's about changing
Nothing ever stays the same
And she said

CHORUS
HOW CAN I HELP YOU SAY GOODBYE
It's okay to hurt and it's okay to cry
Come let me hold you and I will try
HOW CAN I HELP YOU SAY GOODBYE

VERSE 2
I sat on our bed—He packed his suitcase
I held a picture of our wedding day
His hands were trembling—We both were crying
He kissed me gently and then he quickly walked away

PRE-CHORUS
I called up Mama
She said time will ease your pain
Life's about changing
Nothing ever stays the same
And she said

(REPEAT CHORUS)

VERSE 3
Sittin' with Mama
Alone in her bedroom
She opened her eyes
And then squeezed my hand
She said I have to go now
My time here is over
And with her final words she tried to help me understand

PRE-CHORUS
Mama whispered softly time will ease your pain
Life's about changing
Nothing ever stays the same
And she said

(REPEAT CHORUS)

WRITTEN BY *Karen Taylor-Good and Burton Collins;*
RECORDED BY *artists including Patty Loveless,*
Al Jarreau, Karen Taylor-Good, and Melanie.

Although every verse in this example tells a different, complete story, note that each is related to, and clearly leads back to, the same chorus. At the end of each verse it makes sense for the singer to say, "How Can I Help You Say Goodbye" and to repeat the chorus lyric.

Other examples of songs that successfully employ the Verse - Chorus - Verse - Chorus - Verse - Chorus structure include "Get the Party Started" (Pink), "Candle in the Wind" (Elton John), and "Holes in the Floor of Heaven" (Steve Wariner).

Verse - Verse - Bridge - Verse

Note that this structure does not contain a chorus. When using a Verse - Verse - Bridge - Verse structure, the title will almost always appear in one of two places: the first line of each verse or the last line of each verse. While it is acceptable to have your title in either of these places, once that decision has been made, the title will typically appear in the same location of each verse (i.e., the title will either be in the first or last line of every verse). In practice, it is much more commonly found in the last line.

This song form begins with the first verse. The second verse follows. Lyrically, the second verse will develop the story further and introduce new information, and like the first verse it begins or ends with the song title. A two- or four-line bridge (a melodic and lyrical departure or release) follows the second verse. A third verse follows the bridge. Lyrically, the third verse ties the story together, provides additional information, and, in some instances, provides resolution.

It has the same melody as the previous verses and the title will once again be in the same place as it was in the first and second verses.

This song form, shown in the example that follows, is referred to as "A - A - B - A" (A = Verse, B = Bridge).

SAVING ALL MY LOVE FOR YOU

VERSE 1
A few stolen moments is all that we share
You've got your family and they need you there
Though I try to resist
Being last on your list
But no other man's gonna do
So I'm SAVING ALL MY LOVE FOR YOU

VERSE 2
It's not very easy living all alone
My friends try and tell me find a man of my own
But each time I try
I just break down and cry
'Cause I'd rather be home feelin' blue
So I'm SAVING ALL MY LOVE FOR YOU

BRIDGE
You used to tell me we'd run away together
Love gives you the right to be free
You said "Be patient, just wait a little longer"
But that's just an old fantasy

VERSE 3
I've got to get ready, just a few minutes more
Gonna get that old feeling when you walk through the door
'Cause tonight is the night
For feeling all right
We'll be making love the whole night through
So I'm saving all my love
Yes, I'm saving all my love
Yes, I'm SAVING ALL MY LOVE FOR YOU

WRITTEN BY *Gerry Goffin;* MUSIC BY *Michael Masser;* RECORDED BY *Whitney Houston.*

Additional examples of the Verse - Verse - Bridge - Verse song form include "The Way We Were" (Barbra Streisand), "To Make You Feel My Love" (Garth Brooks and Bob Dylan), and "The Song Remembers When" (Trisha Yearwood).

Variations

While the forms previously listed are those that are most often found in popular songs, there are many notable exceptions. A common variation of the A - A - B - A song form adds a second bridge and an additional verse. The resulting song form is Verse - Verse - Bridge - Verse - Bridge - Verse (A - A - B - A - B - A; A = Verse, B = Bridge). When this structure is used, it is identical to the A - A - B - A form; however, after the third verse, there is a second bridge. This additional bridge may or may not contain the same lyric as the first bridge. After the second bridge there is a fourth verse, which most often has a new lyric. In some instances, the fourth verse might repeat the first verse's lyric. As in the basic A - A - B - A song form, each verse includes the title as its first or last line.

Tim McGraw had a #1 country hit with John White's "Red Ragtop," which employed a structure that is not typically used: Verse - Chorus - Verse - Chorus - Bridge - Verse - Chorus. This same variation was used in Avril Lavigne's "Sk8er Boi."

A very small percentage of hit songs begin with the chorus. Brandy and Monica took that structure to the top of the charts with their duet, "The Boy Is Mine." If you choose to start with the chorus it's best to use either of the following structures:

• Chorus - Verse - Chorus - Verse - Chorus

• Chorus - Verse - Chorus - Verse - Chorus - Bridge - Chorus

Starting with the chorus in a song that contains three verses will probably make the song too long for the radio (and for most listeners). If you decide to begin with a chorus, the chorus needs to stand up lyrically without the benefit of having been "set up" by any prior lyric. Sometimes writers start with the chorus to grab the listener immediately, but if your motivation is fear that your first verse won't be interesting enough to sustain the listener to the chorus, rewrite the verse.

Another common variation includes a first verse that is twice the length of the verses that follow. For example, the first verse might be eight lines—a "double" first verse, while subsequent verses are four lines. Or the first verse might be sixteen lines, while later verses are eight lines. However, having all verses consist of sixteen bars is not recommended. It can become boring because verses are not designed melodically or lyrically, like the chorus, to be the catchiest portion of the song.

In her Grammy-nominated, self-written hit, "A Thousand Miles," Vanessa Carlton used a Verse - Chorus - Verse - Chorus - Verse - Chorus structure (A - B - A - B - A - B; A = Verse, B = Chorus) with a variation: her third verse repeated the first verse lyric. Avril Lavigne's first hit, "Complicated" (lyric on page 5) used a similar variation, repeating half of the first verse lyric in the third verse.

Many traditional folk songs were constructed by simply combining a series of verses. This structure, referred to as "A - A - A" (A = Verse) combines three or more verses and does not include a chorus or a bridge. It is rarely used in contemporary music. However, two notable successful exceptions are "The Rose" (written by Amanda McBroom and recorded by Bette Midler) and "By the Time I Get to Phoenix" (written by Jimmy Webb and recorded by Glen Campbell).

EXERCISE: IDENTIFYING SONG STRUCTURES

Learning the craft of songwriting will not compromise or diminish your creativity. It will allow you to express your ideas in a way that can touch millions of people. Now that you are able to identify the components and structures of successful songs, write out the lyrics to three of your favorite songs. If you are writing primarily for artists other than yourself, choose songs that were written by writers other than the artist. However, if you are writing for yourself, with an artist (for his or her project), or for your own band, choose songs that were written by the artist and/or producer in genres similar to your own. Answer the following questions for each song:

- What structure did the writer employ?

- Can you identify each of the sections of the song?

- Where does the title appear?

- How many bars make up the introduction?

- How many lines are in each section of the song?

- How many bars are in each musical section?

- If there is an instrumental solo section, where does it appear, and how many bars is it?

Now, try this exercise for three of your own compositions. Are you using the structures and tools that have proven themselves to be successful?

INTRODUCTIONS, INSTRUMENTAL SOLOS, AND TURNAROUNDS

Musical introductions and instrumental solos are more a function of the arrangement than the basic song form. However, there are some guidelines to follow. On a song demo, no one wants to listen to a long musical introduction. Four or eight bars are sufficient, with eight being the maximum.

> *I like to tell new songwriters that they need to listen, feel, and then analyze the songs that they love. See how they are put together. What kind of sections do the songs have?*
>
> RICK CHUDACOFF (Songwriter/producer for Alison Krauss, Michael Bolton, Smokey Robinson, and Judy Collins)

When a professional is evaluating a song, he or she listens primarily for the melody and the lyrics. Unless the instrumental section includes exciting new chords and melody that are essential to the song itself, it probably should not be included on the demo. There are instances when the instrumental is indeed an integral part of a song's success. The ending of Eric Clapton's classic "Layla" comes to mind. An instrumental solo can also be important for a song that is primarily geared toward the dance market.

If you do choose to include an instrumental solo section, there are several options for its location. In a Verse - Chorus - Verse - Chorus structure the instrumental section typically follows the second chorus and is followed by an additional chorus. In this instance, the solo serves the function of an instrumental bridge. For Verse - Chorus songs that already contain a bridge (Verse - Chorus - Verse - Chorus - Bridge - Chorus), the instrumental section typically goes either after the second chorus or after the bridge. In a Verse - Verse - Bridge - Verse song the solo section generally follows the third verse and is then followed by a fourth verse, creating an A - A - B - A - B - A (A = Verse, B = Bridge) structure, with the instrumental solo serving as a second bridge.

Ask yourself if the instrumental section is critical to the impact of the song. If you are writing material for yourself, and you are a virtuoso musician, you will likely want to write some songs that include a solo to showcase your ability. Similarly, if you are writing for an artist who is known for his or her instrumental ability (for example, Carlos Santana or Bonnie Raitt), it might be a good idea to include an instrumental solo. But if you are writing and demoing songs to pitch to outside artists, instead of investing time and money producing a solo, at that point in the song you might have the singer say, "You can turn off the CD now"— because the executive who is reviewing your song most likely has a huge stack of CDs to screen and probably will stop listening to yours at that point.

The "turnaround" is an instrumental section that can be found in almost all songs. In songs that employ a Verse - Chorus - Verse - Chorus structure, the turnaround is the brief musical interlude that follows the first chorus. Providing an additional melodic hook, the turnaround acts as a segue to lead the listener back to the verse. In the Verse - Chorus - Verse - Chorus - Verse - Chorus structure there will typically be turnarounds following the first and the second choruses. In Verse - Chorus - Verse - Chorus - Bridge - Chorus structures, there might also be a turnaround between the second chorus and the bridge; however, this is not mandatory. In many instances songs go directly from the second chorus into the bridge, without this melodic break.

Songs that are constructed with either the Verse - Verse - Bridge - Verse structure or the Verse - Verse - Bridge - Verse - Bridge - Verse variation may or may not include a turnaround following the first verse and prior to each bridge.

The melody that comprises the turnaround may be based on a musical phrase also found in the verse, chorus, or intro, or it may be a melody that is crafted to occur only in the turn-around. Ideally, it will be catchy and easy to remember. It is most often four bars long; however, it may be eight bars. When a turnaround appears more than once in a song, it is typically with the same melody each time.

If you are having difficulty adjusting to writing within the confines of successful structures, this exercise can ease the process.

1. Choose a favorite song that you wish you had written. If you are writing songs primarily for yourself (as an artist), select a song that was written by the artist (or band) that recorded it. If you are writing songs with the hope that other artists will record them, choose a song that was not written by the artist who recorded it.

2. Using the song you've selected as a template, write a new melody and lyric that can be sung "over" the existing song. Your new song will have the same structure as the song that inspired it.

3. Compose a new melody and chord changes while maintaining the structure of the song you emulated.

STEP 1: CONCLUSION

As you can see, there are no hard and fast rules about song structure and there have been many successful songs that deviated from the structures and variations listed in this chapter. The majority of these exceptions are written by recording artists or their producers. The best thing to do is to learn the structures that are consistently found in hit songs. Then you can choose, on a case-by-case basis, the most effective way to express each of your songs so that they will reflect your vision—while having the best chance of connecting with your audience.

SONG STRUCTURE CHECKLIST

Photocopy this checklist and keep it where you normally write. Each time you finish a draft of a song, check to be sure that it has successfully incorporated the tools and techniques that follow.

- ❑ Song adheres to one of the most successful structures, or one of the variations, discussed in this chapter (check the one that applies):

  - ❑ Verse - Chorus - Verse - Chorus

  - ❑ Verse - Chorus - Verse - Chorus - Bridge - Chorus

  - ❑ Verse - Chorus - Verse - Chorus - Verse - Chorus

  - ❑ Verse - Verse - Bridge - Verse

  - ❑ A popular variation of one of these structures

- ❑ Each verse has the same melody and new lyrics

- ❑ Corresponding lines in every verse contain the same approximate number of syllables

- ❑ Each verse contains four or eight lines of lyric (eight or sixteen musical bars)

- ❑ If the first verse includes a pre-chorus, all subsequent verses also include a pre-chorus section

- ❑ The chorus contains four or eight lines of lyric (eight or sixteen musical bars)

- ❑ Each chorus has the same melody and the same lyrics

- ❑ If there is a chorus, the title appears at least once within it

- ❑ If there is a bridge, it contains two or four lines of lyric (four or eight musical bars)

- ❑ In a Verse - Chorus structure, if there is a bridge, it is between the second and third choruses

- ❑ In an A - A - B - A (Verse - Verse - Bridge - Verse) structure, the bridge is between the second and third verses

- ❑ The bridge (if applicable) does not include the song title

- ❑ The musical introduction is four or eight bars long

- ❑ The instrumental solo (if applicable) is no more than eight bars long

Writing Effective Lyrics

The first time I ever heard one of her records—I mean sat down and actually listened to it—I could not believe it. It was like somebody actually knew how I felt, like she could see inside my heart and say all the things I didn't know how to say.

TESS (a fan, speaking about Dolly Parton)

CHAPTER 2

Developing Great Song Ideas and Catchy Titles

Pull up a chair at a bar next to two women who are drinking and talking. You'll come away with half a dozen song ideas. The most successful thing I've done is to be original in a little way about love. I try to poke my head through a small window or find an angle that's not been beaten to death. I love good titles and original ideas. Lyrically I want to explain my idea in a simple fashion so people who are only half-listening can half-understand, and that works for me.

HARLAN HOWARD (Legendary Nashville songwriter of "I Fall to Pieces," "Heartaches by the Number," "I've Got a Tiger by the Tail," and more than one hundred Top Ten hits)

Simply put, lyrics are the words that tell the story, convey the emotion, and communicate the information from the writer to the listener. The lyricist's job is to provide listeners with the words they want to hear or the words they'd say if they could.

UNDERSTANDING WHAT CONSTITUTES A GREAT IDEA— AND HOW TO FIND ONE

The craft of writing is important, but after you've learned that, then it eventually comes down to who has the best ideas, and a writer today should be asking: How do I put myself in the position to get the great ideas? Writers have to learn to work at finding things to write about—that's a learned condition, finding ideas for hits. There are song gifts, no question, but you've got to be looking for them. When you start with a great title and a fresh approach to an idea that has wide appeal, you're already well on your way to a successful song. A boring, overused idea makes your job much more difficult if your goal is to create something unique. A strong, memorable, distinctive title almost writes itself.

JEFF CARLTON (Vice President and General Manager, Hamstein Music Publishing)

The first step toward writing an effective lyric is starting with a great idea. The vast majority of songs on the radio are about some aspect of love, probably because it is a topic that everyone can relate to. The desire to love and be loved is a basic human need.

The joy of finding love, the pain of losing love, looking for the right love, complaining about the wrong love, missing a past love, hoping for a future love, the fear of losing love, the fear of finding love, cheating on a lover, being cheated on by a lover, wanting to be loved, wanting to be loved differently, and wanting to be loved by someone other than the one who loves you are all prevalent themes in popular songs. It's no wonder that "love" is the most commonly used word in songs—even more than "baby."

Whether the subject of a song deals with relationships, a social issue, a politically oriented message, a religious idea, having a good time, or getting ahead in life, to be commercially viable the idea must appeal to your audience. The most successful songs strike a chord with millions of people.

> *The same notes, chords, and basically the same words have been used since the days of Beethoven and Bach. So I just try to say it in a different way and make the best of what I have to work with. What makes a song a timeless thing? I basically write about love and life because they are always current.*
>
> SMOKEY ROBINSON (Legendary songwriter/artist)

It can be satisfying and cathartic to write deeply personal songs. Many writers also enjoy writing songs that may be poetic, quirky, flowery, vague, or in styles that are not consistent with what is currently being played on the radio. Commercial success is not the only measure of the quality of a song. If you enjoy writing in those styles, don't stop. But if you are hoping to have your songs recorded by artists other than yourself, don't confuse the songs that you write for your own personal satisfaction with "radio-friendly" songs that contain subjects and styles having broad appeal.

> *I hate songs about being a singer or a songwriter. The average listener can't relate to that.*
>
> SHERRILL BLACKMAN (SDB Music Publishing)

Many developing songwriters write songs about wanting to write songs, becoming a famous recording artist, or leaving their small town and moving to a place where they can pursue those goals. While these ideas are very important to the songwriter, the vast majority of people who listen to the radio and buy records do not share those specific dreams—nor do they express themselves by writing songs. While there are exceptions, songs that deal with these topics rarely have universal appeal; they are usually written by the artists who record them. However, it is possible to express ideas that are very personal in ways that satisfy our desire to write about our feelings while still touching listeners who have not had the exact same experience. You can achieve this by answering the following questions:

- What is the essence of the idea?
- What is the emotion at the heart of the idea?
- How can I express this in a way that a wide audience will relate to?

For example, practically all people have fantasies and goals that they wish they could pursue. While a song about becoming a famous songwriter or recording artist has limited appeal, a lyric about following your heart, believing in yourself, and chasing your dreams can indeed speak to millions of listeners, while still capturing the essence of what the songwriter truly feels.

Once you've decided on your subject and determined that it's a topic with potential for wide appeal, one of the most important challenges is finding fresh ways to approach the subject. It's likely that your idea has been written about thousands of times. Finding a new twist or a different angle and expressing it with an intriguing, interesting title is crucial if you hope to set your song apart from the competition. There have been countless songs that express the familiar sentiment, "I wish you would come back and love me again." But only Diane Warren said it in a way that took Toni Braxton to the top of the charts with "Unbreak My Heart."

There are ideas for hit songs all around us waiting to be written. According to hit songwriter George Teren, whose songs have been recorded by artists including Tim McGraw, Britney Spears, and Billy Ray Cyrus, "Ideas are gifts. Sometimes they are phrases pulled out of a conversation, a movie, TV show, or book. Sometimes everything I hear or read sounds like a title."

Potential song titles can be found in everyday conversations, in movies (especially romantic films), on television, on road maps, and in inspirational and funny e-mails that circulate via the Internet. Clay Walker's hit "Chain of Love" was written as a result of a songwriter reading one of those tug-at-your-heart e-mails. Blake Shelton's #1 country hit "Austin" was inspired by an actual message left on an answering machine. The title for Paul Simon's "Mother and Child Reunion" came from a Chinese restaurant menu. Song titles have been known to "hide" in advertisements, newspapers, telephone books, greeting cards, T-shirts, and cartoons.

The title and concept for Jamie O'Neal's Grammy-nominated #1 hit "There Is No Arizona" (written by Lisa Drew, Jamie O'Neal, and Shaye Smith) came from the Stephen King film *Dolores Claiborne*. Lisa Drew had never written a hit song when she watched that movie and saw Jennifer Jason Leigh turn to Kathy Bates and say, "Don't you know there is no Arizona?" Lisa jotted that phrase in her notebook, where it stayed for four years before she cowrote the song that would change her life. Likewise, the title of George Strait's #1 country hit, "Blue Clear Sky" (written by Mark D. Sanders, John Jarrard, and Bob DiPiero), came from the movie *Forrest Gump*. Taking a line of dialogue from a film or a book is not plagiarism when it is used in a different creative medium. The next time you watch a movie, listen closely for either a song title or idea to jump out.

I've heard this said and I believe it's true. One of the most important qualities of being a great songwriter is being a good listener. You'll hear great titles if you shut up and listen. People say them all the time.

HENRY PAUL (Songwriter/artist from the band Blackhawk)

Several times, when preparing for an important cowriting session, I've been less than enthusiastic about any of the titles I've stockpiled and instead have found inspiration at local bookstores. Browse the aisles. There's a good chance you'll find a great song title. Books of quotations, slang, and even titles of novels can be a great source of song titles. I have rarely attended a concert, movie, or play or read a good book without coming up with a song title or idea. Some writers have reported finding song ideas in advice columns such as "Dear Abby," and while watching soap operas and daytime talk shows where guests air intimate details of their personal lives to twenty-five million viewers.

Go to nightclubs, attend concerts, watch videos on television, and, most importantly, listen to the radio. Other writers' songs may spark your own song titles and ideas. Ask yourself how you might have approached their ideas. Many writers report having heard a great line in a song, only to realize that the line they "heard" wasn't actually what had been sung. In many instances, the line that they misheard sparked a new idea.

> *I'm a totally different writer than I was fifteen years ago when I would be inspired by the most lame ideas. When you start off you're just connecting words, but now the song has to have an honesty to it. There are three subjects to write about: life, love, and death. The secret is writing the same old stuff and staying inspired by the simple things. That's probably the secret to life itself—finding the happiness in everyday miracles.*
>
> CRAIG WISEMAN (One of *Billboard's* Top 25 Songwriters
> of the Year; Nashville Songwriters Association International
> and *Music Row* magazine's Songwriter of the Year,
> with over one hundred cuts and thirty charted singles)

One of the most important tools you can incorporate to set your song apart from the competition is a strong, fresh concept. If your lyric is essentially saying, "I love you," why should a publisher, recording artist, producer, or record company executive feel compelled to choose your song over the hundreds of other love songs submitted for consideration? And why should a listener want to hear or buy your song? Those songs that jump out of the pile are the ones with fresh angles, new ways to say "the same old thing," and original concepts. It's not easy to consistently find distinctive, one-of-a-kind ideas and titles, but it is definitely worth the effort.

When pop/hip-hop artist Nelly wrote *IT'S GETTIN' HOT IN HERRE—So take off all your clothes,* this was a completely new approach, a truly novel way to say, "I think you're beautiful and sexy and I'd like to make love to you." Likewise, the lyric for Shaggy's "It Wasn't Me" (excerpt below) was a completely new, attention-grabbing way to approach the subject of getting caught cheating on a lover. The outrageous advice to say, "It wasn't me," regardless of what was witnessed, made for a much more entertaining and unique song than if the singer had simply said, "Oh, baby, I'm sorry I hurt you—please forgive me."

IT WASN'T ME

But she caught me on the counter
"It wasn't me"
Saw me banging on the sofa
"It wasn't me"
I even had her in the shower
"It wasn't me"
She even caught me on camera
"It wasn't me"
She saw the marks on my shoulder
"It wasn't me"
Heard the words that I told her
"It wasn't me"
Heard the screams getting louder
"It wasn't me"
She stayed until it was over

WRITTEN BY *O. Burrell, R. Ducent, S. Pizzonia, and B. Thompson;*
RECORDED BY *Shaggy.*

This is not to imply that the only ways to separate your songs from the pack are by incorporating sexual overtones or outrageous themes. The key is to find innovative ways to express yourself—and original concepts to write about. Additional songs that were built on strong, fresh ideas include "I Hope You Dance" (Lee Ann Womack), "The Rising" (Bruce Springsteen), "Three Wooden Crosses" (Randy Travis), "Calling All Angels" (Train), and "It's Five O'Clock Somewhere" (Alan Jackson and Jimmy Buffett). Give your listeners compelling reasons to select your song—and let one of those reasons be a strong, fresh concept.

> *I want to hear songs my other writers couldn't have written—something*
> *unique and special. I've got to feel something. For me to make a move, the*
> *writer's got to move me, make me cry, or laugh, or dance.*
>
> ALAN BREWER (President/owner, BME Music Publishing; producer)

Like all of the other skills that successful songwriting requires, learning to discern what constitutes a strong title and a great idea takes practice. Through a process of trial and error, the responses you get from friends, family, and music industry professionals, as well as your own emotional reaction to your songs, you will begin to shape your instinct for what makes for an effective title and a powerful idea for a song.

When the idea for "Dear Diary" popped into my head I knew I had hit on a concept that would lend itself perfectly to a song for Britney Spears' young female fans. I even joked with a friend, saying, "I've just gotten another Britney Spears cut—but I haven't written the song, and Britney doesn't know about it yet!" The concept: a girl talking directly to her diary, sharing her feelings about a boy, and asking her diary for advice. It was a fresh, original way to address the insecurities and desires that are experienced by virtually every adolescent girl. The strength of this idea afforded my collaborator, Eugene Wilde, and me the opportunity to write the song with Britney, who provided invaluable insight into the emotional realm of her preteen and adolescent fan base. The lyric wasn't profound, but it was an inventive approach and it spoke to millions of young girls.

DEAR DIARY

Dear Diary—
Today I saw a boy
And I wondered if he noticed me
He took my breath away

Dear Diary—
I can't get him off my mind
And it scares me
'Cause I've never felt this way

No one in this world
Knows me better than you do
So diary
I'll confide in you

Dear Diary—
Today I saw that boy
As he walked by
I thought he smiled at me

And I wondered
Does he know what's in my heart
I tried to smile
But I could hardly breathe

Should I tell him how I feel
Or would that scare him away?
Diary, tell me what to do
Tell me what to say

Dear Diary—
One touch of his hand
Now I can't wait
To see that boy again

He smiled
And I thought my heart could fly
Diary, do you think
That we'll be more than friends?
I've got a feeling
We'll be so much more than friends

Written by *Britney Spears, Jason Blume, and Eugene Wilde;* recorded by *Britney Spears.*

> **Titles are like little promises of an offer that's being made for the next three minutes.**
>
> STEVE BLOCH (Publisher, Writer Zone Music)

Ask yourself, if you had a pile of songs to review, based on the titles alone, which songs would you listen to first?

- "Your Body Is a Wonderland" (John Mayer)
- "Born a Lion" (Ani DiFranco)
- "The Impossible" (Joe Nichols)

or

- "I Love You Very Much"
- "I'm Very Strong"
- "Believe in Yourself"

I would choose the songs in the first set. With nothing else to base my opinion on but a title, I'd expect the songs with the more creative, intriguing titles to be more engaging than the ones with titles that show little imagination or uniqueness.

One-word titles can often be very effective. They are easy for the listener to remember and often have great emotional impact. "Clocks" (Coldplay), "Bitch" (Meredith Brooks), "Snake" (R. Kelly), "Cry" (Faith Hill), "Headstrong" (Trapt), "Intuition" (Jewel), "Feel" (Robbie Williams), "Picture" (Kid Rock and Sheryl Crow), "Beautiful" (Christina Aguilera), and "Unwell" (Matchbox Twenty) have all been hits. Occasionally, a series of nonsense syllables or a new word that the writer creates, like "Bootylicious," "MMMBop," or "No Diggity," can provide a hit title as well. These titles probably resonate with listeners because they're original, catchy, and pleasing to the ear. But most importantly, they're fun to sing.

The strongest titles:

- Grab your attention—"Like a Virgin," "Magic Stick"
- Evoke powerful emotions—"Tears in Heaven," "How Am I Supposed to Live Without You"

- Are unusual—"Soak Up the Sun," "Miss Independent"
- Are intriguing—"Concrete Angel," "Kiss from a Rose"
- Are clever—"Sk8er Boi," "Brokenheartsville"

The most powerful song ideas and titles begin with emotions that come from the heart. If you're trying to fake the emotion, there is probably someone else writing about a similar idea who genuinely feels it—and that's tough to beat. Write about what you care about, what moves you, your own experiences, hopes, fears, pain, and joy. Most of us feel and want the same basic things. Be vulnerable; if you express genuine, honest feelings in your songs, the chances are good that they will touch your listeners.

KEEPING A HOOK BOOK

The "hook" is any part of a song that "grabs" the listener. It might be an instrumental riff that listeners can't get out of their minds, a memorable melodic phrase, a catchy line of lyric that "hooks in" the listener, or a combination of two or more of these elements. The title of a song and its corresponding melody should always be a hook. A song can (and usually will) have more than one hook.

When you get that great title or idea, you'd better have a pen in your pocket, or a miniature tape recorder handy. Be sure to write it down or record it. Even those ideas that you are sure you won't forget can easily get lost along the way—and that title or melody might have been your ticket to a Grammy!

EXERCISE: FINDING ORIGINAL TITLES

Look around you and jot down a list of five objects you see. For instance, I'm looking at a photograph, a grandfather clock, a mirror, a drinking glass with ice melting in it, and a vase filled with flowers. Now, create a song title from each one of the images you see. For example, using the objects listed above, my titles might be:

- "Picture This" (photograph)
- "Tick Tock" (grandfather clock)
- "Just Behind the Mirror" (mirror)
- "Colder than Ice" (melting ice)
- "Yellow Roses" (vase filled with flowers)

Hopefully, you will expand some of your titles into complete songs.

Transfer your lyric ideas to a "hook book"—a list of titles and ideas. I keep my hook book, along with tiny scraps of paper, bank receipts, napkins, and matchbook covers filled with titles and ideas, in a file folder marked "Future Hits."

Under each title, jot down images, premises, or actual lines of lyric. They may or may not make it to your final draft, but they'll help you recapture the initial spark you were feeling when you first got the idea. Bring your hook book to your cowriting sessions and periodically review your titles. You never know when one of them will jump out and demand to be written.

MAKING THE SINGER LOOK GOOD

When evaluating the merits of your song's topic and story, an important question to ask is "Does it make the singer look good?" No one wants to appear in a bad light. With very few exceptions, women don't want to be represented as home-wreckers, immoral, weak, or as victims. The days of Tammy Wynette singing "Stand by Your Man" have been replaced by Destiny's Child's "(I'm a) Survivor," Shania Twain's "(If You're Not in It for Love) I'm Outta Here," and Britney Spears' "Stronger." Instead of presenting themselves as being devastated at the ending of a relationship, female singers are more likely to express that they are finding strength and emotional resources they didn't know they had, and that they're better off without the loser. A strong example of this attitude can be found in Christina Aguilera's "Fighter." The singer tells the man who left her: I should despise you, but instead I thank you because you made me stronger; you made my skin thicker; you made me a "fighter."

It's highly unlikely that any singer, male or female, will want to sing a lyric that presents him or herself as hopeless, an unrepentant drunk, a cheater, or an idiot who doesn't care who he or she has hurt. However, a common theme in popular songs is some variation of "I was a fool to hurt you—and now that I know what a great thing I lost I'm miserable and sorry and will do anything to make things right." In that type of song the singer has learned his or her lesson and is no longer the fool he or she once was.

Honesty makes a great lyric. The willingness to be real and tell the truth.

KAREN TAYLOR-GOOD (Grammy-nominated songwriter,
"How Can I Help You Say Goodbye" and "Not that Different")

Three good rules to follow when writing a great lyric are:

- Write what's real for you.
- Write what you feel.
- Write what you love.

Many fans don't realize that the songs artists sing are analogous to the words in a script that actors recite. The lyrics that come from artists' mouths are often perceived as "real" for those artists. For a performance (either live or recorded) to be effective, the audience needs to believe the singer. Listeners want to be convinced that the artist is experiencing the emotion he or she is singing about. Therefore, the lyricist's job is to give the singer words that are consistent with the image that artist has chosen to present. While some recording artists (particularly in rap and hard rock) cultivate a "bad-boy" or "bad-girl" image that might glorify violence, criminal activity, or sex without emotional involvement, most of the artists who record outside songs do not fit into this category.

Before you begin to write a song, however, ask yourself:

- Will an artist want to say this?
- Will millions of listeners want to hear this?
- Is this an original, fresh approach to this concept?

USING SONGS TO HELP DEFINE ARTIST IDENTITY

The songs artists choose to sing are among the most important elements that define their persona—the image they choose to project. Songs allow the audience to feel as if they know the singer, as if the artist is revealing parts of him- or herself through the lyrics and the attitude conveyed in the music. For example, the songs Shania Twain writes and records play a major role in her audience's defining her as a strong, independent woman, who knows the power of her sexuality and is not afraid to speak her mind. While there may be many additional facets to Shania than just these traits, these are the ones she draws our attention to with songs including "Man! I Feel Like a Woman," "That Don't Impress Me Much," "Don't Be Stupid (You Know I Love You)," and "(If You're Not in It for Love) I'm Outta Here." It would seem quite jarring if Shania were to sing a song that expressed that she was devastated at the ending of a relationship, that she was afraid someone might not find her attractive or desirable, or that she feared she'd never find someone to love her. These ideas are not consistent with the image she has chosen to portray through her videos, costuming, choreography—and her songs.

If you are writing songs that you plan to sing yourself, or songs you are writing for your own band, remember that your songs will send a clear message to your listeners and will make a powerful contribution to the identity you project as an artist. Be conscious of the message your songs are sending and be sure that it is consistent with the image you hope to present.

When writing songs on assignment or for artists other than yourself and when choosing which songs to pitch to artists, it's important to remember that the songs will need to be consistent with the qualities and personality traits these artists are trying to present. Interviews in fan magazines and on artists' Web sites can be terrific sources of personal information that might help you choose topics and beliefs that a specific artist might want to sing about and be identified with.

If you are writing songs for yourself, jot down a list of at least five adjectives and/or phrases that describe the qualities you hope to project. If you are writing songs to target a specific artist (other than yourself), make a list of those characteristics that you believe define this artist's identity.

For example, you might list:

- Wild, rebellious, exuding raw sexuality, fearless, angry

- Sensitive, quiet, a defender of social issues, intellectual, a dreamer

- Wholesome, patriotic, strong moral values, boy- (or girl-) next-door type, squeaky clean

Be sure that the songs you write and pitch are consistent with the identity you (or the artist you are writing for) hope to project.

POINT OF VIEW: DECIDING WHICH "VOICE" TO WRITE FROM

The "voice" or "person" refers to whether the singer is speaking about him- or herself, directly to another individual, or about someone else:

- First person tells about yourself from your own point of view. For example, "I love you."

- Second person tells about the person you are talking to. For example, "You will love me."

- Third person tells about someone else. For example, "She loves him."

Which point of view to write from is a creative decision, determined on a song-by-song basis. In many instances, writing from the first person evokes the strongest emotion because the audience feels the singer is sharing something personal and real.

It would be quite unusual to write an entire lyric from the second-person point of view because we would have to presume to know precisely what another person is thinking or feeling. However, in a "first-person" lyric, it can be quite effective to insert an occasional line from the second-person perspective. For example:

I see you looking at me (first person)

I know I've got what you need (first person)

You know you need it so bad (second person)

I know it's driving you mad (first person)

Third person can be the best way to address a topic about which you, or another singer, might be hesitant to sing, such as cheating on your partner, having an abortion, taking illicit drugs, or engaging in other illegal activities. By telling a story about someone else, any topic can be addressed without the singer having to present him- or herself as the person about whom the story is being told.

Switching point of view (for example, from first person to third) can be confusing for your listeners. Be sure you are clear and consistent about who is talking, and to whom.

USING THE THREE-STEP LYRIC-FOCUSING TECHNIQUE

> *If I have an idea I start singing the idea in my head until I land on something that feels real good with it and I'll build a core around that and then I'll say okay, now I know what needs to be said to get me from here to there, and when I get there it's gonna be good. If you look at "How Do You Like Me Now?" you can see that if you've already got the chorus then you've got to set the song up to explain why you are saying "How do you like me now?" So I've got to take you back to a time when the girl wouldn't listen and she said I'd never get anywhere, and I just start working from there.*

TOBY KEITH (Hit songwriter/recording artist)

The Three-Step Lyric-Focusing Technique was designed to help you focus your idea and craft lyrics that lead your listeners to your title. Both Sting and legendary songwriter Jimmy Webb have been quoted as saying that they always start with a title. The overwhelming majority of lyrics written in Nashville begin with a title. I've written hundreds of songs in various styles. My cowriters have included Grammy winners and some of the most successful and talented writers and artists in the music business, and we almost always begin the lyric-writing process by deciding on a title.

This is not to imply that I never start a song collaboration with a melody, a groove, or a rhythm track—that's perfectly acceptable and works well for many writers. But when it's time to write the lyric we almost always decide what our title will be—before writing the lines. Before a word is written, we'll generally exchange titles, ideas, and "starts" (ideas, lines, or phrases that may or may not eventually develop into a full song) until we settle on the title that excites both of us. Sometimes it can take an hour or more to discuss the merits of and possible directions for each title.

> *I've noticed that all the hit songs that I've written have always started out with a strong concept first—or a title, like "You Give Love a Bad Name" (Child's hit for Bon Jovi).*

DESMOND CHILD (Songwriter whose credits
include hits with Aerosmith, Ricky Martin,
LeAnn Rimes, Cher, Michael Bolton, and Bon Jovi)

You may find that for some songs it works better for you to write in a stream-of-consciousness style, allowing your creativity to flow unhampered with little regard for whether your resulting lyric makes literal sense or tells a cohesive story. Many performing songwriters and bands have great success writing and performing songs with lyrics that are more abstract than those typically sung by artists who do not write their own songs. If you study the lyrics written by artists such as Alanis Morissette, Nickelback, Annie Lennox, Sting, U2, Coldplay, and Leonard Cohen, you will find images that don't always make literal sense, but still manage to evoke powerful emotions in their listeners.

However, if you analyze the lyrics of songs that have been hits for most country artists, as well as lyrics of songs recorded by those pop, adult contemporary, and urban artists who do not write all of their own material, you will see that these lyrics are typically constructed to tell a clear, literal story, or to express a clearly defined emotion. Artists who record outside songs include Celine Dion, Tim McGraw, Whitney Houston, Kenny Chesney, Hilary Duff, Barbra Streisand, Martina McBride, and Faith Hill. If you hope to write for artists such as these it will be beneficial to study the lyrics of the songs they have recorded.

> *When you're writing lyrics for yourself, you know how you want to say things, so you have more latitude. When you're writing for the general market you must cling to the rules of the craft. You're trying to say something for someone you've probably never even met; constructing a well-crafted lyric with one focused thought will give you an edge over the abstract, tangential musing you might enjoy performing—but may be hard for someone else to interpret.*
>
> REGIE HAMM (Songwriter;
> Universal recording artist)

The kinds of lyrics artists write for themselves (or for their own bands) often use abstract imagery, lines with symbolic or hidden meanings, and a nonlinear style of writing to evoke emotion. Examples of these types of lyrics include Train's "Drops of Jupiter," Led Zeppelin's "Stairway to Heaven," Leonard Cohen's "Suzanne," and the Dave Matthews Band's "The Space Between." Songs you hope to pitch to artists other than yourself tend to be more literal, including all the information necessary to convey a clear, concise story in a linear fashion. Neither of these approaches is right or wrong. However, it's likely that one of them is better suited to the artists you are targeting, or for the style and persona you are presenting, if you are writing for yourself.

Whether you are writing for other artists, or for yourself, it will be beneficial to understand how to write a lyric that is focused and clearly communicates what you intend. The main function of the verse lyric is to lead and deliver the listener to your title. If you are using a Verse - Chorus structure, the verse lyric should lead and deliver your listeners to your chorus—which will include the title. In an A - A - B - A form, if each verse begins with your title, the lyric that follows should expand upon and be a logical outgrowth of the title. In an

A - A - B - A structure with the title at the end of each verse, each verse's lyric should lead the listener to, and set up, the title. Attempting to deliver the listener to your title if you don't know your title is like shooting arrows in the dark. You'll have a much better chance of hitting your target if you know exactly what you're aiming for. The steps that follow will help you write lyrics that clearly lead your listeners to one idea—and this idea will be encapsulated by your title and/or chorus.

When I write with a collaborator, we don't literally say, "Let's work on step one... (or two, or three)," but I've noticed that the underlying principles of the Three-Step approach to lyric writing are indeed used by the vast majority of successful songwriters—whether they're aware of it or not.

> *If you can replace your title with another title and it still works—your lyric probably hasn't been written to make your title pay off.*
>
> ALAN BREWER
> (President, BME Music Publishing)

Step 1: Start with a Title

Once you've selected your title, be certain you're very clear about what your title means to you. It can help to pretend that you're explaining what your song is about to someone else by talking into a tape recorder. The bottom line is that you want to have no doubt what your song is about—what the real meaning is—before you start writing the actual lines. If you're working with a collaborator, this is the time to discuss the options and be sure you're in agreement about what constitutes the essence of your song. There is not necessarily one "correct" way to approach your title, but you need to determine what you believe will be the strongest, most accessible meaning of your title.

Define what your title means to you, distill it down to a phrase or two, and write it on the top of your page. For example:

- The multiformat smash "How Do I Live" can be summarized as:
  If you leave, how will I get along without you?
- For "The Wind Beneath My Wings," you might jot down:
  You give me strength; I'm who I am because of you
- For "I Can Love You Like That" you might write:
  I can give you the kind of love described in classic stories and movies

Step 2: Outline the Story

Decide on the ideas and general information that need to be conveyed in the first verse of your song to clearly lead to the title. This is the verse lyric's primary function. There may be many options; however, be certain that the lyric that precedes the chorus supports the title. This is the point in the creative process when you decide what the "story" is—before writing the actual lines.

When you have determined what ideas and information to include in the first verse, decide what additional information will be included in the second verse to develop the story further and lead the listeners to the second chorus. If you decide to add a bridge, outline the idea that you want the bridge to express—prior to writing the actual lines—just as you did for your verses and chorus.

While the function of the verse lyric is to tell the story and lead to the chorus, the chorus' job, lyrically, is to provide a setting to showcase your title. Remember that the chorus is not the place to introduce new, detailed information into the story. It's a summation of your idea, the place to reiterate your title and hammer it home.

Step 3: Write the Actual Lines of Lyric

Now that you know, in a general sense, what information your lyric needs to convey, it's time to begin the process of crafting the strongest lines to express your idea. The tools and techniques described throughout the remainder of this section will help you get your idea across in a conversational, fresh, interesting way, utilizing detail and imagery.

Remember that there are no hard and fast rules in songwriting—what I teach are tools and guidelines based on my analysis of successful songs. With this in mind, understand that there have been many successful songs that do not tell a story in a literal fashion, but instead are built using abstract imagery. While it's true that most of these songs were written by the artists who recorded them, notable exceptions include Tim McGraw's "She's My Kind of Rain" (written by Robin Lerner and Tommy Lee James) and Natalie Imbruglia's "Torn" (written by Phil Thornalley, Scott Cutler, and Anne Preven). Likewise, there have been many successful songs with lyrics that were quite literal that were written and recorded by the artists who wrote them. Examples of these include Michelle Branch's "Are You Happy Now?" and John Mayer's "Your Body Is a Wonderland." So write what you love—but if you hope to hear your songs on the radio, remain aware of the marketplace.

For artists writing for themselves or their own bands—and for those collaborating with artists writing for their own projects, it's worth keeping in mind that you have more latitude to express your ideas lyrically in an abstract, nonliteral fashion—if that is your choice. For you, the sound of the words and the images you choose may be more important than their actual meaning.

When writing lyrics that are not intended to tell a literal story, your job may be to forget about tools and techniques and explore ways to access your subconscious and your deepest levels of creativity. But remember that songwriting is an art of communication and ultimately your goal is to evoke emotion.

WRITING ABSTRACT LYRICS

As in any abstract artistic medium, there are no rules or guidelines for creating abstract lyrics. If your goal is to write lyrics that do not tell a literal story, your job is not to adhere to prescribed tools and techniques, but to open yourself up and leave your internal censor behind. However, it is advisable to avoid predictable phrases, clichés, and over-used images.

Many writer/artists, such as Alanis Morissette, Leonard Cohen, Train, Sting, Creed, Joni Mitchell, Clint Black, Annie Lennox, and many alternative pop, rock, and folk writers sometimes write songs that are abstract, nonliteral, and nonlinear. They seem to be nonrepresentational expressions of the artists' innermost thoughts and feelings. So, what makes some of these lyrics "great" while others remain mediocre? These writers have honed the ability to write words that somehow circumvent our consciousness and get through to our hearts. Their lyrics are a perfect complement to the feelings induced by their music. Although we may not know exactly what these artists' words meant to them, they touch us and evoke a feeling. See where your muse leads you. Explore a wide variety of imagery. You will learn from trial and error which of your abstract lyrics touch you—and your listeners.

CHAPTER 3

Acquiring the Tools for Successful Lyric Writing

I think it was the simplicity and the universal appeal of the lyric that made "I Swear" so successful. The lyric was so simple that everybody could understand it. The message was very clear.

GARY BAKER (Songwriter, "I'm Already There," "I Swear," "Once Upon a Lifetime," and cuts by artists including the Backstreet Boys, Reba McEntire, Joe, and LeAnn Rimes)

The tools of successful lyric writing are skills that can be acquired—with practice, patience, and lots of hard work. These techniques are not a substitute for a powerful idea that excites you and cries out to be written; they are methods to help you successfully convey your ideas to your audience.

EXPRESSING ONE IDEA AND ONE EMOTION

Effective lyrics are crafted in such a way that listeners can clearly understand the story and/or feel the emotion the writer intended to evoke. Keep in mind that the listener may be driving down the interstate and neither have a lyric sheet nor know what you meant to say or what you had in your mind. You only have three to three-and-a-half minutes and probably somewhere between twenty-four and thirty-six different lines of lyric in which to tell your story. That leaves no room for subplots and extraneous details. Ideally, you should be able to express the idea of your song in one sentence, and the lyric needs to stick to that focus. For help mastering this tool, refer to Step One of the Three-Step Lyric-Focusing Technique in Chapter 2 (page 39).

Evoking emotion in your listener is the ultimate goal of songwriting. No matter what you feel when you write a song, if that feeling is not awakened in your listener, you have not successfully communicated. To clearly convey the desired emotion, your entire song should express the same emotion. Your "canvas" is too small to contain varying emotions in different sections. From the opening lines of your first verse, the listener should have no doubt what it is the singer is feeling. It will confuse the listener and fail to elicit the desired emotional response if the singer is happy in the first verse, angry in the chorus, and ambivalent by the bridge.

What I look for in a song is quite simply something that makes me happy or sad, or something that can make me laugh; something that evokes an emotional response; something that moves me. Chances are if it moves one heart, it will move others.

DEBBIE ZAVITSON (Independent publisher/A&R rep)

Effective lyrics clearly let the listener know how the singer feels, but without coming right out and saying it. Instead, imagery is used to help the listener vividly envision the scene and empathize with the singer. For example:

- *She said, "This hurt goes deeper than your words can heal"*
- *Heartache is written in smeared mascara that falls down from her eyes*
- *Sadness hangs over her like a storm cloud in the desert*

These examples leave no doubt about what the character in the song is feeling. Yet, the lyrics never actually say, "She is sad."

MAINTAINING ONE CONSISTENT TENSE AND TONE

If you've chosen a natural, conversational tone for a particular lyric, it is important to use it consistently throughout the song. Do not interrupt a sincere, heartfelt sentiment with an occasional humorous line or a clever twist on words. Likewise, a lyric that is essentially a series of funny twists on words will not work if one or more lines written in a deeply personal, emotionally vulnerable tone are interjected. Effective lyrics maintain one consistent style and tone throughout.

A common pitfall is switching verb tenses. It's an easy mistake to make. Be sure to maintain a consistent tense throughout the lyric.

INCORRECT:
We used to go for walks
Beneath the summer skies
The sun is so bright
All I saw were your eyes

In this example there's an abrupt switch from past tense (*We used to go for walks*) to present tense (*The sun is so bright*), and back to past tense (*All I saw were your eyes*).

CORRECT:
We used to go for walks
Beneath the summer skies
The sun was so bright
All I saw were your eyes

Mixing pronouns is also a recipe for confusion. It is crucial to refer to the subject or object of the song in a consistent manner. The following example illustrates the common problem of interchanging pronouns inappropriately.

INCORRECT:
When I first met her
She was warm and true
Yes, the love that I wanted
I found with you

CORRECT:
When I first met you
You were warm and true
Yes, the love that I wanted
I found with you

or

When I first met her
She was warm and true
Yes, the love that I wanted
Came from out of the blue

If your lyric is written in the first person (speaking directly as the character in the song) be sure that all the pronouns that describe the singer are "I," "me," "my," etc. and that those pronouns that relate to the person the singer is singing to refer to "you." If you choose to write from the third person (telling your listener about the person) be sure to consistently use pronouns like "he," "she," "him," or "her." (Refer to "Point of View: Deciding Which 'Voice' to Write From," Chapter 2, page 36.)

It also needs to be clear to the listener exactly to whom the pronouns refer. If there is any doubt, replace the pronoun with information that clarifies the situation.

INCORRECT:
Mama and Susie went dancing last night
She danced every dance till dawn

It is unclear who danced every dance—Mama or Susie.

CORRECT:
Mama and Susie went dancing last night
Mama danced every dance until dawn

Unintentionally changing tone, tense, or pronouns is a common pitfall. Reread your lyric after you've completed a first draft to be sure that you haven't confused the listener by abruptly changing these elements.

DEVELOPING STRONG OPENING LINES

*I look at the first two or three lyric lines and I know within ten seconds of
listening to the intro whether the song is worth listening to any further. I look
for a wonderful opening line or some imagery that grabs me and moves me.*

JUSTIN WILDE (Publisher, Christmas & Holiday Music; writer, with cuts by artists
including Barbra Streisand, Barbara Mandrell, Ray Charles, and Loretta Lynn)

When I was screening songs for the A&R (Artists and Repertoires) Department at RCA Records in Los Angeles, I'd often take home a box overflowing with submissions by hopeful song-writers, publishers, and artists. During the forty-five-minute drive in the inevitable bumper-to-bumper traffic, I'd try to get through as many songs as possible. I'd pop one into the car stereo and although I'd generally listen through about half of the first chorus, I'd usually draw my conclusions within the first fifteen seconds.

This was all the time I needed to assess the sound of the demo and the opening two lines of lyric and melody. In these few seconds I could pretty much decide if I was listening to something special enough to bring to my boss' attention. Since RCA had a "No Unsolicited Submissions" policy, almost all of the songs I listened to came from major publishers, staff-writers, managers, or entertainment attorneys, so most of them were pretty good. But "pretty good" wasn't good enough when only "exceptional" stood a chance of beating out the competition.

Songs that make it to the next level have to jump out of the pack right from the start with opening lines of melody and lyric that grab the listener immediately. Without a strong opening, the listener will not be psychologically prepared to be impressed with a song. Even if the chorus is a smash, the song will have to overcome a lukewarm initial impression—and it's easier to grab a listener's attention immediately than it is to get it back once you've lost it.

In addition to having a melody and lyric that instantly tell the listener, "This song is special; you're about to hear a hit," the job of your first two lines includes setting the song's emotional tone. By the time listeners have heard the second line of the lyric, they should know what emotion the singer is feeling. Those opening lines need to be unique, fresh, and interesting (both melodically and lyrically) to separate your song from the "pretty good" ones.

In songwriting, as in life, you only get one opportunity to make a first impression. After your initial flow of inspiration, go back and rewrite your first lines to make them as strong as possible, keeping in mind that someone may soon have a finger poised on the eject button, giving you only fifteen seconds to convey that your song is a smash.

Following are examples of attention-grabbing opening lines:

- *Well, I went to bed in Memphis and I woke up in Hollywood*
  "Steve McQueen," WRITTEN BY *Sheryl Crow and John Shanks;* RECORDED BY *Sheryl Crow*

- *He wore that cowboy hat to cover up his horns*
  "Brokenheartsville," WRITTEN BY *Randy Boudreaux, Clint Daniels, Donny Kees,
  and Blake Mevis;* RECORDED BY *Joe Nichols*

Look over a lyric that you've written or are currently working on and jot down the opening two lines. Try rewriting those lines, expressing the sentiment five different ways. Be sure to incorporate fresh, detailed imagery and/or an original angle. Then choose the strongest opening lines—and don't settle for your first draft.

MAINTAINING CONTINUITY

If your intention is to tell a story (as opposed to writing an abstract lyric), each line needs to advance the development of your story with no information gaps. Do not assume your listeners know what you know about the story and characters. Present them with all of the pertinent information if your goal is to successfully communicate. Artists writing for themselves may choose to apply this tool or not, contingent upon whether their desire is to tell a literal story in a given song, or to evoke emotion through the use of abstract imagery and symbolism.

Each line of lyric should flow from the line that precedes it and into the line that follows it. For example:

INCORRECT:

I held you close and said, "I love you"
I was late for work yesterday
The dog was barking when I woke up
This feeling just won't go away

CORRECT:

I held you close and said, "I love you"
And saw my love reflected in your eyes
And in that moment when I kissed you
Baby, there was no doubt in my mind

Although this example does exaggerate the point, it is essential that each line maintain a smooth connection to the lines that come before and after. It is especially important that the last line of each verse is crafted to serve as a "springboard" to deliver listeners to the chorus. That final line of each verse is the link between the verse information and the summation about to be presented in the chorus. For example:

INCORRECT:

VERSE
I held you close and said, "I love you"
And saw my love reflected in your eyes
And in that moment when I kissed you
No matter how hard I tried

CHORUS
I'd found a once-in-a-lifetime love

VERSE
I held you close and said, "I love you"
And saw my love reflected in your eyes
And in that moment when I kissed you
There was no doubt in my mind

CHORUS
I'd found a once-in-a-lifetime love

Note that in the correct example, the last line of the verse dovetails seamlessly into the first line of the chorus. In the incorrect version, there is no logical connection between the meaning of the last line of the verse and the first line of the chorus. Also, when using an A - B - A - B - C - B structure it is important to connect the last line of your bridge lyric to the first line of the chorus that follows it.

INCORPORATING DETAIL, ACTION, AND IMAGERY INTO LYRICS

One of the basic rules of strong lyric writing is "Show—Don't Tell." This is important for all songwriting genres, but it's essential for successful country and rap lyrics. Pop, urban, and other styles of music tend to include lyrics that state how the singer is feeling, but the most effective lyrics in any genre allow the listeners to feel as though they are witnesses to the scene, thereby allowing them to feel what the singer feels. There is no more powerful way to draw listeners into your story than through the use of detailed, specific imagery. A song entitled "She's Lonely" might be expressed with the following "pictures":

- *She stays up all night crying in that big old empty bed*
- *She plays solitaire every Saturday night*
- *She sips her wine at a table for one*
- *She sits alone in the dark, watching the same sad old movie on TV*

The lines listed above make it very clear how this woman feels—without ever saying, "She is lonely." They use action and place the character within a setting evoking far more empathy than lines like:

- *Oh, she's so lonely without him*
- *She feels so blue deep inside*
- *Loneliness is all she feels*
- *Her heart is breaking with loneliness*

When learning how to avoid the common pitfall of telling how the singer feels, it can be helpful to visualize the video for your song. Then use words to "show" the listeners what the singer is "seeing."

The lyric below illustrates several common problems. It tells how the singer feels and uses very general descriptions, as opposed to unique, specific imagery.

THE NICEST PLACE I KNOW

I never owned a house
Now I own one with a beautiful view
I can watch how pretty it is
When it's sunny outside
Or when the moon is out at night
Shining in the sky
I know I'm lucky
Not just because I own this home
But because of what I see
There inside the house

CHORUS
There's my little boy
Who's cute as can be
And my little girl
Who's learning new things every day
And there's also my wife
And what makes me happiest
Is appreciating THE NICEST PLACE I KNOW

I've been many places
Because of my work
I've seen so many places and things
They were more beautiful than I can express
Especially the scenery all through our country
But I always enjoy going back home
To my wife who I love
Home is everything to me
Nothing makes me happier
Than THE NICEST PLACE I KNOW

(REPEAT CHORUS)

I know how good my life is
When I think about all the gifts I've been given

(REPEAT CHORUS)

Compare this lyric, one line at a time, with the following. Note how much more effective it is to include the details and vivid, fresh descriptions.

MY FRONT PORCH LOOKING IN

The only ground I ever owned was sticking to my shoes
Now I look at my front porch and this panoramic view
I can sit and watch the fields fill up
With rays of glowing sun
Or watch the moon lay on the fences
Like that's where it was hung
My blessings are in front of me
It's not about the land
I'll never beat the view
From MY FRONT PORCH LOOKING IN

CHORUS
There's a carrottop who can barely walk
With a sippy cup of milk
A little blue-eyed blond with shoes on wrong
'Cause she likes to dress herself
And the most beautiful girl holding both of them
And the view I love the most
Is MY FRONT PORCH LOOKING IN

I've traveled here and everywhere
Following my job
I've seen the paintings from the air
Brushed by the hand of God
The mountains and the canyons reach from sea to shining sea
But I can't wait to get back home
To the one he made for me
It's anywhere I'll ever go and everywhere I've been
Nothing takes my breath away
Like MY FRONT PORCH LOOKING IN

(REPEAT CHORUS)

I see what beautiful is about
When I'm looking in—Not when I'm looking out

(REPEAT CHORUS)

WRITTEN BY *Richie McDonald, Frank J. Myers, and Don Pfrimmer;* RECORDED BY *Lonestar.*

While both lyrics express essentially the same idea, note how much more interesting, and involving, the second lyric is. It doesn't simply state the facts—it shows the listener the scene by using fresh, detailed imagery in a natural, conversational manner:

- *I never owned a house* vs. *The only ground I ever owned was sticking to my shoes*
- *I've seen so many places and things—They were more beautiful than I can express* vs. *I've seen the paintings from the air—Brushed by the hand of God*
- *There's my little boy—Who's cute as can be* vs. *There's a carrottop who can barely walk— With a sippy cup of milk*

EXERCISE: LEARNING TO TELL THE STORY—NOT THE FEELINGS

This exercise will help you further master the technique of involving your audience, by allowing the listener to "witness" the scene and feel what the singer feels, instead of being told how the singer feels.

In a notebook, list three detailed images that will allow the listener to "see" each of the following. Find ways to paint the scene so that the listener will have no doubt that:

- *He's in love*
- *I'm glad you're gone*
- *I can't get you off my mind*
- *I miss you*
- *I feel like dancing*

The songs are always important (when I sign an artist) because as someone wiser than me said, "It always starts with the song." My main advice to developing writers is to try to tell a story and to create a visual, either with a narrative that the audience can relate to or through evocative imagery and metaphor. Too many writers are lazy in this area, feeling satisfied with using generic and recycled phrases and images we have all heard a thousand times before.

JEFF FENSTER (Senior Vice President of A&R, Island/Def Jam Records)

No one else in the world shares your life experiences, or your unique way of interpreting and processing the events and images around you. Only you have experienced the specific heartaches, joys, fears, and loves that have touched your life. So, while it is true that you cannot write a Diane Warren lyric, a Babyface lyric, or a Jeffrey Steele lyric, they can't write a lyric that reflects your experiences and expresses your distinctive way of looking at the world, either.

Being vulnerable, exposing your pain, fears, hopes, disappointments, and desires in your lyrics is scary. But dig down deep. Avoid using tired old clichés and images that have been heard countless times. Draw on those experiences that are yours, and yours alone, to infuse your lyrics with honesty and individuality. That's what will make them special and give them the power to touch other hearts—and cause publishers, record label executives, and listeners to choose your songs over the competition.

> *Be aware of the market, but don't try to copy what you're hearing. I encourage writers to put a part of themselves in each song, so that it is their own; so that it is something I don't already have.*
>
> JOHN VAN METER (Chief Creative Officer, New Sheriff Music Publishing)

I once collaborated with a writer who seemed to be doodling and drawing stick figures all over his lyric notes. When I asked him what he was doing, he said his publisher suggested that he include more "pictures" in his writing! The bad news is that writing lyrics that include colorful pictures, action, and detail does not come effortlessly to most writers. It is much easier to tell the listeners how you feel than to evoke those feelings with the use of imagery. But the good news is that this is a skill that can be learned and improved with practice—and it can help take your lyrics to the next level.

EXERCISE: INCORPORATING DETAIL, ACTION, AND IMAGERY INTO LYRICS

1. Close your eyes and imagine a scene in which you are about to tell someone that you love him or her. After visualizing the setting in detail, grab your notebook and do the following:

   - Describe where you are. (For example, on the front porch; parked in front of the house in Daddy's old blue pickup truck; wrapped up together in a faded old Indian blanket on the cold, hard basement floor; etc.)

   - If you're indoors, describe the room, including the furniture, using as much detail as possible. (For example, there are two old oak rocking chairs with faded green paisley cushions, side by side in the living room; the last embers of a fire are turning cold in the carved oak fireplace that Grandpa built in 1902; our feet are up on that ugly glass coffee table Mama bought on sale at the Salvation Army thrift shop; etc.)

   - If you're outside, describe the setting in detail. (For example, leaning up against Jimmy's 1972 red Mustang convertible, in the parking lot behind the Longhorn Grill; there's not a single other car left this late; a sliver of a crescent moon is lighting up her face and there's just one star in the sky; the neon sign that says "Best Steaks in Texas" has just been turned off; etc.)

   - Is there music playing? If so, describe it in detail. Is it live, or from a radio or jukebox? Loud or soft? What's the song? Is it fast or slow? What are the instruments? Who's singing? (For example, I could barely hear a scratchy old recording of Nat "King" Cole singing "Unforgettable" coming from the jukebox in the next room; the boombox bass was thumping so loud I could feel the vibrations in my bones; an elderly woman with skin like leather was softly singing a Spanish folk song; etc.) (continued)

- Describe the sounds you are hearing. (For example, crickets; the whisper of the north wind coming down through the ravine; silence as loud as a scream; a whippoorwill singing a love song to his lady; ear-splitting electric guitars; Billie Holiday's voice coming out of an old TV; the sound of her breathing while she sleeps; the echo of high heels on a hardwood floor as she leaves; etc.)

- Describe the weather in detail. Is it windy, rainy, warm, chilly? (For example, it was hotter than July on the bayou; the ache in my bones told me the first snow of the season was on its way; a first hint of spring was in the air; the thermometer said it was 99 degrees but I knew it was a liar; the Santa Ana winds whipped down from the hills; etc.)

- Note the time, explaining how you know what time it is. (For example, the rooster crowed its morning wake-up call; the clock down the hall chimed three times; I heard the midnight train blow its whistle in the distance; the alarm clock said it was 2:22 a.m.; etc.)

- Provide a detailed description of what you're sitting, standing, or leaning on. (For example, sitting on a blanket of soft, warm grass; propped up against Grandma's old blue brocade couch, the one with the frayed gold tassels and the overstuffed cushions; leaning up against a red leather barstool; stretched out on the backseat of a silver limousine; etc.)

- Describe what's happening in your body. (For example, hot tears started flowing from my eyes; my heart was pounding like a jackhammer; I looked down and saw that my hands were trembling; a smile spread all over my face; etc.)

2. Now try this exercise again, this time imagining you're about to tell someone, "It's over."

You probably won't use the majority of the images you come up with in any one song. It would be overkill and there's not all that much room in a three- or four-minute song. But having these details at your fingertips will help tremendously as you learn how to show instead of tell. Until you get used to telling your story with images, it is helpful to begin each song by following the steps of this exercise, as it applies to that song. You may be amazed at your ability to generate these "pictures."

KEEPING IT CONVERSATIONAL

Think Wal-Mart—not Hallmark.

JASON BLUME

The most effective lyrics sound natural, like something you would actually say in normal conversation—not like flowery sentiments you might find in a greeting card. A lyric is not a poem. Well-written lyrics (as opposed to poems):

- Conform to a structure.
- Are concise to accommodate a song length of 3–4 minutes.
- Have sections or specific lines that are crafted to be repeated.
- Are intended to be sung, not read silently or aloud.
- Use rhymes that sound natural (poetry may or may not use rhymes).
- Take into account the actual sound of the words, not just their meaning.
- Are crafted to lend themselves to strong melodies.

Artists who write their own lyrics have much more latitude to include symbolic, abstract, and poetic lines. For example, the opening lines to Madonna's "Ray of Light" work beautifully for this artist's self-written hit, but would probably not be appropriate in a song that you hope to pitch to artists who do not write their own material.

Zephyr in the sky at night I wonder
Do my tears of warning sink beneath the sun

From "Ray of Light," WRITTEN BY Madonna, William Orbit, Dave Curtis, Clive Muldoon and Christine Leach; RECORDED BY Madonna

Read the lyric for "These Days" on page 13 to see an excellent example of a conversational style of writing. It's easy to imagine that the singer would say these actual words when speaking to someone.

KEEPING YOUR IMAGERY FRESH

> *Don't write generic crap.*
>
> GEMMA CORFIELD (Former Vice President of A&R, Virgin Records)

As in every element you include in your songs, it's crucial to use images that are fresh and original. Including detailed, unique, visual images within your lyrics will be one more reason why a publisher, record label executive, or producer might choose your songs over the competition.

> *What I look for in a song is kind of like going on a blind date. You can describe the perfect mate and be given that but still something could be missing. So for me, it's what excites me, makes me passionate, twists my gut in knots... it's a feeling. More technically, (I look for) an interesting lyric. How many ways can you say "I love you" without using the word "love"?*
>
> JUDY STAKEE (Vice President of Creative Services, Warner/Chappell Music Publishing)

If you come up with predictable, obvious lyrics, thousands of other writers will likely have had the same ideas. Stay away from trite clichés and overused phrases and dig deeper to find fresh, new ways to express yourself. If your lyric includes lines such as *Holding hands under the moon, Make a brand new start,* or *Under the stars above,* why should an artist choose yours over the ones submitted by proven hitmakers, the artist's producer—or his or her boyfriend?

A word of caution: While you need to use detailed, specific, fresh images, millions of others still need to identify with your song. Your lyrics will not connect with your listeners if the images you choose are out of the realm of normal experience. For example, when deciding on a unique setting for the story of your song to unfold, the following locations might be effective: at the top of the Ferris wheel; in tenth-grade chemistry class; or in the very last row of the movie theater. Avoid locations that are so unusual that no one will realistically be able to relate to them, such as: sitting by the glow of the nuclear reactor in Chernobyl; albatross hunting in New Zealand; or on the operating table in the cardiac ward. Find that happy medium that straddles the line of being fresh and distinctive, while still sounding natural and conversational.

EXERCISE: FINDING A NEW WAY TO SAY IT

Look over one of your lyrics and circle any words or phrases that state how the singer, or the character being sung about, is feeling. Circle any words that describe an internal state, instead of using imagery to show what could literally be observed. For example, you might circle:

- *She's lonely*

- *I'm blue as can be*

- *She's filled with happiness*

- *I'm furious*

- *He's completely crazy*

Now replace each of your circled phrases with three detailed images that "show" what each of these states looks like. For example, phrases that express *He's completely crazy* might include:

- *He stands naked on the roof and howls at the full moon on frozen winter nights*

- *Last night he whispered to me that he was born on Neptune*

- *He says that the woman who left him twenty years ago talks to him every night through the television*

EXERCISE: USING FRESH IMAGERY

It's important that your lyrics include images that are fresh, detailed, and natural. For example:

Sitting in this place
With these thoughts
At this time
Having this feeling

might be expressed with fresh imagery and detail as:

Sitting cross-legged on the hardwood floor
Thinking of us growing old together
As the grandfather clock chimes two
Your smile whispers a promise of forever

Replace the following title and lyric with detailed, specific images. You might want to repeat this exercise several times, each time using a new title and additional imagery. You may be surprised at your ability to generate "pictures" within your lyrics.

I LOVE YOU

VERSE 1
Here in this setting
In this frame of mind
Doing this stuff
Here's what I want you to know

CHORUS
I love you
This is how much
This is how long I'll feel this way
This is how it feels
So in case you're wondering
I LOVE YOU

VERSE 2
In the future
If you have any doubts
Remember this time
And you'll know

(REPEAT CHORUS)

CREATING A LYRIC PALETTE

As visual artists use a palette of colors to create their art, it can be helpful for songwriters to develop a "palette" of words and images applicable to each song before beginning the process of actually crafting the lyric. Sometimes referred to as "word clustering," this process provides instant access to words and phrases that relate directly to the title. It's an effective way to ensure that your title will have maximum impact and will pay off. A palette of images and phrases for the title "It's Heaven" might include: *angels, golden halos, hell, angel's wings, silver clouds, St. Peter, the pearly gates, harps, eternity,* and *heavenly songs.*

While you certainly won't use all of the related images you come up with, using some of them will add to your title's effectiveness by infusing it with color, detail, and imagery. But remember that the ultimate goal is to evoke emotion. Overloading your lyric with clever images and phrases can make it sound less conversational and more like a novelty song. A lyric palette is an important and powerful tool; use it—but use it sparingly.

EXERCISE: CREATING A LYRIC PALETTE

In your notebook, create a palette of at least ten words or phrases for each of the following titles:

- "Grandma's House"
- "The High School Prom"
- "Daddy's Old Chevrolet"
- "Sunday Picnic"
- "Christmas Back Home"

- "The Midnight Train"
- "Dancing All Night"
- "Louisiana Saturday Night"
- "Halfway to Mexico"
- "Sunset Beach"

AVOIDING REDUNDANCY

"Department of Redundancy Department, how may I be of assistance to help you?" As silly as this phrase may seem, repeating and rehashing the same ideas and images within a lyric is a common problem. To avoid this pitfall be sure that each line:

- Makes a contribution.
- Furthers the development of the story.
- Gives listeners a greater understanding of how the singer feels.

Remember that you have a relatively small number of lines, and only about three or four minutes in which to tell your entire story and evoke the desired emotion in the listener, so there's no room for redundancy. Make every line and every word count.

Harlan Howard, the Irving Berlin of country music, taught me the simple but important art of editing. Every syllable should have a purpose. He told me, "If a songwriter can take out a word in a lyric then it doesn't need to be there, kid."

AMY SMITH HEINZ (Wilderness Music)

AVOIDING PREACHING (UNLESS YOU'RE IN CHURCH)

Sometimes the desire to share a feeling or belief is so powerful that the temptation is to cut to the chase and tell your listeners what they "should" feel. But keep sight of the fact that the goal is to successfully deliver the emotion and message from your heart to the listener's. You can get your point or moral across much more effectively by allowing your story to evoke the feelings, rather than telling listeners what they should feel. Instead, draw the audience into the scene so they can empathize with your point of view and feel what you feel.

When Mark D. Sanders and Tia Sillers wrote Lee Ann Womack's Grammy-winning Country Song of the Year, "I Hope You Dance," their message was expressed as a loving suggestion and a wish for the listener: "I Hope You Dance"—not "Life Is Short So You Better Dance."

When Sandy Knox and Steve Rosen wrote Reba McEntire's hit, "She Thinks His Name Was John," they presented a heartbreaking, detailed story of a one-night stand that resulted in AIDS. The listeners felt they knew the woman in the song. They could understand why she made her choices and were able to share her sorrow. By simply telling a story, that song touched and educated millions of people without ever coming out and saying, "Don't sleep around. If you do, you could get AIDS and then you'll be sorry." No one likes to be told what to do or how to feel, and it's an arrogant stance for the singer to imply that he or she knows all the answers. Avoid preachy phrases like:

- *So don't ever...*
- *You better always...*
- *I'm telling you to...*

WRITING THE DREADED SECOND VERSE

A truly great song has a beginning, middle, and end—just like a good book. The second verse should give me some information, some continuance of the story that I didn't learn from the first verse. When I listen to songs as a producer I always at least listen through the middle or the end of the second verse just to see if the story ever develops. I want to be brought along and have something new unfold to keep my attention.

STEVE GIBSON (Producer of artists including
Aaron Tippin, Engelbert, and Randy Travis)

Many writers find that writing the second verse is their most challenging songwriting task. The second verse's function is to:

- Continue the story.
- Add new information.
- Bring the listener back to the title.

When you read a book, if the second and third chapters reiterate the same information you've already learned from chapter one, it's unlikely that you will keep reading. Without continued character and story development, you would soon lose interest in the book—and it's the same way with songs.

When it's time to write a second verse, it can help to visualize yourself within the scene and allow it to unfold. A guaranteed way to avoid repeating information you've already covered is to ask yourself the following questions:

- Then what happened?
- What else happened?

By answering one or both of these questions in your second verse, you'll avoid the common pitfall of rehashing information from your first verse.

EXERCISE: ADDING NEW INFORMATION TO THE SECOND VERSE

For the following scenarios, craft a second verse that advances your story by answering either "Then what happened?" or "What else happened?" Write each second verse in your notebook.

1. VERSE 1
   I picked you up at eight
   We went dancing
   And as I held you close
   There was no doubt (It was)

   CHORUS
   THE MOST WONDERFUL NIGHT OF MY LIFE
   All of my dreams came true
   THE MOST WONDERFUL NIGHT OF MY LIFE
   Is every night I spend with you

2. VERSE 1
   When I picked up the phone
   I was surprised to hear your voice
   But not nearly as surprised
   As when you said

(continued)

CHORUS
LET'S TRY AGAIN
To love one more time
LET'S TRY AGAIN
And again till we get it right

3. VERSE 1
I tossed and turned all night
In this big old empty bed
I kept remembering
Every single word we said

CHORUS
HOW COULD WE HURT EACH OTHER LIKE THAT
With angry words we can't take back
Can we turn around from where we're at
HOW COULD WE HURT EACH OTHER LIKE THAT

USING RHYMES: WHERE TO, WHEN TO, HOW TO, AND WHY TO

It has been said that rhyming began as a way to aid in memorization, prior to the written word. Rhymes are an important part of successful lyrics. They help us to remember the words, and people who listen to popular music have been unconsciously trained to anticipate rhymes in certain places, although they are probably not aware of it. If your rhymes fail to appear where the listener expects them, he or she will likely feel as though something is missing.

Effective rhyming:

- Helps hold the listener's attention.
- Contributes to making the lyrics easy to remember.
- Provides a sense of completion and satisfaction for the listener.

While rhymes can be an important component of your songs, the meaning of what you say is far more important than the rhymes. It will not work to sacrifice the idea of the lyric or the conversational tone in order to force a line to rhyme. The most effective rhymes sound effortless. You can almost always rewrite a lyric to change the final word of a line that will need to be rhymed, without altering the meaning of the line.

In the example that follows, the writer has written himself into a corner. There are no rhymes for the word "orange."

We walked through fields together
While the sun turned to orange
And as night fell from the sky
A new love...

However, the line can be restructured to end with an easier word to rhyme—without changing the basic meaning.

We walked through fields together
And watched the orange sun
And as night fell from the sky
A new love had begun

Another common pitfall is inverting the natural order of your words to force a rhyme. For example:

If you would give me one more chance
To give you all the love I feel
From now until the end of time
My foolish pride I will conceal

In this example, the natural order of the words in the last line has been inverted and the word "conceal" has been chosen to force the rhyme. In normal conversation you would never say, "My foolish pride I will conceal." By changing the final word of the second line you can avoid the need to settle for an unnatural-sounding rhyme, while still maintaining the meaning of the line.

If you would give me one more chance
To give the love I feel inside
From now until the end of time
I'll put away my foolish pride

Types of Rhymes

Rhymes come in a variety of forms. Perfect, slant, masculine, feminine, triple, and internal rhymes are the primary types writers of popular songs employ.

Perfect Rhymes "Perfect" rhymes are exact rhymes. The sounds of the final accented vowel and the final consonant (if applicable) are identical, while the preceding consonants are different in each of the rhyming words.

For example:

- Tree - Free
- Boat - Coat
- Girl - Pearl

Slant Rhymes While perfect rhymes were required in the era of Irving Berlin, Cole Porter, and the Gershwins, they are not mandatory in current, popular music. Perfect rhymes are still used regularly, but while some purists may insist on them, if you listen to any popular radio station you'll hear they are not required to have a hit song. The option is to use "slant" rhymes, words that invoke a sense of rhyme without rhyming exactly. For example:

- Love - Touch
- Hurt - Were
- Mind - Time

It is perfectly acceptable to use a mix of perfect rhymes and slant rhymes within the same song. Indeed, the majority of popular songs blend several types of rhymes. This adds aural interest.

A common pitfall is using words that appear as though they should rhyme when they are on the written page, but do not actually rhyme when they are pronounced. For example:

- Anger - Danger
- Again - Rain
- Love - Prove

Another common mistake to avoid is the use of pairs of "rhyming" words that are spelled differently, but sound alike. These are not rhymes, but identical sounds, or homophones. For example:

- Blue - Blew
- Through - Threw
- New - Knew

Masculine Rhymes A masculine rhyme is one in which only the last syllable rhymes. This can occur as either a one-syllable word (Boy - Toy) or as the last syllable of a multisyllabic word (About - Without).

Feminine Rhymes Feminine rhymes are two-syllable or "double" rhymes with the emphasis on the syllable preceding the last syllable (Lover - Discover).

Triple Rhymes As the name implies, in triple rhymes, the last three syllables all rhyme (Vanishing - Banishing).

Internal Rhymes Internal rhymes are rhymes that occur within the line (If you feel it's real). They can add extra appeal as long as they sound natural and do not get in the way of expressing the meaning of the lyric. While internal rhymes may be used in every genre of music, they are regularly found in rap songs. Note that internal rhymes do not replace the rhymes at the end of lines, but are used in addition to them.

Rhyme Schemes

The most common rhyme schemes for segments containing four lines employ rhymes that occur at the ends of lines 2 and 4 or lines 1 and 2 *and* lines 3 and 4. Although it is not used as frequently, it is acceptable to rhyme lines 1 and 3 and lines 2 and 4. It is typically not effective in a four-line section to rhyme only lines 1 and 2 or lines 3 and 4.

If a section of your song is comprised of six lines, one option is to treat the first four lines as suggested above and rhyme line 5 with line 6. Another rhyme scheme for verses or choruses that are comprised of six lines rhymes lines 1 and 2, lines 4 and 5, and lines 3 and 6. For example:

1. *I know what's on your mind*
2. *I've known it for some time*
3. *But I promise it's not time for leaving*
4. *I won't let you go*
5. *Girl, until you know*
6. *That baby, it's not time to stop believing*

While it's not important that you learn the technical names of the various types of rhymes and rhyme schemes, it is important that you know how to use them. If your first verse rhymes line 1 with line 2 and line 3 with line 4, your second verse will typically follow the same pattern. Likewise, if your first verse rhymes lines 2 and 4, these lines should also rhyme in your second verse.

It is most effective to be consistent in the types of rhymes used in different verses (i.e., if the first verse contains masculine rhymes, the second verse should contain masculine rhymes). But it is preferable to vary the specific vowel sounds of the rhyming words you use in different sections of a song. For example, if the first verse relies heavily on rhyming "E" sounds (i.e., Free - Tree), you should probably avoid "E" sounds in the chorus. It will also make it easier to find rhyming words if you have a variety of sounds to choose from.

Note that the songs recorded by performing songwriters sometimes include fewer rhymes and fewer perfect rhymes than those songs that are recorded by artists who do not write their own songs. This is especially true in urban, folk/Americana, and alternative rock music.

USING A RHYMING DICTIONARY AND THESAURUS

I initially avoided using a rhyming dictionary and a thesaurus, thinking that using someone else's ideas would compromise my artistic integrity. Then I read an interview in which Stephen Sondheim, Pulitzer Prize-winning Broadway composer and lyricist, said that he regularly uses a rhyming dictionary. If it's good enough for Sondheim.... It's neither realistic, nor necessary to be walking rhyming dictionaries and thesauruses. But why not use every available tool to have the fullest range of words and possible rhymes at your fingertips?

Most of the words listed in a rhyming dictionary or thesaurus will probably never find their way into a song. But some of them may spark an idea that leads your lyric in a new, unexpected direction. The rhymes, words, and phrases you select and how you use them will reflect your own unique creativity. The rhyming dictionary I've found most helpful is Sue Young's *The New Comprehensive American Rhyming Dictionary* (Avon Books, New York). There are also some terrific rhyming dictionaries that can be purchased or downloaded from the Internet for a fee. MasterWriter is an excellent tool that includes a rhyming dictionary, thesaurus, and more.

USING THE LIST TECHNIQUE

Many successful song lyrics are written by using a technique of "listing" a series of examples that relate to, and clearly lead the listener to, the title. This approach, sometimes referred to as the "Laundry List" technique, may be used throughout an entire lyric or in just a portion of it (i.e., the verses or the chorus). For example:

BETTER THINGS TO DO

I could wash my car in the rain
Change my new guitar strings
Mow the yard just the same
As I did yesterday
I don't need to waste my time crying over you
I've got BETTER THINGS TO DO

WRITTEN BY *Terri Clark, Tom Shapiro, and Chris Waters;* RECORDED BY *Terri Clark.*

This chorus lyric was crafted by listing the things the singer could do, followed by a "setup" line (in bold type). The setup line serves as a link between the items in the list and the title, and helps to prepare the listener for the title. The title summarizes the idea and the images in the list. When using this technique, every line does not need to be a part of the list.

Note that the usage of original, detailed ideas within the list adds much more interest than expressing the same idea in a more ordinary way. Compare the above lyric with the one that follows:

I could work or read a book
Watch television or listen to the radio
Call a friend on the phone
Or go for a walk...

"List" songs sometimes use images that are the opposite of the title. In the following lyric the verse is comprised of a list of things you can do, followed by a chorus that says, "But don't...."

ACHY BREAKY HEART

You can tell the world you never was my girl
You can burn my clothes up when I'm gone
You can tell your friends just what a fool I've been
And laugh and joke about me on the phone
You can tell my arms to go back to the farm
You can tell my feet to hit the floor
Or you can tell my lips to tell my fingertips
They won't be reaching out for you no more
But don't tell my heart
My ACHY BREAKY HEART...

WRITTEN BY *Don Von Tress*; RECORDED BY *Billy Ray Cyrus*.

EXERCISE: PRACTICING THE LIST TECHNIQUE

For each of the titles that follow, list five phrases or images that will lead to that title. For the purpose of this exercise the lines do not need to rhyme or have any specific number of syllables. Do not settle for lines that are less than fresh and unique, and don't forget that sometimes the most effective way to set up the title is with a list of images and ideas that are the opposite of the title. (In each instance, one example is included.)

1. "I Don't Think She Loves Me Anymore"
   Example: *I sent a dozen roses and called a dozen times but haven't gotten one call back*

2. "It Must Be Love"
   Example: *It must not be the flu 'cause I don't have a fever*

3. "That's Her Idea of Fun"
   Example: *She drives her Daddy's new Corvette at ninety miles an hour*

4. "Don't Say Goodbye"
   Example: *Say there's one chance in a million*

5. "I Think I Must Be Dreaming"
   Example: *I don't think I died and went to heaven*

6. "If You Said You Didn't Love Me"
   Example: *I would cry a thousand tears*

Examples of other songs that have successfully employed the list technique include "21 Questions" (50 Cent), "7 Days" (Craig David), "I Try to Think About Elvis" (Gary Burr), "If I Ever Lose My Faith in You" (Sting), and "Fifty Ways to Leave Your Lover" (Paul Simon).

LOOKING FOR OPPOSITES AND TWISTS ON WORDS

The first year that I was signed as a staff-writer for Zomba Music I was in awe of the talent of the Nashville lyricists. They seemed to have an amazing ability to find clever twists on words. I thought that those writers must be geniuses. I couldn't imagine I would ever acquire the ability to twist and turn phrases the way they did. I've since learned that finding those clever twists on words is not the result of innate talent, but like so many other aspects of the songwriting process, it's a skill that can be developed and improved through practice.

The first step to using clever twists on words is learning to look for opposites. For example:

- "(I'm a Real *Bad Boy*, but I'm) a Real *Good Man*"
- "*New* Way to Light Up an *Old* Flame"
- "*Don't* Tell Me What to *Do*"
- "Time Has *Come* to Let You *Go*"

You can also create interesting wordplay by using the past tense. For example:

- "You Really Had Me *Goin'*—Now I'm *Gone*"
- "Once I *Held* What He's *Holding*"
- "I Want to *Feel* What I *Felt* Back Then"

The use of opposites is a powerful tool and an important one to master, but use it sparingly. Unless you are writing a novelty song, being overly clever can sometimes distract from the genuine emotion that the song ultimately needs to communicate.

EXERCISE: LOOKING FOR OPPOSITES AND TWISTS ON WORDS

1. For each of the words in the list that follows write its opposite or, if applicable, its past tense.

2. Write a full line of lyric that includes the word and its opposite or past tense.

Example: long (the opposite is short)
For a long time you've been coming up short on love

• Easy	• Will	• Right	• First	• This
• More	• Fast	• Day	• Single	• Weak

To practice this skill, when you are working on new lyrics, circle those words that are especially important to the meaning of your song and ask yourself what each one's opposite (or past tense) is. Although using opposites and wordplay are techniques most commonly used in country music, they can also be effectively used in other types of music, as in Joan Jett's hit, "I Hate Myself for Loving You" (cowritten with Desmond Child).

USING ASSONANCE AND ALLITERATION

I'm very aware of sounds of words as well as what kind of sound is being sung when a note is being held. I don't go overboard. You certainly have to go with exactly what you feel, but you're not going to sing a sound like "it" over a long note. You're going to look for an open vowel sound that a singer can sing. I want to encourage people to be unique, but also to be aware of how things sing.

STEVE DIAMOND (Emmy Award-winning songwriter, "Not a Day Goes By,"
"I Can Love You Like That," "Let Me Let Go," and cuts by artists
including Eric Clapton, Britney Spears, Reba McEntire, and Willie Nelson)

Since lyrics are intended to be sung, their sound is sometimes just as important as their meaning. "Assonance" and "alliteration" are fancy names for specific ways to use the sound of words to add interest to your lyrics.

Assonance is the technique of incorporating the same sounds on the stressed vowels of two or more words to create interest aurally. For example:

- You *say* no *way*
- Hold *on* or I'm *gone*
- This *time* you'll *find* you're *mine*

Alliteration is the use of two or more consonants that have the same sound. Using this tool can help to make a lyric catchier, more memorable, and pleasing to the ear. For example:

- I'm *falling forever*
- Now I'll *never know*
- "The *Way We Were*"

EXERCISE: USING ASSONANCE AND ALLITERATION

Write one full line of lyric for each of the words that follow. In each instance, use the tool of assonance or alliteration to add interest to the line—while still maintaining a natural, conversational meaning.

ASSONANCE	ALLITERATION
Example: Strong	Example: Help
I'm too str*o*ng to go *on* like this	*H*elp me—I'm *h*urting

ASSONANCE
- Light
- Ever
- Dream
- Believe
- More

ALLITERATION
- Kiss
- Sound
- Heart
- Baby
- Give

When alliteration and assonance are used effectively, they sound so natural and organic to the lyric that they are barely noticed. Examples of hit songs that incorporate one of these techniques include: "Love You Out Loud" (Rascal Flatts), "Maybe It Was Memphis" (Pam Tillis), and "Soak Up the Sun" (Sheryl Crow). Alliteration and assonance can add interest to your lyric when used sparingly, but overusing them can distract the listener from your message. Don't lose sight of the fact that the meaning must always be the top priority.

SAVING KEY WORDS

"Key" words are those words that are especially distinctive and memorable within your lyric. They often occur in your title. For example, in "The Wind Beneath My Wings" the key words would be "wind," "beneath," and "wings." Overusing these words can diminish their impact. Using this title as an example, it would probably create maximum impact if you avoided using the words "wind," "beneath," and "wings" in your verses and bridge. Find other ways to express these concepts throughout the lyric—and save these specific words for your title. Likewise, when you incorporate an especially unique or unusual word or phrase within your verse, it is typically best to use this word or phrase only once within the lyric.

WRITING THE BIG PAYOFF LINES

The function of "payoff" lines is to provide a sense of satisfaction and completion for the listener. The payoff, most often found at the end of the chorus, is the line that ties the song together. It provides the emotional punch, or surprise, and adds impact to the lines that precede it. For example:

LESS EFFECTIVE:
I WANNA DANCE WITH SOMEBODY
I wanna feel the heat with somebody
I WANNA DANCE WITH SOMEBODY
Because I like the music

MORE EFFECTIVE:
I WANNA DANCE WITH SOMEBODY
I wanna feel the heat with somebody
I WANNA DANCE WITH SOMEBODY
With somebody who loves me

From "I Wanna Dance With Somebody," WRITTEN BY *George Merrill and Shannon Rubicam;* RECORDED BY *Whitney Houston.*

In the example of the less-effective way to complete the chorus, the listener is left with a sense of "So what?" In Whitney Houston's hit, the payoff line at the end of the chorus raises the lyric to a whole new level by bringing in an additional element to the lyric. When Houston sings, "I wanna dance/feel the heat with somebody" in the first three lines, it means she wants to dance and *anybody* will do as a partner. But the inclusion of the payoff line, "With somebody *who loves me*," brings a new element and additional emotion to the lyric.

WRITING LYRICS TO AN EXISTING MELODY

You may be called upon to write a lyric to a melody that someone else has written, or you may want to write a lyric to one of your own melodies. In either case, there are techniques that can make this process easier:

- Listen to the melody over and over again and ask yourself what emotion it is expressing. Does the melody seem to be happy, sad, angry, wistful, exuberant, timid, or defiant?
- Define the musical style. An urban/R&B song or a dance track will require a different lyrical approach than a folk or a rock song.
- Decide if you are targeting a specific artist or a particular type of artist. For example: a young teenage pop group, a mature female jazz artist, or a hard rock band.

Hopefully, the melody will inspire an idea for a lyric. If not, while listening to your melody, with all of the above considerations in mind, look over the list of titles, concepts, images, and lyrical phrases that you keep in your hook book. One of these may jump out as the perfect mate for your melody—or one of them might spark an entirely new idea.

Sing along with the melody, utilizing nonsense syllables and whatever temporary "dummy" lyrics tumble out of your mouth. Your unconscious may have some terrific ideas, so keep your tape recorder running while you sing along—and don't invite your internal critic.

> *Don't underestimate stream of consciousness. Get on a microphone and make some vowel movements; you'll be amazed how much of the final lyric is in that gibberish.*
>
> KEITH URBAN (Recording artist/songwriter with platinum and Number One hits)

Refer back to the Three-Step Lyric-Focusing Technique (page 37); choose a title and be sure that you are clear about the concept and emotion you are trying to communicate—before writing the actual lines. When it's time to write your lyric you will now have to deal with the additional constraint of your words needing to fit into the existing melody. You may want to add or subtract a few notes from the melody in order to accommodate your words. In some instances this might make your melody even stronger. However, if this weakens the melody, keep working on your lyric. Do not sacrifice a strong melody to cram in, or take away, a few extra words.

Once you have decided on the concept you hope to express, craft takes over. Finding a way to express your thoughts so that they match your melody is like working a jigsaw puzzle. Through trial and error, shift your lyrical puzzle pieces around until you find the perfect fit. The most effective lyrics place emphases on places where we would have them in natural conversation. Whether you are writing to an existing melody or crafting a melody to fit a lyric, be sure that the important words are paired with notes that will allow them proper and natural emphasis. Likewise, you do not want your melody to stress words or syllables that are not the ones you want to stick in your listeners' minds. For example, in Joe Nichols' Number One country hit, "The Impossible" (written by Lee Thomas Miller and Kelly Lovelace), the melodic emphasis falls on the second syllable of the word "im*pos*sible." It would not sound natural to emphasize the word "the." Nor would it be effective if the melody caused the emphasis to be on either the first or last syllable of the word "impossible" because we don't say it that way. Likewise, in Destiny's Child's "Survivor," (written by Beyoncé Knowles, Anthony Dent, and Mathew Knowles), when they sing "I'm a SURVIVOR," the melodic emphasis falls on the second syllable of the word "survivor." It would sound odd and unnatural if the emphasis was on the word "a," or if it had been on either the first or last syllable of the word "survivor."

In a sense, we write a lyric to our own existing melody every time that we rewrite one or more lines of our lyrics after we have decided on a melody. Like all aspects of the songwriting process, this is a skill that will improve with practice and perseverance.

EXERCISE: WRITING A LYRIC TO AN EXISTING MELODY

Copy the lyric of a recent hit song you love and wish you had written. If your goal is to write for artists who do not write their own songs, choose a song that was written by an outside writer. If you are writing primarily for yourself or your own band, select a song that was written by a performing songwriter, or a song that was written by the members of the band that recorded it. This lyric will become the template for a new lyric that you will write.

In crafting your new lyric use the same:

- Basic idea (i.e., positive love song, sad love song, social issue song)

- Song structure (i.e., A - A - B - A, A - B - A - B - C - B, etc.)

- Number of lines in each section

- Rhyme scheme (place your rhymes in the same places that the original song included rhymes)

- Approximate number of syllables in each line

- Tone of the lyric (i.e., clever, heartfelt, conversational, twists on words)

- Style of writing (i.e., literal, abstract, symbolic)

Create a new title, fresh images, and new ways to express the essence of the original lyric—while using the same set of tools that led to success for the writer of the existing lyric.

VISUALIZING A HIT

Part of your job as a lyricist is to get inside the minds of the characters you create in your songs. You need to express what is real for them. You also need to remember that the words that come from your heart and your pen will hopefully be coming out of a performer's mouth someday. The exercise that follows will help you to craft lyrics consistent with the images projected by the artists you intend them for.

EXERCISE: VISUALIZING A HIT

Decide which artist, in your wildest fantasy, you would most want to record your song. If you are an aspiring recording artist, you may be your fantasy artist. If you are not writing for yourself (or your own band), be sure to choose an artist who records outside material. Write down that artist's name.

Close your eyes and visualize a stage in front of an enormous crowd of cheering fans. Hear the announcer introduce your "dream artist" performing his or her Number One smash hit—your song! Pay attention to the details. Notice what the artist is wearing and what kind of accompaniment there is. Then "listen" to the artist singing your song. Let these images "write" your lyric. When the performance is over, soak in the praise and adulation of the fans. Then sit down backstage and have a discussion with the singer. Ask what the artist would want to convey in this song and what words and images he or she would use to say it. Now write down everything you "saw" and "heard." Include specific details—especially any lyric ideas the "artist" suggested.

It can also be effective to imagine hearing your song coming out of the radio. In addition to helping you write a "radio-friendly" lyric, this exercise may also help you create the melody and arrangement. Your fantasy artist may not be the one who ultimately records your song, but if that artist has a proven track record of hits, and you write a song he or she could potentially record, it's likely that song would also be suitable for a variety of other artists who have a similar style.

REWRITING YOUR LYRICS

Be yourself and then keep honing your craft. I know that a great song is rarely written quickly and that it is important to learn how to go back and rework, rework, rework until good becomes great.

KATHLEEN CAREY (Senior Vice President of Creative Affairs, Sony/ATV Music Publishing)

When I teach songwriting classes I often start by writing "Songwriting" on the blackboard. I ask if everyone is there for the songwriting class and when they all say "yes," I tell them that they're in the wrong place. I put a big "X" through "Songwriting" and replace it with "Song *Rewriting*."

Songwriting seems deceptively easy from a distance, but even the most experienced, successful writers work hard at their craft. Jimmy Buffett says that he wrote "Margaritaville" in six minutes, and it's true that, occasionally, the planets line up perfectly and a great song pops out very quickly, requiring little or no effort. Sometimes it almost seems as if a song has come "through" a writer, but a career cannot be based on these rare occurrences. It doesn't happen often, even for the most successful writers. When it does, it's a gift. But the chances of receiving this gift grow as we master our craft and internalize the tools and techniques that so often occur in successful songs.

> *Strip away all the filler. It may take three, four, five, ten rewrites. You don't need five more songs in your catalog. You don't need one more. You need one great one. It's too competitive to let yourself off the hook with lines that are just okay. Dig deep to find that part of you that makes it special and get rid of the things that you would discount if it was another person's song. It's just too competitive.*
>
> STEVE DIAMOND (Hit songwriter/producer)

It is said that Picasso painted up to a dozen versions of each of his most famous works, destroying each one until he felt it was the best it could be. Having to struggle and rewrite (and rewrite and rewrite) doesn't make you a bad writer—but failure to do so might.

My first cut, "I Had a Heart" (written with Bryan Cumming; recorded by Darlene Austin), was rewritten and demoed seven times by my collaborator and me. If I had stopped after rewrite number six, I might still be sitting behind a desk, saying how unfair the music business is, and never knowing that success was waiting just a rewrite away.

The most direct route to success is to rewrite each line of lyric and melody until it's the strongest you can possibly make it. This means that even after you like it, you might still want to try several different approaches to see if you can beat the one you've already got. If not, you can always go back to your original draft.

I still need an objective ear (my publisher or a trusted cowriter) to tell me where I'm hitting the mark, where I'm not, and to inspire me to push myself to do yet one more rewrite, even though it's already "good." In the absence of a publisher or collaborator you can get this input from a songwriting teacher or a qualified critiquing service.

> *I never was great at rewriting. I probably have a lot of songs that were never recorded because of that.*
>
> HARLAN HOWARD (Legendary Nashville songwriter)

When I received a call from my publisher asking me if I'd be willing to write a song to be considered as the end credit of a film (the song that plays at the end of the movie, while the titles scroll across the screen), I said, "Of course." He told me that the film company was looking for a song that lyrically would be inspiring and empowering for the young girls who would be its audience. He described the film's magical, fairytale theme and gave me a musical example of the kind of song they were looking for. There was only one catch. It was Friday afternoon and the song would need to be finished and on its way to New York City by Monday! I hung up the phone and grabbed my pen. (I never use a pencil or erase during the writing process because I never know when I might want to reconsider a line that I had thought wouldn't work—and paper's cheap.) An hour later I had finished a song with the lyric that follows.

AS LONG AS I BELIEVE

There's a fire—inside me
Lighting the way to guide me
To a mountain in the distance
Made of my hopes and my wishes

And I'm gonna do whatever it takes to find it
That's a promise to myself I'll make—just watch me climb it

CHORUS
There's a voice inside my heart
Saying reach out for that star
And don't be afraid to dream
There's a feeling in my soul
Telling me I need to know
That I can do anything
AS LONG AS I BELIEVE

Now the road is—getting clearer
It's waiting for me in the mirror
And when I'm scared—scared to move on
That's when I'll find I can be strong

And even if I take a fall I'll know—at least I tried
'Cause I know I wouldn't have these wings if I wasn't meant to fly

(REPEAT CHORUS)

(As long as I) believe in myself
And have no doubt it's true
There's nothing I can't do

(REPEAT CHORUS)

WRITTEN BY *Jason Blume.*

I was pleased with the work I had done; I knew that, musically, I had captured the feel the film company executive had requested, and lyrically, I'd done a good job of expressing the essence of the film's message of believing in yourself. But as I looked over the lyric, one line jumped out at me as truly exceptional: *I know I wouldn't have these wings if I wasn't meant to fly.* That line was special. Instead of simply stating the message in an obvious way ("I can do anything—as long as I believe"), it conveyed that idea in a more original, interesting, compelling manner. I went back to work crafting a new lyric that would revolve around that one special line. As I worked on rewriting the lyric, I changed the title, and new melodic ideas surfaced; rhythms, chords, and melodies that felt considerably catchier and more emotional than my first attempt. The new version, "Wings," was much stronger than my initial one. The resulting song was chosen to be the end credit theme in the animated DVD/video *Barbie of Swan Lake,* and in addition to having a chance to impart an important message to impressionable young girls and preteens, I was very well compensated. I doubt this story would have had the same happy ending if I had settled for my perfectly crafted first draft. Compare the lyric that follows with my first attempt and you'll see how much fresher and more interesting the rewrite became.

WINGS

I was living in a fantasy
Waiting for somebody to rescue me
But I found a way to light the dark
It was always here inside my heart
No more fairytale pretending
I'll make my own happy ending ('Cause)

CHORUS
If I wasn't meant to fly
I wouldn't have these WINGS
I wouldn't reach up to the sky
Every night—in my dreams
There's a voice inside of me
Saying I can do anything
'Cause if I wasn't meant to fly
I wouldn't have these WINGS

There's a star that's shining down on me
Reflecting everything that I can be
Every journey starts inside my heart
And there's no mountain that's too far
'Cause if I set my mind to it
Whatever it is—I can do it

(REPEAT CHORUS)

To take me farther
Than I ever thought I'd go
Higher than the heavens
'Cause deep inside I know

(REPEAT CHORUS)

WRITTEN BY *Jason Blume;* RECORDED BY *Leslie Mills for Mattel's* Barbie of Swan Lake.

The example listed above is certainly not the only time that rewriting a song has proved to be very rewarding for me. Shortly after Eugene Wilde and I submitted our demo of "Dear Diary" to the executives at Jive Records, I was told that they were very interested in having Britney Spears record the song. However, they felt the sad ending might not be the best approach for Britney's very young audience. (In the original draft of the lyric, the singer finds her boyfriend holding hands with her best friend and tells her diary that she's learned a lesson about how love can break your heart.) The A&R executive suggested that we rewrite the lyric to reflect a happier ending. Being the primary lyricist in the collaboration I wrote four completely new drafts of the lyric. In each version, the singer was still confiding to her diary; however, they each included a different, happier ending. I submitted the rewritten lyrics and kept my fingers crossed.

The lyrics were forwarded to Britney and she had some ideas of her own. The superstar asked my publisher if Eugene and I might be willing to sit down with her and possibly incorporate her ideas into the lyric. Britney's ideas were terrific and I spent an incredible day with her—a day I'll never forget. As you can see in the lyric on page 31 in the final version, the song ends with a bit of realistic uncertainty as the singer confides to her diary that she has "a feeling we'll be so much more than friends." While the ending to the song wasn't exactly "happy," the ending to my story was very happy. "Dear Diary" was included on Britney Spears' Number One, Grammy-nominated album, *Oops, I Did It Again...*, which sold more than sixteen million copies worldwide.

There may be instances when you are asked by an artist, a producer, or a record company executive to rewrite a song. If you feel strongly that rewriting the song will result in your being unhappy with it, you have to decide whether the integrity of the song is more important to you than getting this particular recording. When you have these opportunities, remember that you can always try to accommodate the artist by rewriting—with the understanding that you can revert to your original version if you're not satisfied with your new version.

In the majority of instances, when my songs have been recorded, artists or producers have made changes in vocal phrasing, chords, melodies, and in a few cases, even lyrics. Typically, the first time I learn about these changes is when I hear my song included on the finished album—and it's too late at that point to do anything but smile and say how wonderful it sounds. As the song climbs the charts, I typically grow accustomed to the changes and accept that while they may not have been my preference, they do not significantly detract from the song; the chances are that no one will even notice the changes but me. In fact, when I've been lucky enough to have my songs reach the top of the charts, those changes start to sound terrific to me!

I'm often asked, "But how can they do that? How can they change your songs?" The answer is that technically, artists are not permitted to change your songs without your permission. But the reality is that it's likely that some changes will be made as the result of artistic interpretation. Unless you have considerable clout, arguing about this may cause your song to be dropped from the album and will probably make it very unlikely that this artist, producer, and record label will ever record one of your songs in the future. In some instances, the artist and/or producer may even ask for a cowriting credit for his or her contribution to the song. If the artist has indeed made a major contribution, beyond artistic interpretation, it may be in your best interest to share the credit and resulting royalties. (Remember that 100 percent of nothing equals nothing.) However, this has to be evaluated on a case-by-case basis. If we choose to be professional songwriters, we must accept that when an artist records our song, he or she will likely make some changes to fit his or her style and artistry. If this is not acceptable to you, you have the option of writing for your own enjoyment; you don't have to let anyone record your songs.

EXERCISE: REWRITING A VERSE LYRIC

In your notebook, rewrite each of the following verse lyrics three times. For each rewrite, keep the idea the same, but change the images and the specific words. Feel free to change the length of the lines and where the rhymes occur.

Remember to:

- Use detail.

- Keep it conversational.

- Use fresh imagery.

- Allow the listener to "watch" the scene unfold.

1. *I held you close*
   That first night we danced
   And when I took you home
   I took a chance

2. *There's really good music*
   Where I go on Saturday nights
   Everybody has a lot of fun
   And they're feelin' alright

3. *When you said that you were leaving me*
   The first thing I did was cry
   Then I got really angry
   And then I told you why

MAKING EACH LINE ITS STRONGEST

I once read an interview with legendary songwriter/artist Leonard Cohen ("Suzanne"), in which he said that when he writes a lyric, he might spend the day filling an entire notebook and if one line actually makes it into the song, he's had a good day! At first, that seemed incredible to me, but then I realized that most songs don't have more than eight lines in each of two verses (sixteen); a maximum of another eight lines in the chorus; and at most another four lines of lyric in the bridge. That's a total of twenty-eight lines (although some songs might have a few more or less). Taking twenty-eight days to write a song with each line being an extraordinary line could produce twelve incredible songs per year. It's easier to get one great song published and recorded than a hundred "pretty good" ones.

> *John Huston's words helped me with the craft of powerful rewriting. He believed very strongly that no matter how wonderful a scene is in a film, if it's "off the spine of the movie" it will weaken the film. Sometimes it's very hard to cut out those "darlings," but if you can't or won't do what it takes to make your film powerful, then you are not being true to your art.*
>
> *A song is a three-minute movie playing to an audience with the attention span of a butterfly. Once you break the thread of your story, whether musically or lyrically, you've broken the spell and they fly away.*
>
> BARBARA ROTHSTEIN (Director, MusiCONCEPTS; songwriter with cuts in *The Barney Movie*, and by artists including Bobby Womack, Melba Moore, Kathie Lee Gifford, and Lisa Fisher)

Great songs are rarely written—they're rewritten (and rewritten and rewritten and...). Rewriting is one of a songwriter's most important tools. The exercise on page 75 is designed to encourage you not to settle until each line is the strongest you can possibly make it. And remember that rewriting is not confined to lyrics. Melodies can often be improved by exploring a variety of approaches instead of settling for the first melody we think of.

> *Don't fall in love with your song until it's a hit. Always stay open for possible revision.*
>
> RUSS REGAN (Former CEO, Motown Records)

In his book *Unlimited Power,* self-help guru Anthony Robbins writes that there is no greater predictor of success or failure in any venture than previous successes or failures of similar ventures under comparable conditions. For example, if you are considering opening a cookie store in a shopping mall in a Midwestern city, and cookie stores like the one you were contemplating have fared well in malls in other Midwestern cities with similar populations, that would be a good indicator of likely success. It's similar with songs—that's why I analyze the tools that have contributed to successful songs.

The tools presented throughout this book will help you express your creativity so that it is more likely that your audience will feel those emotions that you intend them to feel. Tools, techniques, and formulas are no substitute for artistry and for accessing and expressing the unique gift that is within each writer. Craft will not take the place of an emotional song idea that starts in your heart and is bursting to get out. When you share your creativity with the world through your songs, you're sharing a part of yourself and affecting those who listen; be sure that each line has been examined and is as strong as you can make it.

Some of these techniques are probably new ways for you to approach the writing process; it's not realistic to expect to master them instantly. But with patience, practice, and persistence, these tools can be successfully assimilated into your own songs.

> *I look for songs that set themselves apart from the pack; a different way of saying things, but something everyone can relate to. Try to bring something new to the game. Even though it is most difficult to find new ideas, that is really the key. Experience new things and see different parts of life. Find a new way to say something—not that you're going to find a new issue to cover on a regular basis, because most songs are about some type of love relationship (the good part, the bad part, or the ugly part). Express how people really feel without being contrived. I think the common factor in the songs I've gotten cut is a real direct link to human emotion: loss, true love, a good time. Find a way to tap into real emotion.*

LYNN GANN (Vice President, Full Circle Music Publishing)

ADDITIONAL LYRIC TIPS

It's best to avoid writing lyrics that cause the singer to tell the character within the song that he or she is singing to what this character would already know.

EXAMPLE:
That first time I kissed your lips the moon was shining down on us

The person to whom the singer is telling this already knows—*because he or she was there.* Instead, add information that the character would not know.

MORE EFFECTIVE APPROACH WOULD BE:
That first time I kissed your lips while the moon was shining down on us I felt like I could fly

Don't write lyrics that require the singer to be a mind reader.

EXAMPLE:
I know that all day long you think about me

This implies that the singer knows what another person is thinking and feeling.

I hope you think about me all day long
I wonder if you think about me all day long

Don't assume the listener knows what you know. If information about your story or characters is not included in the lyric your listeners will not know it. If it's important to you that your audience is aware of specific information, be sure to include it in your lyric.

WHAT IF I ONLY WRITE LYRICS?

An important part of every successful lyricist's job is to find those collaborators who bring out the best in them. Lyricists need to find composers who craft melodies that showcase their lyrics to their best advantage. Publishers and recording artists virtually never review lyrics without a melody, or melodies without a lyric, unless they are submitted by writers with whom they have previously established a working relationship. One of the reasons that publishers deal only with complete songs is that what may appear on paper as only an average lyric may be perfect when paired with just the right melody. This is especially the case in musical styles that are typically rhythm or groove driven, for example, dance, urban, and pop/R&B.

Lyricists can find potential collaborators by joining local songwriting organizations, attending concerts and performances at local clubs, and looking at songwriter Web sites. (See the Appendix for listings.) Never pay to have your lyric or poem set to music—unless you are doing so strictly for your own enjoyment, or to share with family and friends. Companies and individuals that offer a melody-writing service quickly crank out mediocre melodies to dozens of songs per day. Their ads typically run in supermarket tabloids, comic books, and magazines geared to writers, with copy that reads: "Hit Songwriters Will Set Your Lyrics and Poems to Music"; "Lyrics/Song-Poems Wanted"; or "Music Company Seeks Poems and Lyrics for Recording and Publishing. Free Evaluation."

Remember that a fresh, original, "Wow!" melody is a crucial and mandatory component of any successful song. It's extremely unlikely that your lyric will be matched with an exceptional melody by any of these services. If these composers were capable of writing hits, that's what they'd be doing—not churning out ten melodies a day for amateur lyricists who pay them. For additional information about scams see Chapter 14.

CHAPTER 4

Writing for Specialty Markets

Be generous in granting permission for live performances of your "specialty" songs. This is still the best way for other artists to hear your songs and begin performing them.

WAYNE MOORE (Owner, Ducy Lee Recordings; cabaret performer; songwriter/producer of music for television, film, and stage whose songs have been performed by artists including Michael Feinstein, Debbie Reynolds, Jill Eikenberry, Liz Torres, and Andrea Marcovicci)

In addition to writing mainstream pop, country, adult contemporary, and urban songs, there are many other genres songwriters might choose to explore. These include Christian, Latin, Christmas, folk/Americana, bluegrass, comedy, blues, jazz, cabaret, and children's songs. The primary focus of this book is geared to the songwriter who wants to write mainstream radio hits. However, this chapter explores the special considerations a writer should be aware of when writing and marketing songs for auxiliary markets.

When gearing a song to any specific market, it's important to remember that some lyrical and musical elements lend themselves to certain styles of songs and are quite inappropriate for others. For example, while poetic, offbeat, "nonlinear" lyrics may work well in an "alternative" pop or rock song, they'd be out of place in a children's song or a country song. It's important to use vocabulary and colloquialisms consistent with the genre you're writing for. For example, while a rap or hip-hop song might include a phrase such as "chillin' with my homeboy," this would obviously be out of character in a country song. Likewise, some chords and melodies are better suited for particular types of songs. Dissonant melodies and complex chords may be just the ticket for writing an effective jazz song, but are not suitable for a country or folk song.

When writing for specialty markets, the primary motivation needs to be a deep love of the music, because these styles of music are rarely as lucrative as the mainstream markets. But, whether you write commercial pop, country, R&B, jazz, children's songs, New Age, Christmas songs, or Christian songs, or write for any other genre, if you write them because your heart draws you to the music, you'll enjoy success regardless of the amount of money you earn.

WRITING SUCCESSFUL CHILDREN'S SONGS

When my collaborator Karen Taylor-Good offered me the opportunity to cowrite songs for country star Collin Raye's album of children's songs, I had never written a song for that market.

We crafted our melodies and lyrics by incorporating the same tools and techniques that we'd use to write successful songs in any mainstream genre. For each song, we started with a fresh, interesting concept, an idea that we wanted to share with children. While avoiding being condescending, we were careful to choose vocabulary and concepts that would be easy for children to understand. Melodically, we strove to craft beautiful, memorable melodies that relied on simple, short phrases and repetition, those which a child could readily sing along with and remember. Both of our songs were included on Collin Raye's *Counting Sheep* album and I learned that writing for the children's market requires the same skills and considerations as writing for any other genre. The ultimate goal is to write quality songs that successfully communicate lyrically and melodically with your audience.

> *Think about what you want to impart to children. In this market, you have the opportunity to say things of value in a very direct way that the adult market is too hip or cynical for. Start with wanting to say something of importance, wanting to pass something on to children.*
>
> DAVID FRIEDMAN (Composer of songs for *The Barney Movie*, *Aladdin and the King of Thieves*; conductor for Disney's *Beauty and the Beast, Aladdin, Pocahontas,* and *The Hunchback of Notre Dame*)

The market for children's songs includes film, animated television shows, live-action television shows, musical theater pieces, as well as audio recordings. Many writers of children's songs are also performers who record and distribute their own albums. These albums are sold at artists' shows and on the Internet, in addition to being distributed through traditional methods of sales.

Animated family-oriented musical films have, to a large extent, taken the place of live-action movie musicals such as *The King and I* and *The Sound of Music*. Enormously popular animated musical films, including *The Lion King, The Little Mermaid, Aladdin,* and *Beauty and the Beast,* have provided outlets for songs that appeal both to children and their parents. Songs from these films, such as "A Whole New World," "Go the Distance," "Circle of Life," and "Beauty and the Beast," have proven their appeal by becoming pop hits as well. When writing songs for children's films, the writer is creating an actual scene, driven by characters just as in any other musical theater piece. The lyric is crafted to further the story and is told from the character's point of view.

There are melodic and lyrical considerations that must be taken into account when writing songs geared specifically to children. Simple, memorable melodies and catchy, easy-to-sing choruses are found in most successful children's songs. Melodic lines that are crafted by using relatively few musical notes (and corresponding syllables) are easier to remember.

> *When you're writing for kids, just think wonderful songs. Don't think in terms of writing down to a kid. We used the same principles in writing the songs for the Barney scenes as we would in any sophisticated musical. Whatever your principles are, they're going to have to work for children, too.*
>
> BARBARA ROTHSTEIN (Writer of songs for *The Barney Movie*)

Children typically sing between middle C and the A or B above it. For very young children (three to five years old), it's best to use a small melodic range—between five notes and one octave—and avoid melodies that include complex musical intervals. However, when writing for a project that's geared to a wide range of ages (i.e., a Disney musical), it's acceptable and advisable to include some melodies that are more sophisticated.

The subject matter and language must be age-appropriate for children without being condescending. Choose words that your audience can readily understand. Lyrics can be both simple and powerful. Successful children's lyrics typically have a specific, narrow focus. Their stories stick to one idea, follow a thread, and make sense. Likewise, it's best to be very direct in terms of expressing the emotion that's being conveyed. The children's market is not the place for impressionistic, nonlinear lyrics. It's more effective to write: *I like hugs—I like smiles* than *Hugs and smiles are shadows of sunshine on winter snow.*

When writing for this market, it can be fun and effective to sometimes incorporate nonsense words, or words that you've created, such as "super-duper-ific," "happy-yappiness," or "bippity-boppity-boo." A prime example of this is the classic "Supercalifragilisticexpialidocious," from *Mary Poppins.*

Demo recordings of children's songs typically require less elaborate production than their mainstream counterparts. A well-produced keyboard/vocal or guitar/vocal demo that allows the listener to clearly hear the words and melody should be sufficient in most instances. However, as in any genre of music, when recording a demo for the children's music market, if there are musical or vocal elements that you feel are important to the song, include them in your demo.

There are also important business matters to consider when working in the children's market. To approach large film companies such as Disney or DreamWorks, it is necessary to be represented by a publisher or a theatrical agent who represents composers for television, film, and theatrical projects. These companies will rarely do business directly with songwriters. When writing for children's films or television shows, composers are typically paid an up-front, flat fee. They also receive the writer's share of the royalties generated by the sale of audio recordings, as well as performance royalties if the composition airs on television or radio. The writer rarely retains the publisher's portion of the royalties. Composers of music for children's television series are usually paid a weekly salary, as well as receiving performance royalties when the show airs on television.

There are occasions when a children's song, written specifically for a television show or film, is treated as a "work for hire." In these instances, the composer is paid a flat fee with no additional royalties for sales or performances. (See Chapter 11 for a detailed explanation of royalties and works for hire.)

As in all genres of music, networking plays a crucial role in successfully placing songs and generating income in the children's market. Unless your songs are placed in major films, in television shows, on or exceptionally successful albums, writing children's songs is not as lucrative as writing for mainstream radio formats. However, if that is where your heart leads you, it can be deeply satisfying and rewarding.

In recent years, a thriving new market has developed. Sometimes referred to as "tweens," those who are represented by this demographic are six- to twelve-year olds—whose parents account for significant album sales. Radio Disney, with affiliates in thirty-seven markets in twenty-one states, as well as a significant Internet presence, specifically targets these young music listeners. Many of the songs popular in this market are also hits on Top 40 radio. However, artists such as Aaron Carter and Dream Street have sold more than a million albums based primarily on the exposure they receive through Radio Disney—without garnering significant mainstream airplay. Additional artists who have enjoyed great success in this format include Hilary Duff, Justin Timberlake, Kelly Clarkson, and Britney Spears. While these artists are not producing what would typically be thought of as "children's" songs, much of their music appeals to listeners who are under twelve years old.

When writing and pitching songs for very young artists and for those whose fan base is primarily tweens, the music and production tends to be similar to the styles heard on Top 40 radio—however, the lyric content needs to be age-appropriate. Songs about having a crush, going to parties, friendship, dancing, and even falling in or out of love are all appropriate topics. However, overtly sexual references and mature themes should probably be avoided.

WRITING CHRISTIAN MUSIC

Writing lyrics for the Christian music market requires that you either be a Christian or understand Christianity implicitly. The audience can sense insincerity and a lack of biblical knowledge and will not tolerate either one.

REGIE HAMM (Universal recording artist/
songwriter with more than 400 Christian cuts)

Many songwriters enjoy expressing their religious beliefs through their songs. The burgeoning Christian music market provides an outlet for many of these songs. "Christian music" includes styles of music from folk to heavy metal, rap to rock, and everything in between. Reflecting the diversity in gospel music, Grammys are awarded in the following Christian music categories: rock gospel (e.g., Third Day, Jennifer Knapp, Audio Adrenaline); pop/contemporary gospel (e.g., Kathy Troccoli, Newsong, True Vibe); southern, country, or bluegrass gospel (e.g., Gaither Vocal Band, the Oak Ridge Boys, Randy Travis); traditional soul gospel (e.g., The Blind Boys of Alabama, Shirley Caesar, Dottie Peoples); contemporary soul gospel (e.g., BeBe Winans, Yolanda Adams, Fred Hammond); and choral music (e.g., The Brooklyn Tabernacle Choir, The Love Fellowship Choir, Victory in Praise Mass Choir).

What sets Christian music apart is its spiritual message—not the music, the melody, the instruments, the production values, or the quality of the performers. Many Christian artists, such as TobyMac, MercyMe, Third Day, and Jars of Clay, are as contemporary sounding as anything on pop radio.

When I think about the songs that touch me, they're the ones that go beyond the brain to somewhere deep in your soul.

RUSS TAFF (Grammy and Dove Award-
winning Songwriter/Christian artist)

Some writers make the mistake of thinking that their faith and the spiritual message of their songs override the necessity to write well-crafted songs. However, the best and most successful Christian songs present their messages with fresh, memorable melodies, catchy hooks, and well-crafted lyrics—all the same elements found in successful mainstream songs.

Faith and subject matter cannot be an excuse for substandard writing. The thing that makes Christian music unique is its message, not its music.

JIM VAN HOOK (Chairman/CEO, Provident Music Group)
as quoted in *Music Row* magazine.

The three largest Christian music companies are EMI Christian Music Group, Provident Music Group, and Word Entertainment. These companies are based in the Nashville area. EMI Christian Music Group includes Sparrow Records, Star Song Records, Forefront Records, EMI Gospel, re:think Records, Chordant Distribution Group, and EMI Christian Music Publishing. Their artists include Susan Ashton, Avalon, Steven Curtis Chapman, Andy Griffith, BeBe and CeCe Winans, Phil Keaggy, Twila Paris, Newsboys, Charlie Peacock, and Margaret Becker.

Provident Music Group, a division of BMG/RCA Label Group, encompasses Benson Records, Diadem Music Group, Tattoo Records, Verity Records, Reunion Records, Essential Records, Brentwood Records, Ranson Records, and Brentwood-Benson Music Publishing. Their artists include Bob Carlisle, 4HIM, Jars of Clay, Dino, Clay Cross, Kathy Troccoli, Gary Chapman, and Michael W. Smith.

Word Entertainment includes Word Records, Squint Entertainment, the Gospel Music Division, Everland Entertainment, and Word International. Their artists include Anointed, Amy Grant, Sandy Patty, Petra, John Tesh, Point of Grace, Cindy Morgan, Carman, and Shirley Caesar.

The larger Christian music publishing companies sign staff-writers, as well as artists who are also songwriters. As in any genre of music, those publishers that have a large staff of exclusive writers have less need to acquire songs that are written by outside writers. However, there are also smaller publishing companies that have success pitching songs to the Christian market—and smaller independent record labels that successfully operate in this market. The performing rights organizations, or PROs (the American Society of Composers, Authors, and Publishers, or ASCAP; Broadcast Music International, or BMI; and SESAC, formerly known as Society of European Stage Authors and Composers), the Gospel Music Association, the Southern Gospel Music Association, and of course, networking can help you to find these companies.

Christian/gospel music accounts for an estimated 4.5 percent of the domestic music market. In this genre, record sales are typically generated more from touring than from radio airplay.

Many artists sell the majority of their albums themselves, autographing them following performances at concert venues, as well as churches, Christian bookstores, and coffeehouses.

> *As far as getting established as a songwriter or an artist, the Christian market is very different from the pop or country markets. The best advice I can give is to get involved in your local ministry at your church. If you're writing songs and not performing them yourself, find people who are performing in your local area and try to get them to perform your songs. Success has a lot to do with your local ministry—especially if you want to be an artist. Start working at it at a local level in your own church to get people to sing your songs. The cream rises to the top. If you're doing a great job you'll get noticed. Then enter some contests.*
>
> *In the Christian market, lyrics are based on one specific book—the Bible. It's hard to find a new and creative way to say the same things over and over. The writers who do break through are the ones who have an amazing talent. It takes a very poetic person to say what has already been said in new fresh ways, or come up with new ideas of how to put something into music.*
>
> MARTY WHEELER (Vice President Publishing,
> Brentwood-Benson Music Publishing)

While a Top Five pop or country song may earn its writers and publishers $300,000 to $800,000 in performance royalties, an equally successful Christian song may generate only $10,000 to $30,000, to be split among its writers and publishers. This is because there are relatively few radio stations that play Christian music. Those stations that do play Christian music tend to be smaller than the major pop and country radio stations and therefore pay lower licensing fees to the PROs. Some stations broadcast Christian programming only during a portion of the day, or only during specific days of the week, also resulting in lower licensing fees. However, writers of Christian music may earn significant mechanical royalties as a result of sales. With total sales exceeding fifty million units per year, in recent years more than one hundred Christian/gospel albums were certified "Gold" (500,000 copies). At least twenty-five Christian/gospel artists have achieved lifetime album sales exceeding one million copies. (You'll learn more about licensing fees and royalties when you read Step 5.)

Those songwriters (who are not also artists) who earn their living by writing Christian songs tend to be those who procure numerous recordings of their songs on a regular basis—typically by cowriting with successful artists. Many Christian artists write or cowrite some, or all, of their own material; however, some Christian artists rely on outside songs. As in other musical genres, it's very difficult to place a "good" song—but an extraordinary song can still break through.

Any competent music publisher should be able to pitch songs for the Christian music market, provided that he or she is willing to do some research. However, if your primary focus is writing for this market, it is probably best to work with a publisher who is an integral part of the Christian music business. He or she will be more likely to have the personal relationships that are so important to successful song plugging, and will likely have better knowledge of which artists are currently looking for songs, as well as a better ability to discern which songs are best suited for specific Christian artists.

Contests, like those sponsored by the Gospel Music Association, are a good way to gain exposure for Christian music. (For more about contests, see Chapter 14.) It can also help to network with other songwriters and artists at Christian music festivals. (See the Appendix for a listing of Christian music festivals, as well as additional resources for writers of Christian songs.)

For important information about royalties paid for the use of songs in churches, see "Church Copyright License" in Chapter 11.

CRAFTING COMEDY SONGS

The most important consideration in crafting a successful comedy song is that it be funny— and accomplishing that can be a serious matter. Elements that may contribute to making a song funny include a fresh, humorous point of view about a familiar situation; something unexpected; puns; twists on words; outrageous characters; and a story or situation that makes people laugh. There are two types of comedy songs: parodies of existing songs and original humorous songs.

Parodies

Parodies are funny imitations of previously existing material. When writing song parodies, the original melody remains the same as the song the parody is based upon. However, a new, funny lyric replaces the original. For example, Cledus T. Judd turned Deana Carter's "Did I Shave My Legs for This" into "Did I Shave My Back for This," "Weird Al" Yankovic transformed Michael Jackson's "Beat It" into "Eat It," and Sue Fabisch changed "I Am a Man of Constant Sorrow" into "I Am a Mom of Constant Sorrow," with hilarious results.

When planning to write a song parody, it's essential to secure permission from the publishers of the song you are parodying. You must also determine the extent to which you'll be compensated for your efforts. In some instances, publishers may grant the right to allow a parody to be written and recorded; however, they may or may not consent to sharing the performance or mechanical royalties with the writer of the parody. This means that there are instances in which the writer of the comedy lyric earns nothing when the parody is played on the radio, or when recordings are sold. When recordings of the parody are sold or are performed on radio or television, the writers of the original song earn the same royalty as if their original version were being played or sold.

> *The same ingredients that make a ballad a hit song make a comedy song a hit song—a good story, well told.*
>
> RAY METHVIN (Producer/writer of comedy album by Shane Caldwell; songwriter, with cuts by artists including Clay Walker and Chris LeDoux)

If you're a comedy artist, in addition to being the songwriter, it may benefit you to include a parody of a hit song on your own album even if you don't participate in the writer's royalties. If your parody becomes a comedy hit, you'll earn royalties *as the artist* as a result of album sales. However, you can see why it's crucial to reach an agreement regarding royalties. (For additional information about royalties see Chapter 11.)

Original Comedy Songs

Songs in this category are original songs intended to make the listener laugh or smile. They may rely on outrageous situations, puns, twists on words, sarcasm, or other techniques to evoke humor. Some comedy songs are mildly humorous, while others can be described as slapstick—broad, boisterous comedy. As in any successful song, the lyric for a comedy song should be built upon the foundation of a fresh, unique concept—an original angle. Successful original comedy songs include "The Monster Mash" and "Grandma Got Run Over by a Reindeer."

There are several melodic considerations to keep in mind when writing for this market. First of all, keep your melodies simple to allow the listener to focus on the lyric, which is the most important aspect of a comedy song. Second, performers of comedy songs are not typically known for their vocal abilities. Most comedians have a limited vocal range and may not be able to make intricate melodic moves. For this reason, it is best to restrict the melodic range of a comedy song to approximately one octave and avoid tricky intervals that may be difficult for a "nonsinger" to sing.

Artists who record comedy songs sometimes enlist the help of a well-known singer to sing the choruses, while the comedy artist performs the verses—the spoken-word portion. This practice accomplishes two things: it adds to the quality of the recording by letting an accomplished vocalist sing the chorus, and lends a recognizable name to add credibility to the project and encourage radio programmers to play the single. For example, Alan Jackson sang the choruses of Jeff Foxworthy's hit "Redneck Games"; Bill Engvall's country hit "The Sign" featured Travis Tritt.

> *Most importantly, a comedy song needs a new point of view about a familiar situation; something unexpected. And it should get quickly to the point. If you have the opportunity to write "specialty" material for a particular artist, try to write in the distinctive voice of that artist. Ask yourself how he or she would tell the joke if they were speaking rather than singing. Find something true in that performer's life to write about, whether for a comedy song or not, and that truth will resonate with both the artist and the audience. Keep the melody simple so your listeners can focus on the lyrics. It has to be funny.*
>
> WAYNE MOORE (Musical Director and/or writer of material for comedy performers including Joan Rivers, Debbie Reynolds, Liz Torres, and Rose Marie)

The comedy song market is extremely limited. While there are hundreds of successful mainstream recording artists, there are only a handful of well-known artists who record comedy songs. These include Adam Sandler, Jeff Foxworthy, "Weird Al" Yankovic, Cledus T. Judd, Tom Lehrer, Mike Snider, the Capitol Steps, Thom Bresh, Ray Stevens, and Bill Engvall. Many successful performers of comedy songs write or cowrite their own material and few publishers actively seek out or pitch comedy songs. As in other musical genres, networking plays a key role in successfully placing comedy songs with performers, publishers, and recording artists. Performing your songs at writer's nights and encouraging other artists to perform your songs gives them increased exposure. The Songwriters Guild of America (see Appendix) periodically sponsors "Song Mania," a comedy songwriter's night and competition in Nashville. In addition to being great fun, it offers an excellent networking opportunity for writers of comedy songs.

When pitching a comedy song, an elaborately produced, full-band demo is rarely required. In most circumstances, a well-produced guitar/vocal or keyboard/vocal demo is sufficient. Since the lyric is the most important component of a successful comedy song, it's crucial that the words be easily understood. The demo singer's comic timing and delivery will also play a major role in conveying the potential of your song.

Ideas for comedy songs can be found in jokes, films, and on television; on T-shirts, greeting cards, and the Internet; or anywhere else you might find ideas for mainstream songs. Writing effective comedy songs may appear deceptively simple, but it's not easy to make people laugh. If you want to write successful comedy songs, in addition to analyzing hit comedy albums, it can be helpful to study comedy-writing techniques that can be found in books for stand-up comedians and writers in other comedy fields.

WRITING FOLK/AMERICANA SONGS

Folk music encompasses a wide range of musical styles, including songs written by contemporary singer/songwriters, traditional folk, bluegrass, protest songs, Cajun, Celtic, ethnic, and even polka music. Americana refers to the radio format that plays contemporary folk artists, such as Nancy Griffith, John Gorka, John Hiatt, the Chieftains, Lucinda Williams, the Woodys, Gillian Welch, and Patty Larkin. This format also plays bluegrass music and songs by alternative country artists such as Kim Richie, Rhonda Vincent, Nickel Creek, Johnny Cash, and Steve Earle.

Contemporary folk songs are written as forms of personal expression and aren't bound by the same rules that apply to pop, country, and urban/R&B songs. The words, images, and stories that are included in the lyrics of successful contemporary folk songs would typically be considered too personal, poetic, or, in some instances, too controversial for other mainstream genres.

The 1960s saw a resurgence in the popularity of folk music, with artists including Peter, Paul & Mary, Judy Collins, the Kingston Trio, the Weavers, and Joan Baez performing and recording traditional folk songs. However, many of these successful artists also recorded songs by contemporary folk artists such as Bob Dylan, Leonard Cohen, and Phil Ochs. Some of these songs, such as "Blowin' in the Wind," "This Land Is Your Land," "Puff (The Magic Dragon)," and "Where Have All the Flowers Gone," have become such an integral part of our musical milieu that they seem as though they're traditional folk songs. Easy-to-sing memorable melodies, simple straightforward lyrics, and stories that appeal to listeners of all ages and backgrounds have made these songs modern classics.

> *I don't sit down and set up a structure and force a song. I just write what I'm feeling inside but it seems that a lot of folk artists write because they've got to write. Although I don't feel like I'm writing for a "market," fortunately, a market has presented itself for this kind of music, because it really has something to say. It's powerful, personal, and intelligent. Writers in this market strive to come up with uncommon metaphors and unusual lyrics that people find riveting because it's not the same trite sentiment they've heard over and over. In the folk and Americana market the best writers take a few momentous things that happen in people's lives and transform them into real poetry. They're the modern-day troubadours.*
>
> CAROL ELLIOTT (Kerrville Folk Festival performer
> featured on *The Women of Kerrville* album; winner of
> the Wrangler Award for Best Western Song of the Year,
> recorded by Michael Martin Murphey and Bryndle)

The vast majority of folksingers perform their own material. The contemporary folk scene is dominated by performing songwriters who were influenced by traditional folk music and now write and perform their own songs. It's very difficult for a writer who is not a performer to earn a living writing folk songs. Even the most successful folk recordings rarely sell more than 50,000 to 100,000 units, and many very talented artists sell less than 10,000 units. Although artists such as Shawn Colvin and Tracy Chapman have emerged from the folk scene to win Grammys and sell hundreds of thousands of albums, many listeners now consider them pop artists.

Many contemporary folksinger-songwriters earn a large portion of their income by recording their own albums and selling them following performances at folk festivals, coffeehouses, and concerts in private homes (known as "house concerts"), as well as on the Internet.

These artists are not necessarily looking for other artists to record their songs. However, some savvy pop and country artists keep a finger on the pulse of what's happening in the contemporary folk community because some of the most original, powerful songs have emerged from that genre. Bruce Springsteen, Bette Midler, Garth Brooks, Kathy Mattea, Trisha Yearwood, and Rod Stewart are just a few of the mainstream artists who have recorded contemporary folk songs. Often, these songs find their way to recording artists via unconventional routes. While they are occasionally pitched by publishers, more often these songs are stumbled upon by an artist who hears them being performed live at a coffeehouse or folk festival, or in a recorded form on a contemporary folk artist's CD.

> *It's very difficult to make a living in the folk genre. It involves a lot of hard work. In most cases you're doing everything yourself. You're your own booking agent, your own publisher, and manager, and that's a lot of full-time jobs for one person. So know that that's what you want to do and believe in it. Try and write the best songs that you can write—the ones that feel good to you. Don't copy other people's work or try to conform to a certain formula in your writing. While that may work in some markets, it's probably not the way to go in folk music.*
>
> *I just try to write a good song; one that communicates something worth hearing, or feeling, or knowing about, in a way that people can understand—if not on a literal level, on an emotional level. Songwriting speaks to people's hearts even more than their intellects. The brain is only part of the equation. For me, when I'm writing it, a good song makes me think, "Wow—this is cool, I think I'm onto something here."*
>
> BUDDY MONDLOCK (Performer and recording artist
> whose songs have been recorded by artists including
> Peter, Paul & Mary; Garth Brooks; Art Garfunkel;
> Janis Ian; Nancy Griffith; and Joan Baez)

Some publishing companies sign one or more folk-oriented singer-songwriters to acquire songs that might be appropriate for those mainstream artists who occasionally record material that's more left of center. These companies can be found by networking with other songwriters and by referrals from songwriters' organizations.

Folk festivals, such as the Falcon Ridge Festival, the Philadelphia Folk Festival, the Swannanoa Gathering, and the Kerrville Folk Festival, offer an excellent opportunity to network with other songwriters and performers, as well as a chance to hear artists who are successful in this genre. Many of the festivals sponsor songwriting classes, song camps, and competitions that have served as stepping stones for many artists to launch or advance their careers. A comprehensive listing of music festivals can be found at www.festivalfinder.com.

The Folk Alliance Web site (www.folk.org) is a tremendous resource for songwriters and artists in the folk genre. This Web site offers links to folk festivals, as well as to folk societies and organizations, performance venues, song camps and conferences, record companies and distributors, radio stations, print media, agents, managers, promoters, and performing artists. Artists and writers interested in the folk/Americana genre should also be aware of the Americana Music Association (www.americanamusic.org), an advocacy group for professionals in the field. The organization offers a resource guide, as well as excellent networking opportunities through area showcases and a yearly conference held in Nashville.

CRAFTING SUCCESSFUL CHRISTMAS SONGS

Find different ways of saying the same old thing. Before Mel Tormé and Bob Wells wrote "The Christmas Song" you never heard the lines And folks dressed up like Eskimos or Jack Frost nipping at your nose. What a wonderful way to say, "It's cold outside." With the imagery you can feel the sensation.

> JUSTIN WILDE (Publisher, Christmas & Holiday Music; writer and publisher of songs including the five-million-selling "It Must Have Been the Mistletoe," which has been included on thirteen compilation albums and recorded by artists including Barbra Streisand, Barbara Mandrell, Kathie Lee Gifford, and Vikki Carr, as well as cuts with Anita Baker, Toby Keith, Ray Charles, and Loretta Lynn)

It's not surprising that many songwriters dream of writing the next "White Christmas." Irving Berlin's holiday classic has sold more than thirty million copies, making it the best-selling song of all time. A successful Christmas song can generate income for many years and has the potential to be recorded by multiple artists. However, there are far fewer slots for Christmas songs than for nonseasonal songs.

I think the thing about writing Christmas songs is not to reinvent the wheel. Christmas is a time of familiarity, of things you know that bring comfort and nostalgia. I think great holiday songs should reflect that. With that being said, I would say take a familiar theme or structure and try to elaborate on it. One of my favorite sayings is "Watch what everybody else has done—and don't do it." What I mean by that is take the instrumentation, the groove, a singer that may have a voice that lends itself to that style of music—but think of a different way of saying it. For example, "It's Christmas again" could be restated as "It's Twelve Twenty-Five again." Think outside the box lyrically but keep the music familiar.

> GREG BARNHILL (Cowriter, Lee Ann Womack's "Season for Romance" and "Forever Christmas Eve," with additional cuts by Lonestar, Trisha Yearwood, and Brian McComas)

Most fans purchase Christmas albums to hear their favorite artists' renditions of the Christmas standards they grew up listening to, so the majority of the songs recorded on Christmas albums are standards. Anne Murray has recorded three Christmas albums and out of the more than thirty cuts there is only one original song. A large percentage of the original (nonstandard) songs included on Christmas albums are written by the artist, the producer, or another individual "inside" the project. Your Christmas song must be incredible enough to make the artist or producer bump one of the standards or their own original songs to put yours on the album. The competition is fierce because only a handful of artists record Christmas songs each year. There are only so many Christmas images out there, so you have to work extra hard to craft fresh, unique lyrics in order to have your song rise above the competition. However, as in any style of music, the extraordinary songs usually find a way to break through.

What I look for in Christmas songs is the same thing any nonseasonal publisher would look for. If you want a Christmas song to become a standard, it has to have a melody that is so memorable that after you've heard it three or four times you should be able to hum the majority of the melody. It should be something that the average man or woman can sing a cappella on the front porch steps or in a rest home.

JUSTIN WILDE (Songwriter/Publisher,
Christmas & Holiday Music)

Christmas songs are typically recorded from December to July, prior to the Christmas season when they are released. Depending on schedules, some artists record their Christmas album during the Christmas holidays for the following year. If the album is one of those that is recorded live during Christmas, with a choir and orchestra, the songs are typically selected by the previous August or September, which is fifteen or sixteen months prior to the album's release. The bulk of country Christmas albums are completed by the end of May, while pop and R&B Christmas albums are sometimes recorded up through the July prior to their Christmas-season release.

I listen to everything that comes through the door and I've gotten cuts on songs from unpublished writers, but they sent me brilliant material. You have to go through 150 to 200 pieces of junk to find that gem.

JUSTIN WILDE (Songwriter/Publisher,
Christmas & Holiday Music)

Any reputable publisher should be aware of which artists are recording Christmas albums—and should be capable of getting material to those artists, or those who screen songs for them. Justin Wilde's Christmas & Holiday Music is the foremost publisher of holiday music and has placed holiday songs with artists including Barbra Streisand, Anita Baker, Vince Gill, Toby Keith, Johnny Mathis, Tanya Tucker, Melissa Manchester, and The Brooklyn Tabernacle Choir. I'm aware of two writers who published Christmas songs with Justin Wilde's Christmas & Holiday Music as a result of contacting the company after learning about it in the first edition of this book. For song submission guidelines contact Justin Wilde by visiting the company's Web site at www.christmassongs.com.

First, if you look at all the Christmas standards like "Winter Wonderland," "Chestnuts Roasting...," "White Christmas," and all those other evergreens, they have very simplistic, memorable melodies that are easy to assimilate. Kenny Rogers used to say that he looks for songs that the common man can sing along with. So you don't want something with a range over an octave and a fourth. You want to write something that people in high schools and community centers can carry off.

Second, the lyric should function completely by itself without the benefit of melody. When people tell me, "Well, it works with the track," that's a cop-out. If you look at the lyrics of all of the Christmas standards, as well as any of the standards from the golden age of songwriting, they hold up on the written page without a melody.

Third, do not write anything negative unless you are writing a blues song. In a blues song, you can say "My baby left me and I'm lonesome and blue for the holidays." Otherwise, don't bother. In my experience, people don't want to hear about people being out on the street and homeless for Christmas. They want to hear about happy, positive, inspiring stuff.

JUSTIN WILDE (Songwriter/Publisher,
Christmas & Holiday Music)

EXERCISE: WRITING CHRISTMAS LYRICS

When writing a Christmas lyric, many developing songwriters rely on clichés like:

• *The snow was falling*

• *The stockings were hung in front of the fire*

• *The presents were under the tree*

This exercise is designed to help you generate interesting, fresh, unique lyrics for Christmas songs.

1. First, think about a memorable or special Christmas.

2. Jot down your recollections. (For the purposes of this exercise you do not need to rhyme or be concerned with meter.)

3. Compose a list of words, phrases, and images that relate to those Christmas memories. Be specific and be sure to include colors, details, and actions.

4. Incorporate your personal memories into a fresh, original Christmas lyric.

WRITING CABARET SONGS

Cabaret songs are intended primarily for performance in intimate nightclub settings. Occasionally, some of these songs may be recorded or performed in larger venues. However, they're first and foremost conceived as a vehicle for a performer to emotionally connect with his or her audience in a small cabaret, bar, or lounge.

The key to writing cabaret songs is storytelling. A successful cabaret song should be inherently theatrical (without going over the top), drawing the audience into a story that is ostensibly about the performer. For instance, instead of saying I love you, baby, the song could be about the singer meeting the girl, stumbling over the furniture, dreaming of an impossible affair, and then—surprise!—she feels the same way. In cabaret, each song is an "act" unto itself and you have to interest the audience all over again with each new story you tell. Remember that this material will generally be performed live, so clear away the clutter. A simple, catchy melody attached to surprising, personal lyrics makes a song that people want to perform.

WAYNE MOORE (Owner, Ducy Lee Recordings;
cabaret performer and songwriter)

Cabaret songs are not bound by the rules and structures that are typically required for success in mainstream genres—the composer has free rein to express him- or herself. Songs written specifically for cabaret performance often have much in common with the Broadway standards that frequently comprise a large part of cabaret performers' repertoires. Lyrically, they cover a wide range of expression and topics. These songs may be deeply personal, poignant, happy, sad, or funny. But ideally, they evoke some strong emotion.

Songs used in cabaret are diverse and can come from almost any and every musical genre. It is an artist-driven idiom, and material is selected based on each individual performer's taste. Most times an artist will select material that they feel speaks to them and, in turn, will connect with their audience.

Performers will be most likely to record songs that they have been successful singing in concert. So, the key to having your songs recorded is to know what you have that may be right for any given artist, and getting it to them before they are recording. That gives them time to consider your songs and, if you are lucky, they will perform and fall in love with your songs well in advance of any recording dates.

PAUL ROLNICK (Songwriter; award-winning producer
of albums by Karen Mason, Julie Wilson, Lorna
Dallas, Jamie deRoy & Friends, and Deborah Tranelli)

Cabaret shows are typically produced by the artists themselves. Therefore, if an artist falls in love with your song and wants to include it in his or her performance, there are no additional hurdles to overcome. Many performing songwriters in this and other specialty styles produce their own albums partly with the hope that their song will find its way into the hands of other recording artists.

The various PROs handle payment for live cabaret performances differently. If you're primarily writing material that's geared for live performance in a nightclub setting, contact the

PROs to determine which society will best suit your needs. ASCAP's New York office sponsors a highly successful cabaret showcase. (For additional information about PROs, see Chapter 11 and the Appendix.)

> *In cabaret you write songs just for the love of writing and give them to people. It's a more accessible market than the pop and other mainstream markets. There's a lot of brilliant material that comes out of this market. In cabaret you can start from the true reason that we write—for the joy of it. It's different from writing from the point of view of "What do they want?" or "How do I get this cut?" We start from "What is my heart saying?" and "How do I want to say this?" You can use more range of language and emotion in this market. Cabaret can be one of the most satisfying mediums, but it's not lucrative—it's a labor of love.*
>
> DAVID FRIEDMAN (Academy Award-nominated
> songwriter/producer of albums by Nancy LaMott)

WRITING FOR THE LATIN MARKET

It was 13 degrees in Nashville when I received a call asking me to present a songwriting seminar for BMI in San Juan, Puerto Rico. Unfortunately, I learned that the songs I'd be critiquing following my lecture would be in Spanish. Since I don't speak Spanish and had little knowledge of the elements that went into hit songs in the Puerto Rican and other Latin markets, I sadly said that I probably was not qualified to teach the seminar. Luckily, the seminar's organizers felt differently. It didn't take too much effort to convince me that by studying the hit songs on the Latin charts, I'd be able to learn the differences from, and similarities to, successful songs on mainstream radio in the US. BMI agreed to provide interpreters to help with translations, as well as copies of the biggest hit CDs in the Latin market.

When I listened to the albums that were the current Latin top sellers, the first thing that struck me was the wide spectrum of styles that Latin music encompassed. Just as "American" music runs the gamut from traditional country songs to gangsta rap, adult contemporary ballads, Broadway show tunes, grunge rock, folk, R&B, and heavy metal, "Latin" music includes an equally wide variety of styles. The Latin hits included teen pop songs, adult contemporary ballads, pop/rock songs reminiscent of Jewel or Sheryl Crow (but sung in Spanish), funky synthesizer-driven dance music, and songs by quirky, alternative-sounding singer-songwriters—all in addition to the sizzling tropical rhythms I had expected.

Reflecting the diversity of Latin music, Grammys are awarded in the following categories of Latin music: Latin pop (e.g., Juan Gabriel, Jaci Velasquez, Chayanne), Latin rock/alternative (e.g., Juanes, Kinky, Orishas), traditional tropical Latin (e.g., Orquestra Aragón, Plena Libre, Carlos Vives), Salsa (e.g., Celia Cruz, Maraca, Robert Blades), Merengue (e.g., Grupo Mania, Milly Quezada, Manny Manuel), Mexican/Mexican American (e.g., Intocable, Jennifer Peña,

Joan Sebastían), Tejano (e.g., David Lee Garza y Los Musicales, Emilio Navaira, Siggno), and Latin jazz (e.g., Omar Sosa, Jane Bunnett, Caribbean Jazz Project). In addition to the nationally televised Grammy awards, the "Latin Grammys" acknowledge and honor many more of those performers and songwriters who contribute to the Latin music market.

> *The only difference in writing for the Latin market is the language. If you have a favorite artist, study that artist's past productions. Seek contacts through the label copy information. The label copy may list the record company and management company, through which the composer could inquire where and when the next recording is taking place, who the producer is, and where to send the demo. Network, network, network and have many demos available for distribution to those contacts made from networking. If you wholeheartedly want to become a songwriter, "perseverance" is the key.*
>
> DIANE ALMODOVAR (Senior Director, Latin Music, BMI)

To prepare for my trip to Puerto Rico, I began by analyzing the song structures and I found that the majority of the popular Latin songs were constructed using the same structures commonly heard on the radio in the US: Verse - Chorus - Verse - Chorus and Verse - Chorus - Verse - Chorus - Bridge - Chorus structures seemed to heavily predominate.

Next, I examined the rhyme schemes. With a few exceptions, I found that the majority of the hit songs in the Latin market employed rhymes in the same places where I would expect to find them in their American counterparts.

One of the most interesting things I noticed was how easy it was for me to identify the titles of most of the songs—even though I couldn't understand the meaning of their words. As in so many successful English-language hits, the melodies were crafted in such a way that the titles seemed to "jump out" of the songs. (In Chapter 5, you will learn how to accomplish this very important technique.)

When I studied the translations of the Latin hits, I found they had much in common with American songs. The ideas typically had universal appeal (mostly dealing with some aspect of love) and they seemed to possess some unique angle, an interesting title, and a fresh approach. However, in many of the Spanish-language hits there were far more syllables and words per line than would typically be heard in successful English-language songs. The Spanish lyrics I analyzed were often very passionate and poetic. They frequently incorporated images that would be considered too "flowery" and not conversational enough to be effective in the US market. I suspect I learned as much as, if not more than, my students in San Juan. I was introduced to some exceptionally talented Latin artists and songwriters, and I became a fan of some wonderful music.

Most major publishers, such as Warner/Chappell, Sony Music, Universal, and BMG, have Latin publishing divisions based in Miami, Florida. ASCAP and BMI also maintain Miami offices that deal primarily with Latin music. *Billboard's International Latin Music Buyer's Guide* is an excellent resource for songwriters who want to write for the Latin market (see Appendix).

STEP 2: CONCLUSION

Remember that our goal is not only to write and publish hits—but also to write songs that we can be truly proud of. Hearing our songs on the radio is an incredible experience. I hope it will happen for you—and that when it does, you won't cringe each time you hear a weak line on which you could have worked a little harder. So, before pronouncing your lyric "finished," consider the points that follow and decide if your song might benefit from an additional rewrite.

Look at each line of lyric and assess:

- Is this the best way you can convey this idea?
- Is this a cliché?
- Is this a fresh approach—or a line you've heard many times before?
- Does this line give your listener a compelling reason to choose this song instead of the competition?

LYRIC CHECKLIST

Photocopy this checklist and keep it where you normally write. Each time you finish a draft of a song, check to be sure that you've successfully incorporated the tools and techniques that follow:

- ❏ Adheres to one of the most successful song structures
- ❏ Has an interesting title and idea
- ❏ Has a universal theme—not too personal for others to relate to
- ❏ Makes the singer look good
- ❏ Has verse lyrics that clearly lead to the title
- ❏ Contains one focused idea
- ❏ Evokes one emotion
- ❏ Maintains one consistent verb tense
- ❏ Uses correct pronouns
- ❏ Contains opening lines that "grab" the listener and set the emotional tone
- ❏ Maintains one consistent tone and style throughout
- ❏ Uses detail, action, and fresh imagery
- ❏ Sounds conversational
- ❏ Avoids clichés
- ❏ Is not redundant
- ❏ Second verse adds new information
- ❏ Doesn't preach
- ❏ Doesn't "tell" how the singer feels—the listener feels it
- ❏ Bridge (if applicable) adds a new angle
- ❏ Each line logically flows from the previous line and into the following line
- ❏ Employs rhymes in appropriate places
- ❏ Doesn't overuse key words
- ❏ Has a title that "pays off"
- ❏ Lyric has been rewritten to make each line the strongest it can be

Composing Memorable Melodies

The important thing about the melody is that it has something that you can't get out of your mind. It could be two o'clock in the morning and next thing you know you're singing the chorus.

TOMMY LiPUMA (Chairman, The GRP Recording Company; recipient of eighteen gold and platinum records, thirty Grammy nominations, and two Grammy Awards; coproducer, Natalie Cole's *Unforgettable* LP; producer of Anita Baker, George Benson, Diana Krall, and Al Jarreau)

CHAPTER 5

Learning Effective Melody-Writing Skills

The best melodies are simple, easy to remember, and easy to sing along with.
However, the knack is being simple without being run-of-the-mill.

JEFF FENSTER (Senior Vice President
of A&R, Island/Def Jam Records)

I've heard too many publishers and industry professionals say, "The melody's not catchy enough," "It's not 'hooky' enough," "The melody's just not memorable"—but they have never told me how to make it catchier, "hookier," or more memorable. Webster's defines "memorable" as something that is easy to remember—and worth remembering. In Chapters 5 to 7, you'll learn there are specific tools and techniques that you can use to craft catchy, memorable melodies that communicate the feeling you intend to evoke.

This section of the book is geared to songwriters who, like myself, have little or no musical training. While it's true that Sheryl Crow earned a degree in classical music, this is the rare exception. Musical training is definitely not a prerequisite for writing hit melodies. Indeed, many hit songwriters, publishers, and recording artists cannot read music. I've attempted to study music theory several times, but it never quite makes sense or sinks in. Nonetheless, this lack of training has not stopped me from writing melodies to hit songs. The chapters that follow identify and explain the elements of successful, memorable melodies in nontechnical, plain English.

WRITING A CAPPELLA

A cappella means without instrumental accompaniment. Writing a cappella means composing melodies in your head, without a guitar or a piano. For me (and for many of my songwriting students), many times it's been the ticket to crafting the strongest melodies.

When I was just beginning my career in Los Angeles, my father accompanied me to a songwriting workshop during one of his visits. The guest speakers were Jay Livingston and Ray Evans, writers of standards including "Que Sera, Sera," "Silver Bells," "Mona Lisa," and the theme from the classic television show *Mr. Ed.* After watching these two pros musically punctuate their points from their perch at the piano, my father said he didn't think I could possibly write hit songs because of my limited musical knowledge and inability to play the piano.

I couldn't deny that outside of the clarinet lessons I took as a child, I had very little musical training or knowledge of music theory. When I attended my first songwriting workshop, I was indeed one of those who raised their hands when the instructor asked, "Who writes lyrics only?" I didn't play piano or guitar, so I assumed that meant I could not write melodies. I was confusing the ability to play a musical instrument with the ability to compose catchy, memorable melodies in my head. I've since learned that they are two distinct and very different skills.

Over the years, I've taken a few guitar lessons and learned some basic chords. But like so many developing songwriters, I made the mistake of composing melodies by strumming chords and allowing them to lead me to the next predictable notes that sounded good with those chords. I wrote lots of boring, uninspired melodies this way. Needless to say, none of them brought me any closer to writing a hit song.

Then I tried a new approach: I accepted that I was probably never going to be a very good guitarist or keyboard player, but I wasn't willing to let that hold me back. My solution was to try writing a melody by simply singing it into a portable tape recorder. After all, most individuals do not have a piano or a guitar in their shower or their car, yet they still have the ability to sing a memorable melody in the shower, or while driving on the highway. It's melody that people sing and remember—not chords. The number one melodic pitfall developing songwriters fall into is first playing chord changes on their keyboard or guitar, and then imposing melody onto these chord progressions. If the melody works well with the chords, it's likely that the result will be a "perfectly crafted" melody, but not necessarily an inspired one. Melody is not secondary; it is often the primary reason why a song gets recorded—or not.

> *First and foremost, a great melody makes a great song; something that connects emotionally. Don't let the craft get in the way of the passion.*
>
> STEVE LUNT (Senior Director of A&R for Jive Records; songwriter with cuts by artists including Britney Spears and Cyndi Lauper)

I'm not implying that finding the most effective chords is not important. The chords that accompany a melody, sometimes referred to as "harmonization," have a considerable impact on how the melody feels and the emotions it evokes. Try crafting the strongest, catchiest, freshest, and hookiest melodies and rhythms you're capable of—and then find the chords that work best to support those melodies and bring out the "colors" you hope to emphasize. I'm not willing to let my limitations in figuring out chords and playing a musical instrument stop me from writing hit songs. I tend to collaborate with songwriters who are better than I am at figuring out the chords that will best support our melody.

For songs I've written alone, I sometimes hire a guitarist or keyboardist to bring forth the chords I hear in my head, if those chords are complex and beyond the very limited scope of my knowledge. I ask the musician to play me all of the appropriate options and when I hear them, I recognize the chords I had in mind. The process rarely takes more than thirty minutes and does not constitute collaboration; the fee you pay will be the musician's full compensation. However, it's important to communicate this information up front. On the other hand, if you are writing melody and lyrics to a preexisting music track (bass, drums, and chords), this will likely be considered a collaboration. In some styles of pop music, and in urban, dance, hip-hop, and R&B, the groove, the chord changes, and the track itself are typically crucial components to a song's success; it could be argued that in these genres, they are more important than the lyric.

Some writers find that writing to a drum track helps inspire them—especially when working on up-tempo songs and styles of music that rely heavily on the rhythm and groove (e.g., dance, R&B, urban, and hip-hop). You can create drum tracks of your own by using an inexpensive drum machine or by purchasing CDs that contain drum tracks in various tempos and styles. (See "Drum Tracks for Songwriters" in the Appendix.)

My first success as a songwriter came when I had a song recorded by the 5th Dimension. The song was called "On Love Tonight" and I wrote 100 percent of it without ever touching a musical instrument until the melody and lyric were finished. I could clearly hear the chords in my head, but had no idea what they were or how to play them. I enlisted the help of a friend who was a step ahead of me in the chord department to translate what I heard in my head. He observed that I had employed modulations (key changes) and implied chords that were quite unexpected and unorthodox. I have no doubt that the freshness of the melody was a big factor in getting that song recorded. Knowledge of music theory can be helpful, and you should study it if you're so inclined. But I've managed to have success by simply singing melodies that sounded good to me—without knowing what the next chord "should" be according to classic music theory. Remember:

- Playing a musical instrument is not a requirement for writing a hit song.
- Knowing how to read music is not a prerequisite for writing great melodies.
  (You just have to be able to hear them in your head and find a way to get them out.)
- Knowledge of music theory is not necessary to compose successful songs.

I know that writing a cappella works. Still, I was amazed to learn that singer-songwriter Seal had composed and arranged his Grammy-winning smash hit "Kiss from a Rose" by singing all of the instrumental parts into a multitrack tape recorder. Stephen Sondheim, a proficient pianist and composer of some of the most richly textured and complex melodies on Broadway and in popular music, has said that he often chooses to compose his melodies without the aid of an instrument. Sting has also been quoted as saying that he frequently writes his melodies a cappella. If it's good enough for Sting, Seal, and Sondheim....

EXERCISE: WRITING A CAPPELLA

- Write three original catchy chorus melodies by singing into a tape recorder without using any instrument. (For the purpose of this exercise, do not write an accompanying lyric unless you choose to after you have finished your melodies.)
- Write your next five songs a cappella before deciding if this is an effective way for you to strengthen your melody writing.

After attending more workshops than I can count, and writing (and rewriting) hundreds of songs, I have gone from believing I am "only a lyricist" to writing melodies for hit songs by singing them into a tape recorder. Although I've become a much better guitarist, I still rarely use an instrument when writing melodies. When I teach songwriting workshops the comment I probably receive most often is that the participants are relieved and validated to learn that they do not need to be able to play an instrument or figure out chords in order to write hit melodies. Many of them felt they were the only ones writing melodies without the benefit of an accompanying instrument—or that doing so would be impossible. To all of you who are "instrumentally challenged," like me, I hereby grant you permission to write hit songs, lyrics and melodies—without using an instrument.

Since writing melodies (or writing melodies without an instrument) may be a new experience for you, be patient with yourself. It's unrealistic to expect to master this skill with the first few attempts. The fact that you may not be an expert melody writer today does not preclude the possibility of composing hit melodies in the future—whether you play an instrument or not.

EXERCISE: TRYING A NEW APPROACH

This exercise is all about shaking things up and getting out of our creative ruts by trying a different approach to our songwriting.

- If you typically write by beginning with a lyric, start a new song by writing the melody first (or vice versa).

- If you usually write your melodies while accompanying yourself on an instrument, start a new song a cappella—even if you are a proficient musician.

- If you play keyboards and guitar, but typically write by using only one or the other of these instruments, try writing a new song while accompanying yourself on the instrument you don't usually use for this type of song.

- Another time, write a new song by beginning with a drum track.

You may be surprised at how your writing will be affected by the way that you approach the writing process.

KEEPING IT SIMPLE AND SINGABLE (K.I.S.S.)

Remember that your goal as a songwriter is to deliver your idea from your heart to the listener—both lyrically and melodically. Your objective is to communicate. But when composing melody, the language available to us is comprised of notes, rhythms, and chords—instead of words, images, and rhymes.

Many developing songwriters make the process of melody writing more difficult than it needs to be. They make the mistake of composing complicated melodic lines that are too intricate for a nonsinger to retain. It's impossible for the average listener to remember or sing melodic phrases that are excessively long and complex. For example, it's easier to remember "I love you" than "I want you to know that there's no doubt in my heart whatsoever that there's a feeling I want to share with you and you can always know that no matter where I am I love you." It's easier for listeners to remember and sing whatever melody might accompany the simple phrase "I love you" than any melody that could correspond with the rambling second phrase.

If your audience does not connect emotionally with your melody, your melody has not done its job—and it's easier for listeners to feel an emotional connection to a melody they can easily sing and retain. Remember the acronym K.I.S.S. (Keep It Simple and Singable).

> *While it's true that country music is known for the meaningful lyrics in the songs, you need to remember that the melodic hook is just as important. Great lyrics need a great melody.*
>
> PAIGE LEVY (Senior Vice President of A&R, Warner Bros. Records)

USING HYMNS AND CHILDREN'S SONGS FOR MELODIC INSPIRATION

> *There is no question in my mind that if a nonperformer feels comfortable whistling, singing, or sharing a piece of music with their neighbor it's going to linger.*
>
> NOEL PAUL STOOKEY (Peter, Paul & Mary),
> as quoted in *Performing Songwriter* magazine.

Elton John has said that at times he has drawn inspiration for his melodies from hymns. I thought about why that might be the case and concluded that hymns have melodies that are intended for "nonsingers" to sing. Almost anyone can sing "Amazing Grace" or "Rock of Ages." They have endured throughout the years largely because they are easy for millions of nonsingers to remember and sing along with. Isn't that a primary goal of popular songwriting?

Likewise, classic children's songs from "Twinkle Twinkle Little Star" to "Mary Had a Little Lamb" and the theme song for *Barney*, can be powerful melodic models. I've even written a very successful verse melody based upon the notes that children sing when teasing each other with "Na-Na-Na-Na-Na-Na."

Children's songs are easy to retain and to sing because:

- The phrases are short and concise.
- They employ melodic and/or rhythmic repetition.
- The melodic intervals (the space from one note to the next) tend to be close to each other and, therefore, are easy to remember.

- The melodies contain symmetrical phrases (as explained in Chapter 6).
- They are not excessively wordy.

Try incorporating these tools into your songs—whether you are writing for children or not.

MAKING IT OBVIOUS WHERE THE TITLE GOES WITHOUT THE LYRIC

After hearing a melody one time, there should be no doubt in the listener's mind where the title will occur within the song. The portion of melody that contains the title needs to jump out and separate itself from the rest of the melody. This can be accomplished by any of the following techniques, or by a combination of more than one of them.

ALTERING THE RANGE, VARYING THE RHYTHMS, AND INSERTING PAUSES

A common technique to make the title stand out is to have some of the notes that accompany the title be higher or lower than the rest of the melody. An example of the title being higher than the surrounding melodic phrases can be found in "Over the Rainbow." Sing through a verse of that classic song and you'll see that the title line includes notes that are indeed higher than the notes in the rest of the song.

A rhythm that is different from the rhythms employed in the rest of the song can also effectively set your title apart. For example, if the lines surrounding your title are composed primarily of notes that are held for a full beat or more (quarter notes, half notes, or whole notes), crafting a title with shorter notes (eighth notes and sixteenth notes), thereby creating a choppier rhythm, will help differentiate it from the rest of the song (and vice versa).

The title can also be differentiated from the rest of the melody by employing a brief pause or a "stop" immediately preceding the melodic phrase that encompasses the title. A strong example of this technique can be found at the end of the chorus in Diane Warren's "How Do I Live," which was a hit for both Trisha Yearwood and LeAnn Rimes.

EXERCISE: MAKING YOUR TITLE JUMP OUT

Write a chorus melody and lyric, being sure to include your title at least once. Rewrite your melody three different ways, making sure each time that your title "jumps out."

- Compose the musical phrase that accompanies the title by including notes that are either higher or lower than the other lines in the chorus.

- Assign a rhythm to the title that differentiates it from the other lines in the chorus.

- Insert a pause or a stop immediately prior to the title.

MARRYING THE MUSIC TO THE LYRIC: PROSODY

To achieve prosody, the melody should sound as if it is happily married to the lyric it accompanies, and vice versa. A melody that makes the listener feel happy should accompany a lyric that has a positive, pleasant message. Likewise, a lyric that conveys sadness should be expressed melodically with notes, chords, and musical phrases that evoke a similar feeling of sadness. Minor chords typically contribute to a sad-sounding melody, while major chords can have the opposite effect.

> *Great melodies are simple, memorable, and enhance the mood and emotions set forth in the lyric.*
>
> GEORGE TEREN (Writer of country hits including "Real Good Man" and "Busy Man," as well as cuts with artists including Britney Spears, Trisha Yearwood, and John Michael Montgomery)

Tape recording your melody, without any lyric, can help you be sure that your melody and lyric work together. Either play your melody instrumentally (or have someone play it for you), or sing it a cappella using a nonsense syllable, like "la" or "ooh." Listen back to the melody and ask yourself what feelings it evokes. If it's not consistent with the emotion of the lyric, it's definitely time for a rewrite.

Certain words typically imply higher notes, while other words tend to go with lower notes. For example, it would sound wrong if the word "low" was assigned a high note when Garth Brooks sings Bud Lee and Dewayne Blackwell's "I've Got Friends in Low Places." Likewise, words like "fly," "soar," "up," "high," and "sky" often best convey their intended emotion if they are sung on high notes. Additionally, it's best to avoid pairing crucial melodic moments with words such as "a," "it," "the," or "and," which convey little emotional impact.

According to Michael Hollandsworth (President, Full Circle Music), "It's the total combination of lyric and melody that makes a song a hit." Although the lyric and melody may have been rewritten many times, ideally the final version of your song should sound as though the words and music fit so perfectly together that the listener cannot imagine another melody accompanying that lyric, or another lyric working with that melody.

VARYING THE RHYTHMS

Rhythm is determined by the lengths of notes and rests (for example, whole, half, quarter, eighth, and sixteenth notes or rests), how they are combined, and how they relate to each other. Tempo, or the speed at which notes are sung or played, is an additional component of rhythm. Rhythm is not contingent on the pitch of the notes, or where they are within the scale (for example, C, D, E), but is based solely on their lengths. It is what you would hear if you tapped out your song with your hands or on a drum.

One way to achieve different rhythms in different sections of your songs is to use different numbers of syllables and words. This is sometimes referred to as changing the "lyric density." For instance, a chorus that follows a very wordy verse might be differentiated from the verse by using fewer words (and, correspondingly, longer notes) per bar of music. The use of different rhythms in the various sections of a song helps to maintain the listener's interest. Using similar rhythms in the verses, choruses, and bridge tends to be boring and makes it difficult for listeners to differentiate the chorus from the verse. For example, if your verses are comprised primarily of long, held-out notes (i.e., half notes or whole notes), your song will have added contrast if your chorus takes a more rhythmic approach, using shorter notes (i.e., quarter notes and eighth notes), or vice versa.

If you do a study of hits on the radio, you'll hear that the majority of them incorporate different rhythms in the various sections of each song. Examples of songs that successfully vary the rhythms to differentiate the verses from the chorus include "A Thousand Miles" (written and recorded by Vanessa Carlton), "99.9%" (written by Greg Barnhill and Billy Austin, recorded by Brian McComas), and "Unbreak My Heart" (written by Diane Warren, recorded by Toni Braxton).

When it's time to craft a bridge, explore rhythms that will set your bridge apart from the choruses or verses that surround it. For example, in "Over the Rainbow" think about how different the rhythm is in the bridge section compared with the verses. The opening line of its verse (*Somewhere over the rainbow bluebirds fly*) contains ten syllables and ten corresponding notes. In that same amount of space (four bars), the opening line of the bridge (*Someday I'll wish upon a star and wake up where the clouds are far behind me*) contains nineteen syllables and corresponding notes. The result is a sense that the bridge provides a melodic and rhythmic departure from the rest of the song.

CHOOSING THE APPROPRIATE MELODIC RANGE

My voice instructor in college used to say that just as we have ten fingers, we should have ten notes that we can comfortably sing. Most professional singers will be able to sing an octave and a third (ten notes) without any difficulty. An example of an octave and a third would be the distance from middle C on a piano to the E an octave above. Most professional male singers can comfortably sing from a low C to F above middle C. Most female singers can sing from a G below middle C to a high B. (Of course, many singers exceed this range.) If all of this sounds incomprehensible, don't despair. Have someone who's more comfortable with music theory plunk out the notes of your song and see if what you've written is within "normal" range.

It is perfectly acceptable to craft a strong, catchy melody that uses less than ten or eleven notes. In fact, if a song is considerably more than an octave and a third, you risk getting into a situation where singers who want to record your song may not be capable of singing it. Be aware that if you write melodies that significantly exceed an octave and a half, only a handful of singers in the class of Celine Dion, Barbra Streisand, Martina McBride, Andrea Bocelli, Reba McEntire, Josh Groban, or Mariah Carey will be capable of comfortably singing them.

On the other hand, songwriters who might have a smaller-than-average vocal range must be careful to avoid the trap of writing only the kind of melodies that they themselves can easily sing. Remember, you are writing for professional singers who will hopefully use your melody to showcase their vocal abilities. Craft melodies that will intrigue and challenge a skilled vocalist, without being something that only Pavarotti would be comfortable singing.

CHAPTER 6

Using Repetition Effectively

A great rock song, a great country song, or a great folk song are three different beasts. What makes a great song varies from genre to genre. There are some eternal truths, however. First the song must be memorable. When you walk away from that record or from that radio station, a great song is one that you remember. The song must have something unique about it, either its point of view, its melodic structure, or its hook—something about it has to stick out in your mind. If it says something profound, to me that's the best. It is important that a song touches you and makes you feel something, whether it's hilariously silly, profoundly sad, deeply touching, or profoundly depressing.

ROBERT K. OERMANN (Music journalist; judge, *Nashville Star* television show)

A successful melody touches listeners and stays with them. It communicates the emotion that the composer felt and wanted to convey when he or she wrote it. One of the most effective ways to connect with your listeners is by using the tool of melodic and rhythmic repetition. Nothing contributes more to a melody's being "memorable" than incorporating notes, rhythms, and phrases that repeat.

It's common sense that it's easier for listeners to remember a melodic phrase that they've heard over and over again than one that they've heard only once. Studies conducted by the advertising industry have determined that it takes approximately five exposures to an advertisement before the average listener retains its message. Similarly, our melodies will have the best chance of being remembered if we provide repeated exposure. Repetition can be employed by repeating a melodic phrase exactly, repeating the same notes while the accompanying chords change, or by repeating a rhythm while altering some or all of the actual notes of the phrase. Melodic or rhythmic repetition may be exact or may be just close enough to evoke a sense of repetition.

KEEPING YOUR PHRASES SHORT AND CATCHY

On my first visit to Nashville, when I played one of my songs for a music industry executive, his comment was, "Y'all have enough words in this verse for a whole album!" That meeting was a turning point in my development as a writer. The proverbial lightbulb went on over my head. It was the first time I grasped the idea that it was virtually impossible to compose lines of catchy, memorable, easy-to-sing melodies if their lyrical counterparts had too many words and syllables.

I began analyzing the hit songs on the radio and found that an overwhelming majority of them were comprised of short, melodic (and corresponding lyric) phrases. Of course, songwriting is not an exact science and there are some exceptions. But over and over again I found that most hit songs contain melodic and/or rhythmic fragments that repeat and usually are comprised of less than ten notes (or syllables), and sometimes as few as two or three notes.

One of our goals is to write melodies that are memorable—and this means melodies that are easily remembered. It's much easier to retain small amounts of information than long, complex ideas—and this concept also applies to melodies. If you were asked to repeat a three- or four-note melodic phrase, it would likely be easy for you to do. However, if the phrase contained ten or more notes, it would probably be impossible for you to remember and repeat it after having only one chance to hear it. This is probably why telephone numbers are recited in short segments. For example, you would probably not say that your phone number is 6152950463; you'd be more likely to say, "My number is 615-295-0463." It is easier to remember three short bits of information than one long, complex one.

I learned another valuable lesson about melodic repetition and the impact of short melodic phrases from Kevin Richardson, a member of the multi-Platinum-selling pop group, the Backstreet Boys. I was cowriting a song with Kevin and Gary Baker and felt we were writing a hit when Kevin said he thought something was wrong with the melody. He said that the chorus seemed to have "too many sections" and that their previous hits had been more simple and straightforward melodically. Kevin was right. The chorus needed additional repetition to make it as easy to remember as the band's biggest hits.

We deleted the second half of the chorus (a rhythmic and melodic departure from the first section) and replaced it with lines that repeated the rhythm that we had established in the first half. Here is the resulting chorus lyric for the song "Back to Your Heart":

(Tell me)
The words to say
The road to take
To find a way
BACK TO YOUR HEART

What can I do
To get to you
And find a way
BACK TO YOUR HEART

WRITTEN BY *Jason Blume/Gary Baker/Kevin Richardson;*
RECORDED BY *the Backstreet Boys.*

Every line in the chorus lyric contains the same number of syllables—four. The simplicity and repetition of the short, melodic phrases contributed significantly to the song's success, as people could not get it out of their heads—and our song was recorded by the Backstreet Boys on their twenty-three-million-selling *Millennium* album, which was named *Billboard's* Album of the Year.

While you will not want to use short phrases and repeating rhythms exclusively, incorporating short phrases that repeat into sections of your songs will make your melodies easier to remember and sing. It may take some practice to get comfortable with composing this way, but this is a skill that can be acquired. As you master this technique, you'll be amazed at how much catchier and more memorable your melodies become.

WRITING SYMMETRICAL PHRASES

Writing lines that have the same numbers of notes, with stresses and emphases in the same places, is a tool that will help you craft melodies that are easier to remember. Counting the number of syllables in each line of your lyric will have the same effect as counting the number of individual notes in the corresponding melodic phrases. It is impossible to craft melodic or rhythmic phrases that repeat exactly, if each line contains a different number of syllables.

Some of the most effective melodies employ a technique that can be referred to as "call and response." When portions of melodies are crafted using this tool, the lines seem to "answer" each other melodically. The reason these lines seem to answer each other is that they are symmetrical; they mirror each other by containing the same number of syllables.

Within a song, the entire verse or chorus may use repeating phrases—or there may be rhythmic and/or melodic repetition of several lines within the verse or chorus. There are no hard and fast rules about how much or where to use repeating phrases. As you study and analyze hit melodies you will become aware of the prevalence of this tool.

Many hit writers approximate this effect by writing lines with similar, but not the exact same, numbers of syllables. For example, in Stacie Orrico's "Stuck" (written by Stacie Orrico and Kevin Kadish), the first line of the chorus—*I hate you*—which contains three syllables (and three corresponding notes) is followed by *But I love you,* which is comprised of four syllables and notes. In this instance, the word "but" acts as a pickup note to the second line. Therefore, the overall sense of rhythmic and melodic repetition is retained, despite the fact that the two lines do not contain the exact same number of syllables. However, if line one contained three syllables (and notes), while line two contained five or more, it would be impossible to create a sense of repetition.

The chorus of Destiny's Child's hit "Survivor" contains a series of phrases that have the exact same numbers of notes (and corresponding syllables). With only one exception, each line contains five syllables. This technique helped create an exceptionally catchy and memorable melody and rhythm. The numbers following each line show the number of syllables (and corresponding notes) in that line.

SURVIVOR

I'm a SURVIVOR (5)
I'm not gonna give up (6)
I'm not gon' stop (I'm) (5)
Gonna work harder (5)
I'm a SURVIVOR (5)
I'm gonna make it (5)
I'm a SURVIVOR (5)
Keep on survivin' (5)

WRITTEN BY *Anthony Dent, Beyoncé Knowles, and Mathew Knowles;*
RECORDED BY *Destiny's Child.*

EXERCISE: CRAFTING LYRICS THAT LEND THEMSELVES TO CATCHY MELODIES

PART 1

Here are some examples of lyrics that "answer" each other with rhythmic repetition by using the same number of syllables in key lines:

How do I live without you (7 syllables)
Answer: *How do I breathe without you* (7 syllables)

You are my dream (4 syllables)
Answer: *All that I need* (4 syllables)

With a look (3 syllables)
Answer: *With a touch* (3 syllables)

In your notebook, for each of the lines in this exercise, write the next line of lyric, using the same number of syllables as the initial phrase. Note that for the purpose of this exercise it is not necessary to rhyme these lines. For example:

The past is past (4 syllables)
Answer: *What's done is done* (4 syllables)

• *If that's the way you want it* (7 syllables)

• *If this is a dream* (5 syllables)

• *Say the words that I want to hear* (8 syllables)

• *Hold me* (2 syllables)

• *I never meant to hurt you like I did* (10 syllables)

(continued)

PART 2

Write the next two lines of lyric, using the same number of syllables as the two-line phrase. For this part of the exercise, be sure to rhyme the second line you write (line four of the section) with the original second line.

For example:
I love you so much (5 syllables)
And I want you to know (6 syllables)

Answer:
These two loving arms (5 syllables)
Will never let you go (6 syllables)

- *Tell me that you love me* (6 syllables)
  If you really do (5 syllables)

- *Hold me close* (3 syllables)
  And swear that it's forever (7 syllables)

- *All I want to do is dance with you* (9 syllables)
  All night long (3 syllables)

- *Show me* (2 syllables)
  How you feel (3 syllables)

- *There's a place down the road* (6 syllables)
  Where everybody goes (6 syllables)

- *I wouldn't stop loving you if I could* (10 syllables)
  And I don't want to try (6 syllables)

- *One sweet* (2 syllables)
  Hot night (2 syllables)

- *High-heeled boots* (3 syllables)
  Skin-tight dress (3 syllables)

- *Give me a call* (4 syllables)
  If I ever cross your mind (7 syllables)

- *Don't ever stop* (4 syllables)
  Whatever it is that you're doing (9 syllables)

PART 3

Compose a melody for each of the four-line lyrics that you have written. Note how the use of symmetrical phrases make your melodies easy to remember.

CHAPTER 7

Acquiring Additional Melody-Writing Techniques

I am melodically driven, so the first thing that will catch my attention is a great and unique melody. Sometimes I'll listen to a song twenty times before I know what it's about.

FRANK LIDDELL (Carnival Music Publishing;
producer, Lee Ann Womack)

Few songwriters would assume that every word of their first draft of a lyric is the very strongest it could possibly be. Most writers take it for granted that rewriting a lyric will almost always be necessary if the goal is to write the most effective, creative lines possible. The same holds true for melody writing. The odds of every note, rest, rhythm, and chord of your first melodic draft being the very best that you can possibly write are infinitesimally small. We've all heard it said that songwriting is 10 percent inspiration and 90 percent perspiration. This applies just as much to composing melodies as it does to lyrics. The strongest melodies start as inspiration, but are then scrutinized and rewritten until they are the best the composer is able to write.

Although for some songs, the story contributes more to the song's success than the melody does, even "lyric-driven" songs require memorable melodies that showcase their lyrics if they are to become hits; no one walks down the street humming a lyric. Many songs, especially in the fields of pop, dance, and urban/R&B, seem to become hits largely on the strength of their melody and/or groove. While the lyrics to some of these songs may seem trite and inconsequential on paper, when paired with just the right melody, they contribute to the overall success of the song. A lyric like Kylie Minogue's "Can't Get You Out of My Head" (Cathy Dennis and Rob Davis) may not be profound, but it has done its job if it propels listeners to the dance floor.

A good case can be made that without a catchy, memorable melody, listeners might never get an opportunity to hear the lyrics of any song—because it would never get on the radio. The bottom line is that settling for the very first melody that pops into your head sells you and your song short. Such an effort is unlikely to lead you to success. Melody is crucial, not secondary, to a song's success. Put at least as much time and effort into writing your melodies as you put into your lyrics. It's easy to get accustomed to a melody, and many songwriters have a hard time coming up with alternatives. The tools that follow can help you explore your melodic options before deciding which is the strongest.

USING FRESH RHYTHMS

Few tools help transform a "good" melody into an "I've-got-to-cut-this-song" melody as well as incorporating fresh, unique, unpredictable rhythms. While it's obvious that rap, R&B, and reggae music are built upon a foundation of catchy rhythms, when you analyze your favorite songs in pop, country, adult contemporary, Christian, and other musical genres, it's likely that you'll hear catchy rhythms that contribute to the songs' successes.

Incorporating fresh, attention-grabbing rhythms into your songs can be accomplished by rewriting—exploring a variety of different ways to phrase your melody—before settling. Listen to songs that have successfully used rhythms that demand to be listened to and incorporate equally compelling rhythms into your own songs. The section that follows ("Breaking the Lines") will teach you a technique that will help you rewrite your rhythms.

For excellent examples of songs that incorporated exceptionally fresh rhythms, listen to Faith Hill's "This Kiss," Jason Mraz's "The Remedy (I Won't Worry)," Avril Lavigne's "Complicated," Lonestar's "Amazed," Nelly Furtado's "I'm Like a Bird," Nickelback's "How You Remind Me," and Rascal Flatts' "These Days."

BREAKING THE LINES

It can be helpful to look at the various places where you might place pauses to separate a line into smaller melodic segments. For example, let's look at different ways to approach the title "If You Really Love Me."

1. One option is to craft a melody that does not include any pauses or emphases in it. Rhythmically, each syllable of the lyric has a corresponding note of equal value (i.e., all eighth notes).

If - You - Real - ly - Love - Me

2. A second rhythm to try when crafting a melody for this title is to assign a longer note value to the first word, "If" (i.e., a dotted quarter note, while all other notes are eighth notes). Holding it out longer will add emphasis to that word.

If - You - Real - ly - Love - Me

3. Another place to break up the line would be after the word "You."

If - You - Real - ly - Love - Me

4. You might emphasize the word "Really" by assigning a longer note value to its two syllables and adding a pause after that word.

If - You - Real - ly - Love - Me

5. Another option is to emphasize the word "Love" by assigning a longer note value to that word.

If - You - Real -ly - Love - Me

While every note of melody is important, it's essential that your hook be the strongest melody you're capable of composing. Of course, a line of lyric that contains many syllables will present more places to break up the line than a lyric with only one or two syllables. But even a line with very few syllables can be expressed rhythmically in a variety of ways by turning one-syllable words into multisyllabic words.

You - ooh - ooh - ooh - ooh

The intention of this example is to illustrate that the melody for each segment can be written with an almost infinite number of different rhythms—regardless of the number of syllables (and corresponding notes) it contains.

TRYING DIFFERENT NOTES

When rewriting your melodies, try a variety of notes with each of the various rhythms. For instance, using our previous example, a melodic phrase that assigns an eighth note to each syllable might be expressed with the following melodies:

There are an infinite number of combinations of notes and rhythms. If you attempted to try all of them you'd never finish a song. But your songs will improve as you experiment with various melodies for each section of your song before settling on the one that best conveys the emotion of your lyric in a catchy, memorable way.

LEARNING TO USE NONSENSE SYLLABLES

Using nonsense syllables (sounds that have no meaning) can be an effective tool to add interest to your melodies. The first line of Peter Frampton's classic hit "Baby, I Love Your Way" wouldn't have nearly the same melodic impact without the "Ooh" that precedes it. Blackstreet added an additional hook to their mega-hit "No Diggity" by including a section that repeats *Hey-yo, hey-yo, hey-yo, hey-yo,* and the hook of Anne Murray's classic "I Just Fall in Love Again" is actually sung *Oh—I just fall in love again.*

When they are used effectively, we barely notice that a song includes nonsense syllables—they simply sound like a natural part of the melody and lyric. "Genie in a Bottle," the hit that launched Christina Aguilera's career, includes a pre-chorus section that is largely based on the sound "Oh—Oh—Oh—Oh—Oh." The catchiest, most memorable part of the song that first skyrocketed Britney Spears to the top of the charts, ". . . Baby One More Time," is the line *Oh, baby, baby* that begins the song and several of the verses. Sounds like "Ooh" and "Oh" can be added either once or several times to help craft a catchy melody. While it will not be appropriate for every song you write, it is one more tool to keep in your "toolbox" to help you craft the catchiest, most memorable melodies.

REPEATING WORDS OR PHRASES

Repeating a word or a phrase can also add interest to your songs. For instance, in the example given earlier in this chapter, "If You Really Love Me," you might craft a hook that sings: *If you really-really-really love me* or *If you really love-love-love-love me.* The Dixie Chicks had a Number One hit with *Ready, ready, ready, ready—READY TO RUN.* David Bowie had great success by repeating just a part of a word: "*ch-ch-ch-ch-ch*anges" and Van Morrison repeated the word "love" in "Crazy Love," a song that's been recorded over and over (*She gives me* love-love-love-love).

You certainly will not want to use nonsense syllables or repeating words or phrases in all of your songs, but it is important to remember that you have them as options. When experimenting with various melodic alternatives, inserting a nonsense syllable or repeating a word may be just the ticket you need to make your melody special.

LEARNING THE POWER OF SEQUENTIAL INTERVALS, ASCENDING NOTES, AND DESCENDING NOTES

Writing melodies that are memorable can be much easier when you build them by using sequential intervals—notes that are consecutive. For example, the sound of C - D - E will be easier to remember than C - F# - B♭. Notes that are close to each other on the scale seem to go together naturally. Order makes sense to the brain and is easier to retain. For those readers who are as nontechnically oriented I am, think of the melody of the popular childrens' songs "Mary Had a Little Lamb" and "Twinkle, Twinkle Little Star." You'll notice that the intervals, the distance from one note to the next, is quite close. Most of these notes are one "step" apart.

Notice that each note is only one note away in the scale from every other note, or is a repetition of the same note. The only exception is the interval that goes from C to E♭. Repeating notes can also help to make a melody easy to remember.

Using notes that descend in succession can help create a melody that is memorable. One notable example is "The Christmas Song." Think of the classic melody that accompanies *Chestnuts roasting on an open fire*. The distance from the note sung on "Chest" to the note sung on "nuts" is an entire octave. However, most of the rest of the phrase is made up of notes that descend one step or musical interval at a time in a logical sequence.

It can also be quite effective to build melodies by including a series of notes that ascend in sequence. It would be terribly boring if all melodies were crafted using sequential notes, but using some notes that either ascend or descend in succession can make a melody easier to remember. Another tool to try when writing and rewriting your melodies is using melodic phrases that alternate between ascending and then descending. The chorus of Vanessa Carlton's Grammy-nominated "A Thousand Miles" uses this technique. The first melodic phrase of the chorus (*If I could fall*) goes up and seems to be "answered" by the second phrase (*Into the sky*) which comes back down the scale. This technique is used very effectively throughout most of this chorus, and can be found in many successful songs.

EXERCISE: INCORPORATING SEQUENTIAL INTERVALS, ASCENDING NOTES, AND DESCENDING NOTES

For each of the following lines of lyric:

- Compose a melody based primarily on notes that are either one note above or one note below each other.

- Compose a melody that includes notes that ascend in succession.

- Compose a melody that includes notes that descend in sequence.

- Compose a melody that ascends—and then descends.

Note: when using this tool, it is not necessary for every note in the melodic phrase to conform to this technique. Use this as a starting place, then be creative.

- *I don't think I love you anymore*

- *I'm gonna fly you to the moon*

- *Why can't we still be friends*

- *I've got a feeling that I'm dreaming*

- *What's going on in your heart*

VARYING THE TEMPO AND TIME SIGNATURE

I've had covers in a ton of different genres—pop, jazz, folk, salsa,
cabaret, rap, R&B, and I think that's because a great song translates
into different genres. One of the ways I test new songs is to sing
them in different feels.

JANIS IAN (Nine-time Grammy nominee)

The tempo refers to the speed at which a melody is performed. When exploring different melodic options it can be helpful to try your song at various tempos. Bonnie Raitt's heart-wrenching, Grammy-winning ballad, "I Can't Make You Love Me," was initially written with an up-tempo bluegrass feel—and your song that you thought would be a terrific ballad may make an even better mid-tempo or up-tempo song. Likewise, it can be beneficial to try your song in different time signatures. A song that you had intended as a waltz (3/4 time) may be even stronger in a more straight-ahead 4/4 time signature.

EXERCISE: APPLYING DIFFERENT TEMPOS AND TIME SIGNATURES

- Take an existing song (either one that you've written or a radio hit) and try singing it at a new tempo. If it was originally a ballad, try speeding it up. If it was conceived as an up-tempo or mid-tempo song, try it as a ballad.

- Now sing the same song in a new time signature (e.g., as a waltz).

FINDING THOSE MAGIC MOMENTS: THE UNEXPECTED NOTE OR CHORD

Imagine hearing "Send in the Clowns" by Stephen Sondheim without that wonderful, distinctive, high note that accompanies the word "my" (in bold type below):

Isn't it rich
Isn't it queer
Losing my timing this late
*In **my** career*

Now imagine Garth Brooks singing "I've got Friends in Low Places" without dipping down to the very low note that corresponds to the word "low." In both instances, that single, special note provides one of the most memorable, "magical" moments in the songs. According to an article in *The New Yorker* magazine, legendary producer David Foster refers to this as "the money note." He said that he came up with the expression during a recording session that he was producing with Barbra Streisand. When Streisand hit a particularly powerful high note and wanted to know how it sounded, Foster responded, "That sounds like money!"

When rewriting your melodies, consciously look for those places within your songs that might benefit from a fresh, unexpected chord, rhythm, or note that is out of the ordinary. When used effectively, those tools grab the listener's attention, add interest and uniqueness to the melodies, and bolster the emotion that the composer is trying to evoke.

> *Generally speaking, there is something about the songs I can get cut that separates them from the other songs—a unique idea or a unique melodic passage.*
>
> JOHN VAN METER (Chief Creative Officer, New Sheriff Entertainment)

In some instances, prosody will dictate the most effective way to insert a "magic moment" into the melody. For example, in "Friends in Low Places" it was natural for songwriters Dewayne Blackwell and Bud Lee to give the singer a low note to sing on the word "low." Likewise, words like "top," "up," and "fly" will lend themselves to being sung on a note that is higher than the surrounding notes.

There needs to be something about your song that sets it apart if you want to rise to the top. A special melodic moment is often the ticket. You have a multitude of melodic options to explore to take your melodies to the next level—from good to WOW! But don't insert "magic moments" into your melodies with a proverbial crowbar. Use them only where they genuinely support the melody.

EXERCISE: INCORPORATING MAGIC MOMENTS

Writing the strongest melodies involves conscious decision making and lots of rewriting. Think about the places where you can include "magic moments" to bring your melodies to the next level.

- Listen to a favorite album and note the unexpected "magic" melodic moments.

- Sing the chorus melody of a song you've written and explore where you might incorporate a special note, rhythm, or chord to add to the emotional impact of the melody. It might help to write down the lyric first and see if there are words like "up" or "down" that lend themselves to a higher or lower note.

- Try at least three different options and repeat this exercise with several of your existing songs.

USING SIGNATURE LICKS

Listeners can usually identify a favorite hit song on the radio within the first few moments of the instrumental introduction. This is because the recording begins with a catchy, melodic phrase unique to that song. This instrumental hook, or signature lick, is often included in the song's introduction, at the turnaround (between the end of the first chorus and the beginning of the second verse), and again at the outro (the end of the song).

Sometimes, the signature lick is the same, or very similar to, a melodic line used elsewhere in the song. This added hook often reiterates or evokes the melody that accompanies the song's title, the first line of the chorus, the last line of the chorus, or the opening line of the verse. It's also acceptable to have a signature lick that is a totally separate melodic entity, not appearing in any other section of the song.

The majority of rap songs incorporate these catchy melodic hooks. Since the verses to these songs are spoken in rhythm, including the "extra" melodic hook makes the songs more memorable and distinctive. However, signature licks are also widely used in all styles of popular songs. They are an important tool that help make your song instantly identifiable and give the listener one more reason to choose your song instead of the competition.

EXERCISE: COMPOSING SIGNATURE LICKS

Compose two different signature licks for a song you've written but have not yet demoed. If you are unable to play these melodic phrases on an instrument, sing them a cappella into your tape recorder.

- Have the first lick be a melodic line that is the same, or similar to, a melody already within your song.

- Create an alternate signature lick using a melody that is not found elsewhere within your song.

- Decide what instrument you want to play your signature licks on when you record your demo.

INCORPORATING MODULATIONS

Changing the key within a song is called "modulating." Modulations, or "mods," are often an effective way to increase the emotion, provide a sense that the song is building, and allow a singer an opportunity to show off his or her range. A classic example of a modulation can be found in Celine Dion's version of Eric Carmen's "All by Myself." When Dion performed this song at a televised awards show the result was electrifying. An additional example of an especially effective modulation can be found in Whitney Houston's version of the Dolly Parton song "I Will Always Love You" at the beginning of the third the chorus: pause, drumbeat, and then "Iiiiiieeeeeei-iieeii will always love you."

Barry Manilow was well known for incorporating modulations and some people associate "mods" with being *schmaltzy,* sounding "too adult contemporary," "too *Star Search,*" or over-dramatic. However, Faith Hill's crossover smash, "The Way You Love Me" (Keith Follesé and Michael Dulaney) contained several modulations that added to the song's uniqueness and distinct flavor. Modulations have been part of many additional successful songs.

The best modulations sound natural—not forced. They typically raise the key one full step, although it is not uncommon to modulate a half-step or even a step and a half. A "cold" modulation refers to going from the original key to the new key without the benefit of any passing chord or melodic segue. The other option is to set up your modulation by inserting a chord that connects the original key with the new one. Ideally, this chord, often referred to as a "passing chord," provides a smooth transition into your new song's new key. Effective modulations should not seem jarring to the listener—and using a passing chord can help avoid this common pitfall.

In songs that use a Verse - Verse - Bridge - Verse structure, the modulation typically occurs at the beginning of the second verse. This technique has been especially effective in traditional country songs. In songs that employ a Verse - Chorus - Verse - Chorus - Bridge - Chorus structure, the modulation most often occurs in one of three places:

- After the first verse, at the beginning of the first chorus.
- After the second verse, at the beginning of the second chorus.
- After the bridge, at the beginning of the third chorus.

The last option is the one most often used. Modulating from the verse into the chorus is not typically done, but Diane Warren used this technique very effectively in "Unbreak My Heart" (recorded by Toni Braxton). Writers sometimes modulate from each verse into the chorus if they feel they might have failed to create a chorus that has "lifted" and differentiated itself sufficiently from the verse. If you decide to modulate from your first verse into your chorus (the first example), it is likely that you will want to modulate back down to the original key for the second verse. Otherwise, your key will keep getting progressively higher. For example, if the first verse is in the key of C, the first chorus would modulate up one full step to the key of D. Unless you modulate back down, the second verse would be in the key of D (same as the first chorus) and the second chorus would modulate to the key of E. This would probably make your melody excessively rangy for most singers.

There's no right or wrong way to incorporate modulations, nor is there a rule about when they should or should not be used. You can always try a modulation and then decide if it improves—or detracts from—your song. This tool is not one that you will likely incorporate into the majority of your songs. But keep it in your proverbial tool box and occasionally it will be just the ticket to propel your song to the next level.

Choose a song you've written that has a Verse - Chorus - Verse - Chorus - Bridge - Chorus structure. Incorporate a modulation into this song in two different ways.

1. Raise the key of the first chorus one full step from the first verse. Return to your original key for the second verse and modulate back up to the second chorus.

2. After your bridge, raise the key of your last chorus one full step.

You can decide on a song-by-song basis whether this is an effect you like. You might not use modulations often, but in just the right spot, they can be a very powerful melodic tool.

AVOIDING PLAGIARISM

A common concern among songwriters is whether our melodies are truly original, or we are unconsciously "borrowing" from other songs. Sometimes our fear is unwarranted, but other times it may be real. How can you tell? If you've got that nagging feeling that you've heard your melody somewhere before you "wrote" it, play it *without the lyric* for friends and relatives who may be knowledgeable about popular songs. Without the distraction of the lyric it may be easier to recognize the melody that inspired yours. If several people fail to identify your melody as belonging to another song, you're probably safe. But if you do determine that you've inadvertently copied another melody, use the rewriting techniques previously discussed in this section to change your melody sufficiently so that, while it might be *reminiscent* of another melody, it is not identical.

THE MELODY TEST: CAN YOU WRITE EFFECTIVE MELODIES?

The ultimate test of whether a melody is powerful and memorable is its ability to stand up on its own. If you want instrumental versions of your hit songs to play on Muzak, they will need to have melodies that do not require the benefit of a lyric to sound like a hit. Sing your melody into a tape recorder—without the lyric. Either use a nonsense syllable like "la" or try humming. When you listen back, be objective and ask yourself the following questions:

- Are there extra notes crammed in to make the lyric fit?
- Does it sound as though notes (or syllables) are missing?
- Is this the strongest melody you could have written—regardless of the lyric? Or does it sound like the melody was written to accommodate the lyric?
- Does your melody incorporate fresh, catchy rhythms?

- Does your melody sound as if it is following predictable chord changes— or do the chord changes support a catchy, memorable melody?

- Does your melody evoke an emotion all by itself?

One of the primary reasons any song evokes a powerful emotional response is because of its melody. Let the melodies of the songs that move you be your teachers. Analyze those songs you love, noting how their melodies were constructed and which of the tools discussed in this chapter were incorporated. Remain open to exploring the full spectrum of melodic and rhythmic possibilities before settling for one that may not be the very strongest you're capable of writing. After you've rewritten and have multiple versions, how do you know which melody is the best? It's probably the one that you can't get out of your head a day or two later.

EXERCISE: ANALYZING HIT MELODIES

The purpose of this exercise is to learn how your favorite melodies were constructed, then to incorporate those tools that contributed to your favorite songs into your own melodies.

1. Choose a song that you love—in a style in which you hope to write. If you are writing primarily for yourself as an artist, choose a song that was written by the artist who recorded it. If you are writing for artists other than yourself, select a song that was not written by the artist, the producer, or anyone else "inside" the project.

2. Get a copy of the song and a notebook. Analyze the techniques successfully used by the composer by answering the following questions:

   - What song structure did the composer implement?

   - How many bars of music are in each verse, chorus, and bridge?

   - Is there a pre-chorus? If so, how many bars is it composed of?

   - How many bars comprise the primary melodic phrase (i.e., the hook) in each section?

   - How much melodic repetition was used, and where?

   - Is the melodic and rhythmic repetition exact, or are phrases similar?

   - Is the melody comprised of intervals that are close to each other?

   - Are there varied rhythms in different sections of the song?

   - How much range is required to sing this song?

   - Are there unexpected, fresh melodic intervals or chords?

WHAT IF I WRITE ONLY MUSIC?

If you write only music, remember that finding a lyricist who can generate those words that sound as if they were born to match your melodies is as much a part of your job as is writing those terrific melodies. Publishers, recording artists, producers, and record label executives review only completed songs. Your job is to network and find those collaborators who can transform your melodies into hit songs.

For those who are primarily, or exclusively, composers, here's some good news: if you excel at your craft you will be in demand. There are many more lyricists who are looking for melody writers than vice versa. While it's true that the vast majority of urban, rap, and hip-hop artists write or cowrite their material, many of them write to music tracks—keyboards, bass, and drums that have no melody, only chords and rhythm. Composers who are able to create exceptional tracks in these genres should have many opportunities for collaborations. For suggestions regarding finding cowriters, see "What If I Write Only Lyrics?" (page 78) and "Collaborating" (page 204).

Some composers choose to write instrumental music—music that is intended to be performed without lyrics. It is extremely rare for an instrumental song to become a hit on the radio; most of them have been theme songs from films, for example, the themes from *The Godfather, Romeo and Juliet,* and *Chariots of Fire.* Additionally, instrumentalists such as Kenny G and Dave Koz tend to write their own songs. However, there is great demand for music in television and films and these areas are outlets that any instrumental composer should be aware of.

The individual in charge of selecting music for a television show or film is known as the "music supervisor." Writers of music for television and movies almost always provide finished pieces of music, as opposed to rough demos. These instrumental compositions, or segments of them, are often used as background music and are typically produced in home studios by writers who also perform the music on synthesizers. Music libraries are companies that collect music from a variety of different composers, and then offer music supervisors an enormous variety of instrumental cues to choose from. For information about placing your compositions with music supervisors and music libraries, see "Pitching Instrumental Music" in Step 5 of this book.

STEP 3: CONCLUSION

Writing memorable, unique melodies does not typically happen by chance or without effort. With practice and persistence, the tools described within this book can help you to write the kinds of melodies and rhythms that demand attention. Using the techniques previously discussed, try writing at least five different melodies for each section of your songs (i.e., verse, chorus, bridge) before deciding which one you feel is the strongest. Wouldn't you be willing to do this if you knew that your success was contingent on composing the very strongest melodies? Well, it might be. Melody truly is that important. Infuse your melodies with something that is fresh and truly special. If you fail to do so, why should a listener (i.e., a publisher, producer, recording artist, or record label executive) choose your song instead of the excellent competition? Writing well-crafted, but predictable melodies is analogous to writing lyrics that consist of tired old clichés, and images and concepts that we've heard far too many times before. This won't get you on the charts—or into the hearts of your listeners.

For additional information about melody techniques, listen to *Writing Hit Melodies with Jason Blume* (instructional CD available at www.jasonblume.com).

MELODY CHECKLIST

Photocopy this checklist and keep it where you normally write. Each time you finish a draft of a song, check to be sure that you've successfully incorporated the tools and techniques that follow:

- ❏ Easy to remember and sing

- ❏ Not too "wordy" to be melodic

- ❏ Obvious where the title goes (without a lyric)

- ❏ Rhythmic and/or melodic phrases repeat

- ❏ Melody and lyric seem to go together (prosody)

- ❏ Rhythms are varied in verse, chorus, and bridge

- ❏ Not too much range for singers to sing

- ❏ Phrases are short and catchy

- ❏ Melodic phrases are symmetrical

- ❏ Contains a "magic" moment (fresh, unexpected note or chord)

- ❏ Contains sequential, logical intervals

- ❏ There's no doubt where the chorus is

- ❏ Bridge (if applicable) adds a new musical dimension

- ❏ Includes a signature lick

- ❏ Incorporates fresh, interesting rhythms

- ❏ Is accompanied by the most effective chords

- ❏ Has been rewritten to make each line its strongest

- ❏ Melody holds up without the lyric

Producing Successful Demos

The demo is very important. If people tell you they can hear it through a guitar/vocal, don't believe them. Try to make the demo as close to a record as you can. With most of my songs, the artists and producers have tried to come close to the demo. The songwriters are the "true producers." The artists and producers reproduce what we produce. If you can get a great demo you can get a great record.

WAYNE PERRY (Hit songwriter with cuts by artists including Tim McGraw, the Backstreet Boys, George Strait, Toby Keith, and Joe)

CHAPTER 8

Learning How and When to Record a Demo

When it's time to make the actual demo that will be used to pitch, there are very few, great songs that can make it with a demo that uses only a guitar and a vocal—and most of those are written by writer-artists who have the rare ability to sit down and play a guitar to sell a song. Being able to do that is a much rarer talent than being a hit songwriter. To play a song for an artist, a full demo is what's normally needed in order to compete with what's going on out there.

MICHAEL HOLLANDSWORTH (President, Full Circle Music)

"Demo" is an abbreviated form of the word "demonstration"; an effective demo literally demonstrates your song's potential. Ideally, it provides the listener with all he or she needs to hear to determine the song's hit potential and appropriateness for his or her needs. Different types of songs require varying types of production to convey the song's possibilities.

When I began writing songs, I had no clue what constituted an effective demo. I couldn't imagine how I would ever acquire the skills—or the money—to produce one. I could barely pay the rent for the tiny room I was living in, so initially, I would look for collaborators who owned home studios where we could demo the song for free. If they could also play all the instruments and sing the song, that was even better. At that point, hiring a studio, an engineer, musicians, and vocalists—and knowing what to tell them to do—seemed as likely a possibility for me as flying. But, like everything else in songwriting, learning how to produce successful demos was part of a long process that included trial and error, and lots of practice.

HOW TO KNOW WHEN YOUR SONG IS READY

Few things break my heart more than hearing an elaborately produced, expensive demo of a song that I know will never stand a chance of being legitimately published or recorded. The writer has not only spent time and money unnecessarily, but will likely have grown attached to the song "as is." (There seems to be a direct correlation between the amount of money spent on a demo and the songwriter's refusal to do additional rewriting—especially if the demo sounds terrific to friends and family.)

The very first step in the demo process is being sure that the song itself is ready. But how can you be sure? Put your song under the proverbial microscope. Ask yourself if you can honestly say that each line of lyric and melody is the strongest and freshest you're capable of. Use the lyric and melody checklists provided in this book to see if you're hitting the mark. When you're confident that your work is as strong as you can make it, it's time to get some additional opinions. In order to play the song for others and to objectively evaluate it yourself, you'll need a rough recording of your song—a "work tape." (More about recording work tapes in Chapter 9.)

You can get song critiques from a variety of sources. There are songwriters' organizations throughout the US and some of them provide peer critiques and periodically bring in music industry professionals to their meetings (see Appendix). The Songwriters Guild of America (SGA), the Nashville Songwriters Association International (NSAI), and Taxi are among the organizations that offer their members professional song evaluations through the mail. You may also be able to get a professional opinion by attending workshops and classes. If you have already established relationships with music publishers, and you trust their ability to recognize your song's potential in a rough version, ask if they would be willing to share their opinion. But, do not send a rough work tape as your first introduction to a music industry professional. You'll want to make your best first impression with a well-produced demo recording.

If you cowrite, ask your collaborators for their honest opinion of your work. You might set up a support group to review each other's songs, using the lyric and melody checklists included in this book. Using the checklists helps evaluators objectively specify your song's strengths and weaknesses, avoiding hurtful, unproductive comments like, "I just don't like it," or "It doesn't sound like a hit." Unfortunately, friends and family are not generally qualified to determine if your work is meeting professional standards. The goal is to get as much objective, professional input as possible before investing money in a demo.

A word about critiques: Not all evaluators (even professionals) are equally skilled at identifying the areas that need work, or at determining the merits of songs. Some publishers and other industry professionals may be able to spot a hit instantly, but may be at a complete loss to express why your song doesn't meet the criteria. After receiving a critique of one of your songs, if you instantly feel, "Wow, she's right! Why didn't I see that?" or "That would make the song so much stronger," you will obviously want to make the suggested revisions. But, if you feel strongly that the critique is off-base, allow a few days to pass (to recover from being told that your "child" is not quite as perfect as you thought) and ask yourself if there are any elements of the critique that resonate as true. If you strongly disagree with what has been said, and you have a legitimate basis for your feelings, get additional opinions before making any changes. Ultimately, you'll want to write the very strongest songs—while also pleasing yourself.

You may need to repeat the process of rewriting, recording a work tape, and receiving critiques several times before you decide that your song is ready for a demo. Not every song warrants the time and financial commitment of a demo. Most professional songwriters do not record a demo of every song they write. You may decide that a particular song is simply one more step in your journey of honing your songwriting skills, and it is not in your best interest to produce a demo.

IDENTIFYING WHAT'S RIGHT FOR YOUR SONG

I fully produce my demos. It seems that nobody can hear them otherwise. The days of the piano/vocal are gone.

FRANNE GOLDE (Writer of songs on Grammy-winning albums and cuts with artists including Whitney Houston, Faith Hill, and Celine Dion)

You've gotten positive feedback on your song and have decided to proceed with recording a demo. What's the next step? There are two primary considerations: What does this particular song require and how much money can you afford to spend? Songs in various genres require different amounts of production and instrumentation to convey their potential. In preparing for this book, I interviewed many successful songwriters, music publishers, A&R executives, and record producers. One of the questions I asked them was what qualities they felt were important in a demo. Almost all of these music industry professionals concurred with my own experience: a demo of a ballad does not generally need more than a professionally produced guitar or keyboard and an excellent vocal, but an up-tempo song usually requires additional instrumentation. That doesn't mean that a ballad might not benefit from additional embellishment, or even a full-band demo—but it's not mandatory, the way it is for most up-tempo songs. If you are writing an up-tempo, groove-oriented dance song, your demo better include those elements that will make the listener want to dance. For demos of up-tempo songs, it's almost impossible to get the feel of the song across without including a rhythm section (bass and drums), in addition to other instruments.

The demo is very important, but has to be decided upon on a song-by-song basis. A great ballad doesn't need as much as a full-on dance song.

JUDY STAKEE (Vice President, Creative Services, Warner/Chappell Music Publishing)

You may be lucky enough to find an A&R person or a record producer who has the rare ability to hear your song's potential from a very rough demo. But he or she will have to play that same demo for the artist (who will play it for his or her spouse), the artist's manager (who will play it for her boyfriend), the other A&R executives, and the record label president. The chances are between slim and none that all of these people will be able to hear what a great song you've written if it's represented by a poorly produced demo. A successful demo gives the listener an indication of how a song might sound if it were fully produced.

AVOIDING "THE BIG LIE"

A great demo can get an average song cut. A poor demo can keep a great song from getting cut.

GEORGE TEREN (Hit songwriter)

Early on in my career, I used to tell myself over and over: "But this song is so wonderful, surely, they'll be able to hear how great it sounds even though my demo isn't very good." But it's not true. Most music industry professionals who review songs are deluged with song submissions. They have neither the time, nor the ability, to envision how your song might sound if your demo had been produced differently. It either sounds like a hit or it's on to the next song.

While a big part of your demo's job is to get your song published or recorded, it also serves another crucial purpose. Since songwriters are rarely invited to an artist's recording sessions, your demo is your representative there. The music on that CD is your only opportunity to share with the artist and producer your vision of how your song should sound. If you envision a specific guitar lick, a unique vocal harmony line, a particular combination of instruments, or a special string part that you feel is important to your song, it needs to be included in your demo. Music publishers, A&R executives, recording artists, and record producers are not mind readers. Finished master recordings often sound remarkably like the song's demo. If those elements that contribute to your vision for your song are included on your demo, there's a very good chance they will be on the finished recording. If they are not on the demo, there's virtually no chance that the publisher, record producer, or recording artist will imagine what you are hearing.

I used to resent being forced into the position of "record producer"—especially since I knew that my skills were very limited in that department. I felt it should be enough that I had written a song with a strong melody and lyric. Why should I be obligated to spend money I didn't have to present a "finished record" on a silver platter to a professional who should be able to hear my song's potential even if I sang it a cappella? In the real world it doesn't work that way and my energy is better spent honing my demo-production skills than complaining about the way I wish things were. To compete with the professional competition, I've learned to produce the very best demos my budget and skills allow.

DISTINGUISHING BETWEEN SONG DEMOS AND ARTIST DEMOS

To determine what level of production your demo will require, you need to be clear about what function your demo is intended to serve. If your demo is intended as a tool to get your song published and ultimately recorded by an artist other than yourself, it is considered a "song demo." But, if the demo's purpose is to demonstrate your potential as a recording artist, it is considered an "artist demo"—and it will need to meet even higher standards. Typically, the vocals are mixed louder on a song demo than they would be on an artist demo, or on a song you might hear on the radio. This is done to ensure that a listener who is considering recording your song can clearly hear the words and melody. On the other hand, the musicianship, clarity, and overall production values of an artist demo often approximate those of a finished master recording (one that would be included on an album). Most importantly, the vocal performance in an artist demo needs to be nothing less than perfect. The pitch, tone, and emotion of the vocals must be excellent.

Many aspiring recording artists spend tens of thousands of dollars and hire well-known producers to help them record their artist demos. In these instances, the producer helps the artist find songs and uses his or her expertise to create a demo that is indistinguishable from a master recording. Many of these producers choose to work with artists because of their strong belief in the artist's potential. There is no shortage of producers (many of whom have formerly had major hits) who now earn their livings by producing demos for artists. But unfortunately, in some instances, the only ability an artist needs in order to contract the services of these producers is the ability to write a check. Within the industry, these deals are often referred to as "custom sessions," and while many producers indeed provide a legitimate service, some custom deals fall under the category of "scam." For additional information about custom deals, see "Avoiding the Scams" in Chapter 14.

While you may not need to invest a fortune, if your goal is to produce a demo to secure a record deal as an artist, you need to present a demo that will sound like a hit—with no excuses or apologies attached. But remember, success can be achieved one step at a time. If the most you can afford is a professional recording of your voice, accompanied by a guitar or a keyboard, don't despair. This may be enough to attract a publisher, producer, or other industry professional who may be able to help you get to that next level—if your talent is exceptional.

> *I like for a demo to effectively put across the "intent" of the writers. The style of music often dictates the type of demo. Many country songs can be very effective in a guitar/vocal demo, whereas an urban or R&B piece may need loops and more production techniques to translate the groove intended by the writers. In general, I'd much rather get a simple demo of a song rather than a poorly, but more produced, version.*
>
> RICK CHUDACOFF (Hit producer/songwriter)

I can't count how many times I've heard an artist say, "But if you could just hear me play live...." While it's important for an artist to have the skills to present an exciting live performance, there's a problem with that thinking. Since it is a recorded product that is played on the radio and purchased by the consumer, the record label executive needs to hear how the artist sounds on a recording. It's true that a handful of artists have been signed to record deals based on a live performance in a record company president's office. But it's a rare artist who has the kind of connections that can facilitate that kind of meeting. It's also a rare performer who can convey the full extent of his or her artistry without the trappings of a band and the enhancements a professional recording studio can add.

As with a song demo, the amount of production and instrumentation on the artist demo depends to a large extent on the genre of music. An acoustic-oriented folksinger, a rapper, or a country singer may require far less embellishment to convey his or her potential than a Euro-techno dance, rock, or funk band. But even the majority of acoustic-oriented artists are signed to record deals on the strength of a demo that showcases them in their very best light.

The one instance in which it might be best to use a live recording (as opposed to a demo produced in a recording studio) is when the demo is intended exclusively to help you secure work as a live performer. According to Wind River Recording artist David Roth, "People who book folk venues have told me they often prefer live demos to fully produced CDs. It makes sense because someone who books live performances is more interested in how you sound and relate to a live audience than how you can use studio musicians and studio tricks to sound good."

MEASURING UP TO THE PROFESSIONAL STANDARD

Prior to the first time I heard demos of songs that had gone on to become hits, I had no idea of the quality of the demos my competition was producing. I was amazed at how much the demos sounded like finished records. The musicians were excellent, and I couldn't believe the demo singers didn't have their own record deals. Most of the time, the catchy, instrumental hooks on the record had come straight from the demo. The final product usually had vocal harmonies in the same places the demo had used them. With the exception of the sound quality and the vocalist, sometimes it was hard to differentiate the demo from the hit record.

My first demos were recorded for free in friends' basements. The musicianship was mediocre at best, and the vocal performances were even worse. When I pitched those demos, no matter how well-written the songs might have been, from the opening notes I was sending a message loud and clear: "This song is from an amateur." Whether you are producing a guitar/vocal song demo or a full-band artist demo, your demo needs to be a clear, professional-sounding recording with top-notch musicians and the best vocalist you can possibly hire. We'll discuss this in more detail later in this section.

Many songwriters own equipment that allows them to produce their demos at home. One advantage to this is that they can take their time and explore various arrangements and sounds for their songs—without budgetary concerns. However, the best synthesizers and recording equipment will not produce "radio-friendly" licks unless the writer/producer can envision and perform them. Therefore, some songwriters who own home studios hire professional musicians to play on the demos they produce at home.

The most important part of the demo is being able to hear the lyrics and melody, whether it is just a guitar/vocal work tape or a full demo.

MIKE SISTAD (Nashville Director
of Member Relations, ASCAP)

KNOWING HOW MANY TRACKS ARE NECESSARY

Virtually all professional recordings are made on multitrack recorders. Some of these use tape; however, this mode of recording has almost completely been replaced by machines that record digitally, directly onto a computer hard drive. These machines are able to record multiple instruments and sounds, while keeping each individual sound separated on different "tracks." Different multitrack tape recording machines have the capability to record 4, 8, 12, 16, 24, or 32 tracks. For some albums, these machines are linked together to provide the artist and producer with 96 tracks or more. With the use of computers, the number of tracks available is tremendously increased; it would not be unusual for a professional album to be recorded using 120 separate tracks. But for a demo you will rarely need more than 24 tracks. Depending on the type of demo you are producing, you may need far fewer.

Drums may be assigned 16 tracks or more so that each sound (hi-hat, crash cymbals, kick drum, snare, etc.) can be isolated. Having each instrument (and vocal) on its own track allows the engineer to adjust the reverb, equalization, and other effects. (If this sounds incomprehensible, don't panic. You don't need to be an expert in this area—you just need to hire a competent recording engineer.)

How many tracks do you need for your demo? The standard answer I've always heard is that what is recorded onto the tracks is far more important than the actual number of tracks. That's true. No amount of tracks will turn a mediocre song into a great one. However, using multiple tracks will allow your engineer to make the instruments and vocals that are recorded sound their best. If you are producing a demo that will consist of a guitar and a vocal (with no harmony vocals), you probably don't need more than 4 tracks. If you are recording a seven-piece band and three background vocalists, you may need 32 tracks or more. Of course, part of your decision will be based upon your budget.

DETERMINING BUDGETS

> *You don't need Platinum-record credits to record a guitar/vocal demo, but neither do you want an inexperienced engineer and poorly maintained studio when the session musicians are on the clock. When selecting studios, engineers, musicians, and vocalists, keep in mind the difference between price and value. The difference in price between mediocre and excellent quality is sometimes small, but mediocre quality will seldom be of great value.*
>
> HERB TASSIN (Studio owner/recording engineer whose clients include Art Garfunkel, Diamond Rio, and Pam Tillis)

Producing demos can be expensive. A professional, full-time songwriter may spend $15,000 or more per year on demos. Many staff-writers receive a demo budget from their publisher. Other staff-writers who own their own studios may have the estimated costs of their demos factored into the advance they receive from their publishers. Your primary costs will be for studios, engineers, musicians, vocalists, tape (if you are using a tape-based recording format), and CD costs. The cost of each of these can vary greatly, depending upon their quality or credentials. It also depends on what part of the country you live in.

It is important to decide how many musicians you will need to hire in order to have your demo reflect what you hear in your head (e.g., is this particular song crying out for a saxophone, a steel guitar, or a cello?). This decision will help you determine how many tracks you will require in a studio.

It costs far less to rent studio time in a 4-track or 8-track studio than in a studio with 32-track capability. Studio rates may be quoted per hour or as a "day rate" and may or may not include an engineer. Depending on your location, a competent 8-track studio in someone's basement may cost as little as $25 per hour, including an engineer. The best 32-track studios cost in excess of $250 per hour. However, there's no reason to spend that much for a demo. Most cities have 24-track studios available for $50 per hour or less. This should be sufficient for even the most elaborately produced demo. Note that many studios will offer a discounted rate during off-peak hours.

One of the recording engineer's responsibilities is to effectively capture the sounds of your instruments and vocals on tape or digitally. This requires selecting the most appropriate microphones and positioning them to best record each instrument and vocalist. The engineer is skilled in operating the recording console and the equipment that will add "effects" (e.g., equalization, echo, or reverb) to each sound. It's also the engineer's job to mix the instruments and vocals together, placing each in its appropriate place in relation to the other sounds.

Many small studios are owned and operated by recording engineers who include their services in the price of the studio. If you need to hire an engineer, ask the studio manager to recommend someone who is familiar with that particular studio's equipment. Then ask to hear samples of the engineer's work before making your decision. The cost of hiring an engineer can range from $10 per hour to more than $100 per hour depending on the individual's skill level and credentials. In most circumstances, a competent engineer for a demo costs in the range of $25 to $45 per hour. Similar to studios, engineers sometimes offer a "day rate," as opposed to a price per hour.

It's often most cost-effective to record more than one song during a recording session. Some musicians charge a fixed fee per song; however, musicians who are members of the American Federation of Musicians union (AFM) are paid per hour, usually in a three-hour block—not per song. Therefore, when employing musicians who are union members, it will cost you the same amount of money for musicians whether you record one song or six songs in a three-hour recording session. "Union scale," the amount paid to musicians who are AFM members, varies from city to city. The AFM, which has offices in most major cities, provides listings of professional local musicians.

In Nashville, it's not unusual for professional songwriters to record the music tracks for five or six country songs in one three-hour period. The vocals are then recorded and the tracks mixed during another session. When songs are recorded this way, the complete demos generally cost in the range of $350 to $850 per song. Whether you're at the high or the low end of this range depends on how many musicians you hire, the credentials of those musicians, the quality of the studio, and how many songs are recorded in the three-hour block. I don't recommend recording multiple songs during one session until you gain some experience in demo production. Trying to cram in as many songs as possible with the time clock ticking is very stressful and can result in compromising the quality of all the song demos recorded.

To reduce the cost of their demos, many developing songwriters hire musicians and vocalists who are not affiliated with the musicians' and singers' unions. There are tremendously talented musicians and singers who are not union members—and they perform on countless, terrific demos. Typically, however, the most successful players and vocalists—those with major album credits—work only through the union and command higher fees.

"Cartage" is an additional expense you need to calculate into your budget. It refers to having musical equipment and instruments delivered and set up. Many musicians haul their own equipment and do not charge any additional fee. However, it's quite common for successful drummers, keyboard players, and guitarists to have a company or individual move their instruments and equipment from one gig to the next, set it up, and break it down. The fee varies from $60 to $200. When calculating your demo budget, ask the musicians you are hiring if there are additional fees for cartage, and how much those charges will be. You may find that you don't require all of the instruments and equipment a musician would typically have delivered to the session; determining this may save you cartage fees.

The cost of blank tape, if applicable, and CDs also needs to be included in your demo budget. The type of equipment available at the recording studio you choose will determine the format of the tape you need to purchase (if any). When recording directly into a computer, no tape is required. Studios with tape-based formats almost always provide blank multitrack tape, CDs, and digital audiotapes (DATs) if they know in advance that you wish to purchase them. However, most studios add a surcharge for providing that service. You will save money if you supply your own tape. Be sure to ask the studio what format is required. (For additional information about tape formats, see Chapter 10.)

If a piano is one of the instruments you plan to record on your demo, one more cost to factor into your budget is the fee to have the piano tuned for your session. While a piano used at home or for writing songs may not need to be perfectly in tune, professional-sounding recordings require the piano (and all other instruments) to be perfectly tuned. Many studios hire a piano tuner prior to the beginning of each recording project. The fee for this is typically $60 to $100.

For urban and pop music demos, it is much more common to hire one musician to program the drums, bass, and keyboard parts on synthesizer. This is frequently all that is required to produce a full-sounding demo. Depending on the song, you may also choose to add a guitarist. It may sound as though hiring one or two musicians should be less expensive than hiring a full band, but that is usually not the case. Building a music track by programming one sound at a time can be very time-consuming. Professional-quality demos of urban, R&B, or pop songs usually cost at least $500 per song and it is not uncommon for successful professional pop writers to spend more than $1,200 per demo. A developing, unpublished songwriter should not be spending this kind of money unless his or her last name is Rockefeller, Getty, or Trump. You certainly want to present your songs in their best light, but until you secure a publisher to absorb your demo costs, or begin generating income from your songs, you probably don't need to spend more than $350 to $500 per song demo. Excellent demos of ballads can be recorded for significantly less than this amount.

The amount of money you spend recording a demo of your song is affected by the amount of time you take to record the instruments and vocals. In preparing a budget, always factor in a "cushion." When Murphy wrote his famous law ("If something can go wrong—it will"), he must have been producing demos. There will inevitably be a vocalist who can't quite get the harmony right, a musician who needs an extra twenty minutes to nail his solo, an equipment failure, or an engineer who accidentally erases the last note of your song. Or, it may just take you longer than you'd anticipated to convey to the musicians what you'd like to hear. As you produce more demos and practice the skills required for producing demos, you will get better at them and will require less time in the studio.

DECIDING BETWEEN SELF-PRODUCING AND DEMO SERVICES

Deciding whether to produce your own demo or to hire a demo service is similar to deciding to either hire a contractor to build an addition on your house or build it yourself. Assess if you have the time, skills, and inclination to hire a studio, recording engineer, musicians, and vocalists; purchase tape; and oversee and make decisions regarding every aspect of the recording and mixing process. Consider also whether the quality of musicianship you need in order to be competitive is available in your hometown. Using a top-quality demo service based in a major music center gives you access to professional musicians and vocalists who are skilled in recording for the current market. Due to supply and demand, studios, musicians, and vocalists in cities with thriving music scenes may cost less than they would elsewhere. If you are self-producing your demos, it may be cost-effective and worthwhile to make periodic trips to record in one of these cities.

Because of the volume of demos they produce, demo services are often able to produce a demo less expensively than the writer could on his or her own. They can also take the guesswork out of your budget by quoting a flat fee per song. Many demo services work via the mail. Songwriters send a work tape and lyric sheet, and the demo service returns a finished demo. Some songwriters prefer to be included in each aspect of the creative process and are not comfortable being "out of the loop." They may choose to produce their demos themselves.

When turning your song over to a demo service, it's important to let them know what you want. Provide as much detail as possible—and be specific. Instead of saying, "I want it to sound country," try "I'm looking for a contemporary, pop/country feel along the lines of Faith

Hill's 'Cry.' I want to include electric guitars and an organ sound like they did on that song." If you've always imagined an acoustic guitar playing the instrumental solo in a specific song, don't assume the demo service will know that. If you hear three-part vocal harmonies on your choruses, be sure to specify that, too. It can help to send a copy of another song that has similar instrumentation or the same "groove" or feel that you're hoping to capture on your song. Of course, it's not realistic to send a demo service a copy of a Madonna song that may have cost $35,000 to produce as your example, and expect your $500 demo to sound the same. But it will give the producer and musicians a direction to pursue.

On your work tape, include any instrumental hooks that you want on your demo. If you're unable to play them, sing them a cappella into a tape recorder. Let the demo service know whether you want a male or female vocalist and specify the style you want. Again, it's important to be specific. There's a world of difference between the styles of Janet Jackson, Beyoncé, and Mary J. Blige, yet they could all be considered female R&B singers. The more information you provide a demo service, the better the odds are of your demo sounding the way you imagined.

A listing of excellent, reasonably priced demo services can be found at www.jasonblume.com. As in any business, the best referrals usually come as a result of networking. When you hear a demo that sounds great, ask the songwriter how he or she produced it. Was it produced by a demo service? Were live musicians used, or was it programmed on computers and synthesizers? Who is the singer? Who played those great electric guitar parts? You can often get referrals to demo services by calling songwriter organizations in the major music centers. NSAI maintains a limited listing of Nashville-based demo services. They also recommend purchasing a copy of the *Nashville Red Book*, a comprehensive music business directory that is available in Nashville bookstores and at the NSAI office. There are similar directories that list musicians' services in New York and Los Angeles (see Appendix).

Be wary of any company that promises to either publish or include your songs on an album—contingent upon your paying them to produce demo recordings. While some legitimate publishers may indeed require you to re-demo a song in order to bring it up to the professional standard, they will typically absorb the cost. However, some shady individuals and companies earn their livings by producing exorbitantly priced demos—with assurance that the new demo will result in your song being published or included on an album. These companies are essentially overpriced demo services. They fall under the category of "scams" and acquire their clients based on false hopes and promises. You can protect yourself by keeping your demo budgets within the guidelines presented within this chapter—and by remembering that legitimate publishing companies do not solicit unpublished writers and do not earn their livings by producing demos.

To write successful songs and produce effective demos, you don't have to be an expert in every aspect of the songwriting and demo process. What you do have to do is honestly examine your strengths and weaknesses. Concentrate on the tasks you're good at, while working with professionals in those areas where you need help.

EXERCISE: PLANNING TO RECORD YOUR DEMO

This exercise is designed to help you practice the skills necessary to produce a successful demo.

1. Select a song you've written, but have not yet demoed, and answer the following questions:

   - What type of demo would be best to show your song's potential (i.e., keyboard/vocal, guitar/vocal, programmed synthesizers, or live full band)?

   - What instruments do you want to use?

   - How many tracks will be required?

   - Do you feel competent to produce the demo yourself, or would you hire a demo production service?

2. After you've answered these questions, research what it will cost to produce the demo you have in mind.

CHAPTER 9

Preparing to Record Your Demo

When a writer is prepared, it makes everything easier and more efficient in the studio. Some people are continuing to write when they bring the song into the studio. Part of the creative process includes possible rewrites at any time, but you should have had enough critiquing to know that the song is finished. The lyrics should be typed and you should have plenty of copies. You need a work tape that is in tune and in tempo so that it's possible to decipher what is intended. It doesn't have to be polished, but if it doesn't have a consistent meter and a consistent pitch then it's going to be a real guessing game to decipher what the song really is.

BRYAN CUMMING
(Studio 23 recording studio)

The more time you spend preparing for your demo, the less aggravation and expense you're likely to encounter in the studio. Always reconfirm your appointment with the studio, engineer, vocalist, and musicians several days prior to the recording session. It's important to listen to your song repeatedly and either jot down notes or tape record your melodic ideas so you won't forget them. Expressing your ideas to the musicians as clearly as possible avoids the risk that they won't know what you have in mind.

Producing demos takes a lot of time and involves many individual tasks. It's not uncommon for me to finish writing a song in only a few hours, and then spend twenty hours preparing for and recording the demo. When producing your own demo, you need a work tape, chord charts, lyric sheets, an arrangement, and the proper key for your demo singer—all prepared before the recording session.

PREPARING LYRIC SHEETS

A "lyric sheet" is the document that contains the words to a song. Type your lyric sheet as in the example that follows on page 145. Note that the only information included on the lyric sheet is the song title, the lyric itself, the writers' names, a contact address, a telephone number, a fax number (if applicable), an e-mail address, the copyright symbol, and the year of copyright

*D*REAMER'S MOON MUSIC

9 Music Square South, PMB 352, Nashville, TN 37203; (615) 665-2381; JBSongdoc1@aol.com

IF IT HADN'T RAINED

I hope you don't mind if I
Stand in your doorway and I
Wait till this storm passes by
I'm soaked right to the skin and
I guess you can't believe it
When the radio says "hot and dry"

These shoes are never gonna be the same
But suddenly I have no complaints

> IF IT HADN'T RAINED
> I bet we would have never wound up here together
> Oh, I sure do love this weather ('cause)
> IF IT HADN'T RAINED
> I wouldn't be here wonderin'
> If that's my heart or thunder
> I feel poundin' in my veins
> Oh - IF IT HADN'T RAINED

Thank you for the offer
To lend me your umbrella
I promise that I'll bring it back real soon
To show my appreciation
I hope you'll let me be takin' you out
How 'bout Sunday afternoon

Is that a rainbow reachin' cross the sky
Could this be love - or have I lost my mind

> (Repeat Chorus)

When I left for work I never did imagine
I'd be dancin' in the rain with the puddles splashin'

> (Repeat Chorus)

JASON BLUME
CLAIRE ULANOFF

Dreamer's Moon Music/Zomba Songs Inc. (BMI)/Planet Happy Publishing (ASCAP) ©2004
Contact: Jason Blume (615) 665-2381; JBSongdoc1@aol.com

registration (for example, ©2004). It is not appropriate to include any additional information (e.g., vocals performed by Maris Goldberg and the Teens Three, or demo production by Virginia Rice); nor is it proper to include a description of the song (e.g., "mid-tempo pop song" or "positive love ballad").

If your song was copyrighted more than a year or two ago, I suggest showing the copyright as the current year; no one wants to think he or she is being pitched an old song that you haven't been able to get recorded in years. If the person to whom you've sent your song decides to record or publish it, you can inform him or her, at a later date, that it was originally copyrighted in 1987. In the event that the song is published, also include the publishing information and writers' performing rights affiliation, for example, Dreamer's Moon Music (BMI).

When you record your demo, be sure to bring enough copies of the lyric sheets for you, your collaborators (if applicable), and the recording engineer, as well as an extra copy for your singer, in case he or she has forgotten to bring one. It's a good idea to double-space your singer's copy so that he or she will have room to add notes, symbols, or numbers above the words.

RECORDING WORK TAPES

A work tape is a rough, bare-bones recording of a song. Its purpose is simply to allow the listener to hear the words and music. A guitar or piano and a vocal will be sufficient. Your work tape may be recorded onto a portable, handheld tape recorder at home. If you are unable to play an instrument or sing the song well enough to accurately get the melody on tape, hire someone to do that for you. If you do employ someone else to record your work tape, the process should not take more than an hour, or cost more than $25 to $50 per song.

The instrumental and vocal performances do not need to be perfect on a work tape; it is not a demo and will not be used to pitch the song. But, it is important that the melody, chords, and timing be accurate, because you will use this recording to have your song critiqued. In the event that you decide your song is ready for a demo, your musicians and singers will listen to the work tape in order to learn the song. By the way, although you might copy this rough recording onto a CD, it is still typically referred to as a work "tape."

WRITING CHORD CHARTS

The chord chart of a song is usually referred to as simply "the chart." This is the music your musicians read in order to know what to play. Chord charts are not to be confused with "lead sheets." A chord chart shows the chords for each measure of a song. Lyrics and actual notes are not included. A lead sheet includes every note of the melody, as well as the corresponding chords and lyrics. (Sheet music is an example of a lead sheet.) A lead sheet is neither required nor expected by the musicians or vocalists at your demo session.

Prior to your recording session, clearly write out the chord chart for each song or hire someone to do that for you. For an individual to write a chord chart for you, he or she needs to hear either a live performance or a work tape that includes the chords.

In the event that you have written a melody, but are not able to figure out or play the accompanying chords, you can hire a musician to generate the chords as described in Chapter 5, "Writing A Capella," page 100. This is typically done for a flat fee and does not ordinarily constitute a collaboration.

If you employ musicians who are members of the musicians' union, it is standard for the musician who is designated as "leader" on the session to generate the chord charts at no additional charge. (He or she will earn an additional fee as the session leader.) If you hire someone to write out your chord charts, expect to pay $20 to $35 per song. Photocopy the charts and bring enough copies to the session for each musician and engineer, as well as for yourself and any collaborators. This way you can all follow along.

THE NASHVILLE NUMBER SYSTEM

In Nashville, chord charts are prepared using a method called the "Nashville Number System." In this system, which is totally unique to Nashville, each chord is assigned a number, which is determined by its distance from the root chord. The advantage of this system is that it allows the musicians to transpose (change keys) with little effort. For instance, if the key of C seems too low for the singer, the charts still work perfectly in any other key.

For example, in the key of C: C = 1, D = 2, E = 3, F = 4, G = 5, A = 6, B = 7. Sharps and flats are designated by a sharp or flat symbol preceding or following the number. For example, in the key of C: C# = #1 (or 1#); E♭ = ♭3 (or 3♭). A minor key is designated by a dash (-) immediately following the number, or a lowercase letter "m." In the key of C: C minor = 1- (or 1m); F# minor = 4#- (or 4#m).

There are many more symbols and intricacies involved in the Nashville Number System. If you're interested in mastering this method, read *The Nashville Number System* by Chas Williams, *Nashville Numbering System* by Neal Matthews, or *A Complete "How To" Guide for the Nashville Number System* (book and audiocassette) written by Todd McCoig and Mark Honeycutt.

Whether you need a conventional chord chart or one that uses the Nashville Number System, if you are unable to generate it yourself, there are lots of professionals who can do that for you. If you are using a demo service they will provide the chord charts. Be sure to keep a copy of your charts; they may be requested in the event that an artist wants to perform or record your song in the future. On pages 148 and 149, you can compare a standard chord chart with one that uses the Nashville Number System.

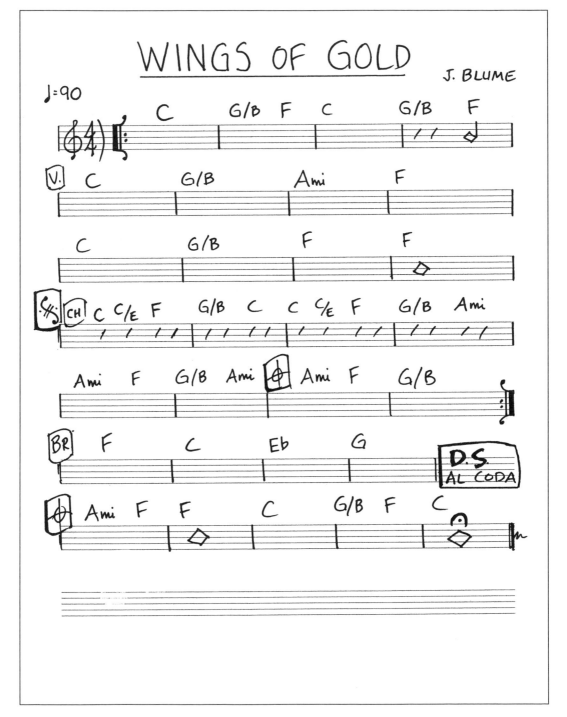

Sample Nashville Number System Chord Chart

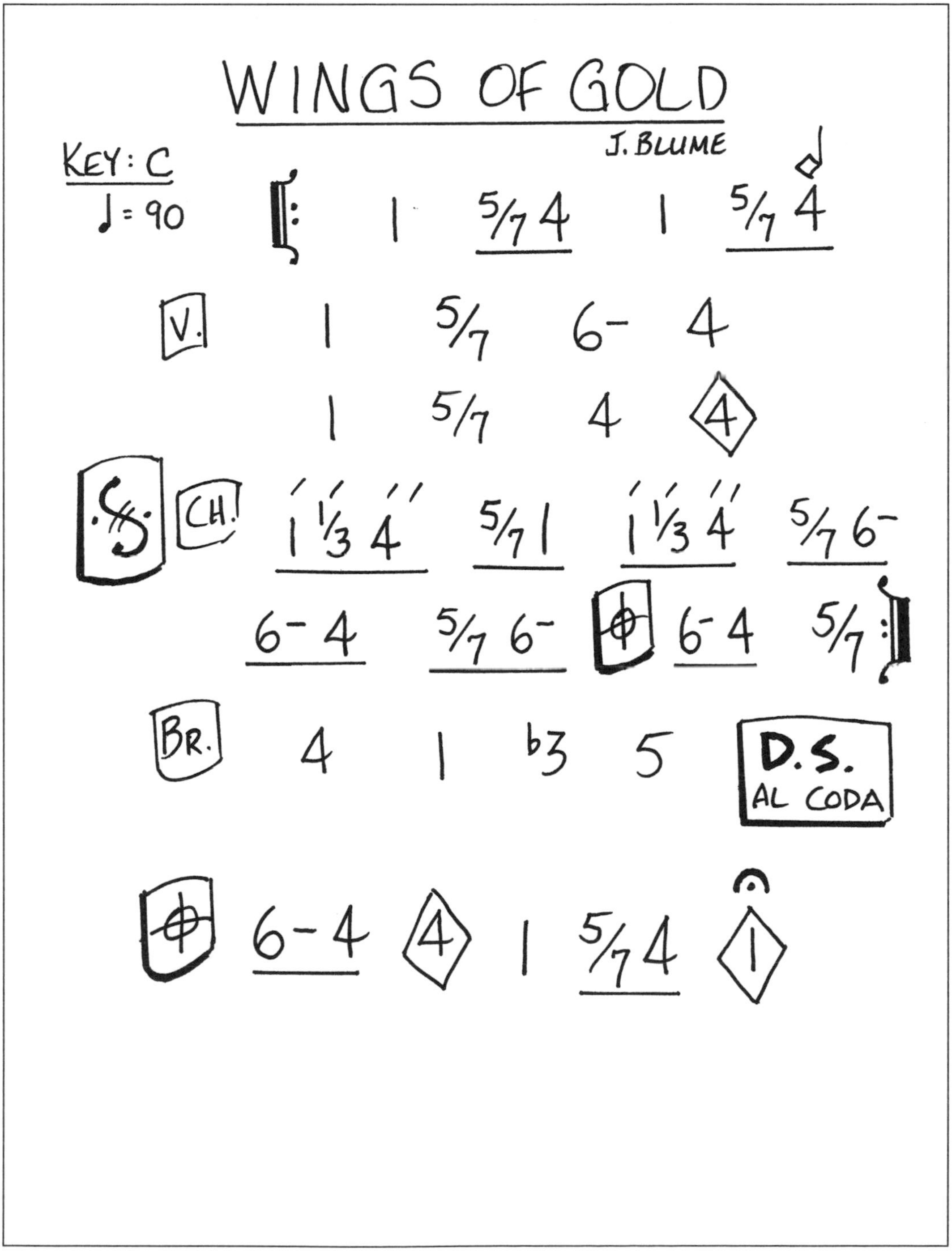

DECIDING ON AN ARRANGEMENT

A song's arrangement refers to the way the different sections of the song are "arranged" in relation to each other to build a complete song. For example, a song can be arranged as follows:

8-bar instrumental introduction

Verse 1

Chorus

4-bar instrumental turnaround

Verse 2

Chorus

8-bar instrumental solo

Chorus

Repeat chorus

Fade

The other crucial aspect of an arrangement is deciding which instruments will play which parts (e.g., will the lead solo be played by electric guitar or synthesizer? Will the primary sound be keyboards or guitars?). You do not need to write out the specific notes that each musician will play. Your musicians create their own parts based on the input you provide them and your chord chart. That's partly why it's so important to hire the best musicians your budget allows. The players bring not only their technical prowess, but also their ability to create parts that enhance your song and make it more "radio friendly."

The best musicians can make your song sound the way you'd always hoped, or even better. However, they need to know what you have in mind. If you want the guitar or the keyboards to take the "fills" (little instrumental phrases that fill in the bare spots where the vocalist is not singing), you've got to let the musicians know. They need to hear any specific instrumental melodic phrases you want them to play—and you can sing them a cappella if you are not able to play them.

> *A great arrangement provides an imaginative setting for the song with tasteful use of the instruments at your disposal and a certain amount of simplicity. It should enhance the tune, rather than just state it.*
>
> TOM SCOTT (Grammy-winning arranger who has recorded with artists including Barbra Streisand, Paul McCartney, and Joni Mitchell) as quoted in *The Recording Industry Career Handbook*

It doesn't take musical training or extensive technical knowledge to express how you envision your song—just plain English, some thought, and planning. It can also be tremendously helpful to let your musicians hear a recording of another song that has the feel or instrumentation that you imagine for your song. If you have a specific signature lick in mind, include it on your work tape, or sing it a cappella for the musicians. You can compose these identifiable melodic phrases in advance, or you can ask the demo musicians to play a catchy lick during the introduction. Whether you compose them yourself or have your demo musicians create them, signature licks need to be included on your demo to give your song its best shot. (For more about signature licks, see Chapter 7.)

Here are the notes I brought to the studio regarding the arrangement for one particular song:

Start with an eight-bar intro

First four bars of intro—just acoustic guitar (fingerpicking the signature lick)

Second four bars of intro—bring in the full band, repeating the signature lick

First verse—keep it sparse—mostly acoustic guitar with piano fills

Build into the chorus

Chorus—make it huge—have gritty electric guitars carry it

Four-bar turnaround—just like the second half of the intro

Second verse—have acoustic guitar take the fills; add electric guitars

Second chorus—even bigger than the first

Fade on repeating choruses (use signature lick)

When the musicians ask you a question regarding the arrangement (e.g., "How do you feel about changing the G chord on the fourth bar of the chorus to a G sus?"), if you don't understand, ask them to play it for you. Similarly, if you need to hear how it would sound to have the keyboard play the fills in the second verse, ask the musicians to play them for you.

DETERMINING THE PROPER KEY

The key refers to pitch—where you place your song on the musical scale. It determines how high and low the notes will go. The only way to know what key to record your demo in is to ask the vocalist. Singers don't have one particular key that they always sing in. It's determined on a song-by-song basis, depending on range and mood. Some songs sound best with the vocalist singing at the top of his or her vocal range. Other songs sound more pleasing using the singer's lower notes. Before your singer selects a key, you need to communicate whether you'd prefer the song to be belted out near the top of the singer's range, or sung softly, near the bottom of his or her vocal register.

Get a copy of your work tape and lyric sheet to your singer at least a week prior to your recording session. Include all the pertinent information the singer needs to know regarding your session (i.e., the address and telephone number of the studio, your home telephone number, your cell phone number, directions to the studio, and the day and time of the recording session). This gives the vocalist ample time to learn the song and to choose the key that works best. If neither you, nor your singer, are able to determine the key, have him or her sing you the song where it's comfortable. Tell the musician who is preparing the chart what the singer's first note is and he or she will be able to figure out the key. If you don't play a musical instrument and don't know what the first note is that the vocalist is singing, record it. (Be sure you have good batteries in your tape recorder. Otherwise, when you play it back for the musicians, the pitch may be altered.)

You need to know the key prior to having the charts written, unless you are using the Nashville Number System. It's a good idea to have the vocalist sing you a verse and a chorus of your song (even over the phone) in the key he or she has chosen, to ensure that it sounds like what you intend, because your vocalist may not be in the studio when the musical tracks are being recorded. For a *song* demo (as opposed to an *artist* demo) the singer typically shows up to record his or her part after the musicians have finished, or even on another day. The songwriter sings a rough, "scratch" vocal so that the musicians will be able to create parts that work well and don't "step on" or interfere with the vocals. If you are not comfortable singing the scratch vocal, you need to arrange for either the vocalist who will be singing the demo or someone else to be at the tracking session to do so.

HIRING THE BEST MUSICIANS

When I recorded my first demos in Nashville, I was living in Los Angeles, but was signed to a staff-writing deal in Nashville. The Nashville style of producing demos was totally foreign to me and I had no idea which musicians were the best. My publisher produced at least my first twenty Nashville demos, while showing me the ropes. (If you don't have a publisher to teach you how to produce demos, you might enlist the help of a more experienced songwriter, or an aspiring producer.) One thing I observed was that the musicians my publisher hired had a higher level of talent and professionalism than anyone I had previously worked with. I could hardly believe what they were capable of.

These demo players were the "A Team"; they were often booked a month or more in advance and played sessions like mine ten to fifteen times per week. They knew just what to do to make the songs they recorded sound like those on the radio. In a three-hour recording session, they transformed six songs they had never previously heard into what sounded like finished records. They added catchy instrumental licks and rhythms that took my songs to the next level and beyond. The musical charts the session players read show only chords—not specific notes to play—unless they are recording a television or movie score. What separates the good players from those who are at the top of their profession is not necessarily their technical proficiency, but their ability to craft the licks and catchy parts that contribute to a song sounding like a hit.

Surprisingly, many of the top musicians will gladly play demo sessions on the days when they're not booked for "master sessions" (to record albums). After I had recorded at least a dozen demos with the musicians mentioned above, I was at a friend's home in Los Angeles and picked up a copy of the latest Garth Brooks album. I could hardly believe my eyes. Three of the players from my demo sessions were on Garth Brooks' album! Musicians who have played on my demos have recorded with a list of artists that reads like a "Who's Who" in the music industry: Celine Dion, James Taylor, Barbra Streisand, the Eagles, Billy Joel, Patty Loveless, George Harrison, Shania Twain, Bette Midler, Brooks and Dunn, Reba McEntire, Monica, Lonestar, Faith Hill, George Strait, Natalie Cole, Randy Travis, Rascal Flatts, Billy Ray Cyrus, Alan Jackson, and many more.

It may not be financially or geographically feasible for you to work with musicians of this caliber right away. Hiring the "best" means the best that you can afford and have access to at this point in time. No level of musicianship can change a poorly written song into a great one. But presuming that you've written a strong song, the creativity and expertise that professional musicians can contribute can make the difference between a demo that sounds "pretty good" and one that gets a "Yes!"

SELECTING THE RIGHT STUDIO

There are several factors to consider when choosing the studio that will best serve your needs: the number of tracks required; whether you're using a live band versus synthesizers; the equipment available; and your budget. The number of tracks you need immediately narrows your choice of studios. If you are recording a full band and multiple tracks of vocals, you probably want a studio with at least 24-track capability. A guitar/vocal or keyboard/vocal recording obviously requires fewer tracks.

Some studios are set up to accommodate recording many musicians at the same time. If you are working with a live band, you need a facility that has a room large enough to comfortably fit your musicians and their gear. Isolation booths (small soundproof rooms) keep the sounds of the acoustic instruments (e.g., acoustic guitar) and any instruments that are recorded by placing a microphone in front of a speaker (e.g., electric guitar) from "bleeding" into each other. You need a studio that has an isolation booth for each acoustic instrument that will be recorded at the same time (e.g., piano, acoustic guitar, fiddle). Some studios consist of one small room designed to record synthesizers and vocals. If the musical tracks of your demo consist exclusively of electronic keyboard parts, this type of studio may best suit your needs.

Most studios are glad to provide prospective customers with a list of the equipment included in the price of the studio rental. Top-quality microphones and equipment that can achieve a variety of effects (e.g., reverb units, pre-amps, autotuners, finalizers, compressors, etc.) play a big role in shaping the sound of your demo. You don't need to be able to operate or even understand the specific functions of these items. That's your recording engineer's job. But before deciding on a studio, check with your engineer to be sure that the equipment available is sufficient to produce the professional sound you require.

Budget limitations play a major role in selecting your studio. "You get what you pay for" definitely applies to recording studios. However, studio prices are often negotiable. A savvy studio manager will often offer a bargain rate rather than leave the studio empty. It pays to shop around. While you certainly want the best-sounding demo you can comfortably afford, your budget will probably dictate whether that means recording in a converted garage or in a posh setting with a hot tub. The most important consideration is "How does the music sound?" Get referrals and then visit a studio in person before booking it. Ask to hear samples of demos that have been recorded there. If the studio price also includes a recording engineer, ask to hear demos that were recorded by the engineer you'll be working with. It's also important to ascertain that your engineer is experienced in recording the genre of music you want to record; an engineer who works primarily with hard rock bands may not be skilled in achieving the sounds required for a hip-hop or country song.

LEARNING TO SPEAK "MUSICIAN"

For those songwriters with limited knowledge of music theory, trying to explain what you want your musicians to play can be a frustrating, difficult experience. Failure to accurately convey what you have in mind is even more aggravating. When producing a demo, if you can't find a way to express what you envision for your song, you won't get it. It often feels as though the musicians are speaking in a secret language. The words sound familiar but they make no sense. (e.g., "On that fourth line of the second ending, when the E over G switches to the tonic, what about adding a diminished seventh?" Or in Nashville, "What do you think about changing the four-split-one minor to a fifty-five eleven sus with a diamond?"). I used to feel intimidated and embarrassed by my ignorance. Now, I remind myself I have different skills and talents that are important and valid. In the many years that I've been producing demos I've learned quite a bit, but I may never be able to speak "musician" fluently. I don't have to—but I do need an interpreter.

You're a creative person. Use everything you have in your verbal arsenal to explain what you want—in plain English. Then ask one of your musicians to act as your interpreter. Confide to him or her that it's difficult for you to understand the technical jargon. Have your interpreter explain the things you're not clear about, and don't be afraid to ask the band to play you examples of what they're talking about. Remember that you are the employer and your musicians hope to please you so that you will hire them again and recommend them to other songwriters. Having an "interpreter" in the studio may take a little longer, but you'll be far more likely to come out with a demo that represents your vision for your song—and you'll be learning in the process.

CHOOSING THE BEST VOCALIST

No single element can make or break your demo as much as the singer. A singer who has problems with pitch or timing, or who is not up to the professional standard, distracts the listener from your song. On the other hand, an extraordinary vocalist can wring every drop of emotion from your words and music and play a big role in "selling" your song.

I'm a good singer. I've sung on television shows, been a lead singer in several bands, recorded my own album, and performed professionally in nightclubs. But I'm rarely the *best* vocalist I can find to demonstrate the full potential of my songs. When selecting a demo singer, I've learned to put my ego aside and act in the best interest of each song. When I demo a country song, I want a genuine country vocalist: someone who naturally adds the phrasing and embellishments that help my song sound like the real deal. Likewise, when choosing a singer for an urban song, I want someone who lives and breathes that genre—not someone who is *trying* to sound as if he or she does.

Each song has its own particular needs. Choosing a demo singer is like casting a role in a film or a play. A great actor will not be suited for every role, and a great singer is not necessarily the right singer for every song you write. Norah Jones is an amazing singer, but I wouldn't hire her to sing a traditional country song or a hip-hop demo.

When you hear a great singer on someone else's demo, ask for that singer's phone number. In Nashville, the American Federation of Television and Radio Artists (AFTRA)—the singers' union—holds periodic showcases where you can hear live performances by some of the best demo singers out there. If you are near a major music center, you can probably hear great singers performing in local clubs. You can also get recommendations from recording studios and demo services. Professional vocalists are glad to provide sample CDs that show their range and various styles.

> *The vocalist is the most important (part of the demo), because they are selling the song.*
>
> JUDY STAKEE (Vice President of Creative Services,
> Warner/Chappell Music Publishing)

Some of today's demo singers will become tomorrow's superstars. I once critiqued a song demo with a vocal by a then-unknown teenager who later changed her name to Pink. Among the artists who sang demos in Nashville while waiting for their big break are Garth Brooks, Alan Jackson, Joe Diffie, and Trisha Yearwood. (I know someone who has framed the invoice he received in the early 1980s from superstar Trisha Yearwood, requesting $35 payment for singing a demo!) "Nashville Star" winner Buddy Jewell estimates that he sang more than four thousand demos over a ten-year period before becoming a successful recording artist. I remember seeing Faith Hill singing background vocals for a songwriter performing in a small Nashville café. This is the caliber of vocalist that is required to compete with the professionals.

Many developing writers also have aspirations to be performing artists. It can be especially difficult for them to accept that they are not the best vocalist to sing a particular song. Nonetheless, it's no coincidence that when I began hiring professional demo singers to record my songs (instead of singing them myself), I began getting publishing offers. I've worked with many developing songwriters who are good, but not great, singers. I've seen the hurt looks when I told them they needed to hire professionals to sing their demos. My suggestion to writers in this category is to hire the best singer you can find. After your professional singer has recorded his or her vocals, record your own version for your friends and family, and for your own enjoyment. But when it's time to pitch your song, use the version that gives your song its best shot.

Just as studio musicians are expected to come up with their own parts (within a song's chord changes), session vocalists typically create their own background vocal parts. To play it safe, confirm that your singer will also sing the background vocals. Background vocals, sometimes referred to as "harmony vocals" or BGVs, can significantly add to (or detract from) your song's hit potential—especially in urban, pop, R&B/pop, and hip-hop music. A singer's ability to generate great-sounding background parts is an important consideration when selecting a session vocalist.

Using singers with "star potential" can have additional benefits. Hit songwriter Wayne Tester told the following story: "I wrote 'A Place for Us' with Jimmy Scott, who writes for Chrysalis Music, and he knew the artist Kim Hill. He got Kim to come in and sing on the demo and she really liked it. She played it for the producer. He really liked it and they cut it. It was her first single on Starsong/EMl records and stayed at Number One for two weeks on the Contemporary Christian charts."

The price of hiring a professional demo singer varies in different areas. The going rate in Nashville currently averages $85 to $125 per song for a lead vocal and background parts on country demos. Some vocalists charge separately for lead and background vocals (e.g., $75 for a lead vocal and $25 for a background), so be sure to clarify exactly what is included in the fee you are quoted. Pop, rock, and R&B vocalists may charge double these amounts or more, because demos in these styles often require additional background parts and take longer to record. Supply and demand also affects the price. Nashville is crawling with up-and-coming country singers, but top-notch pop, rock, and R&B singers are harder to find there. Similarly, a great country singer in Los Angeles can charge much more to sing a demo than he or she could in Nashville.

Demo singers command the highest prices in Los Angeles and New York. The best studio vocalists in these cities earn $250 or more per song. While that may seem like a lot of money, a great singer's contribution to your demo is worth every penny. A pro vocalist also saves you time (and therefore money) in the studio. He or she will arrive prepared (having already learned your song), and will deliver a professional performance quickly.

When I book a singer for a country song demo session, my expectation is that he or she will have learned the song in advance and will be able to sing the lead vocal, plus one or two background vocal parts, within approximately one hour. Since pop and urban songs typically require additional background vocal parts, I allot two to three hours to record vocals in these styles. It is not unusual for a session singer to record twelve or more tracks of background vocals for a pop or urban song. He or she typically doubles, or triples, each of the harmony parts to "fatten" them up. I expect that his or her pitch and timing will be excellent—even though my recording engineer will likely use a computer to tune the lead vocal to make it perfect.

Don't let your ego, or the cost of a professional singer, convince you to settle for second best. You can't afford *not* to hire the best vocalist available.

USING TECHNOLOGY TO CAPTURE THE BEST VOCAL PERFORMANCE

Your demo singer has most likely learned your song from a rough work tape, so he or she will need to get used to singing with the fully produced track, which will probably sound quite different. I typically allow the singer to run through the song several times until he or she seems comfortable with it. Then, for a song demo, I record several "takes" of the lead vocal and choose the one I like best. At this point, I ignore the other versions and, listening to the vocal I plan to use, I note on a lyric sheet which lines are not quite right. These lines might have wrong phrasing, pitch problems, an incorrect melody, a lyric that was sung wrong, or they may be lacking in emotion. One line at a time, these lines are "punched," meaning the singer goes back and sings just these lines until they are as good as they can be.

Background vocals are recorded after the lead vocal is finished and tuned. Unless I'm recording a song where I want the vocal to seem raw and edgy, (e.g., blues, hard rock, reggae, or folk) I have the engineer tune the lead vocal even though it may sound great to my ear. Technology has made inexpensive computerized tuning widely available and, therefore, industry professionals have come to expect perfect vocals—anything less will distract the listener and identify the writer as an "amateur." Programs such as ProTools, Antares AutoTune, Digital Performer, and Logic can tune a vocal in just a few minutes and should be available at any professional studio.

Not every demo singer is right for every song. If, after twenty or thirty minutes, you feel that this singer is not capable of generating the sound you had in mind, there's no use in frustrating everyone involved—and running up studio bills. If you've done your homework and chosen carefully, this should be a rare occurrence—but it does happen occasionally. In these instances, I thank the singer and let the person know that he or she is a terrific singer—but just not right for this song. I ask if the singer would be comfortable accepting a portion of his or her regular fee. If the singer hopes to work for me in the future, he or she will wisely agree to this.

When recording an artist demo, it's crucial to have the vocal sound the very best you are capable of. To achieve this, a process called "comping" the vocal is typically used. Comping is slang for compiling, and the process essentially involves choosing individual lines from various vocal takes to create one great lead vocal. Here's how it works: Similar to recording a vocal for a song demo, the singer records multiple versions of the lead vocal; each version is recorded and saved onto its own track. When there are several excellent takes from which to choose, one track is selected and each weak line on this take is punched and re-recorded until it is as strong as it can be. Unlike recording the vocal for a song demo, this process is now repeated two or three more times on different tracks, so that you get three or four different, complete lead vocals—each one the result of punching lines to make it sound its best.

Sometimes it can be effective to have the singer approach the various takes differently. For example, one version might have a tougher attitude, while a second version expresses more emotional vulnerability. A third version might be sung harder and louder, while a fourth version might explore the softer qualities of a vocalist's voice. Each line and approach is evaluated and the very strongest lines, those that best convey the emotion and phrasing, are pieced together by the engineer to create one perfect vocal. Your final lead vocal might include the first two lines from version one, the next line from version three, the fourth line from version two, etc. Note that compiling from more than three or four different vocal tracks becomes complicated and is not recommended. By the time you listen to take number four or five, it's likely that you'll forget how take number one sounded.

In the event that a line might have been a little ahead of or behind the beat, when recording on computer programs such as ProTools, Radar, or Logic, in addition to tuning, the recording engineer can also shift the location of the vocal to help it lock into the "pocket." These and similar programs are capable of cutting and pasting the digital information that has been recorded (your vocals and instruments), just as you might copy, move, or edit text in a computer document. This allows a recording engineer to copy a line that was sung exceptionally well in one chorus into one or more of the other choruses. This technique is called "flying" a vocal. It can also be used to move or tune any instrument. The vocals on most major artists' albums (including those who are terrific singers) are recorded using these tools—and your vocal will be expected to measure up.

DECIDING WHETHER TO USE A MALE OR FEMALE VOCALIST

In many instances the decision as to whether your song is best served by a male vocalist or a female vocalist is clearly dictated by the song's lyric. Some songs contain lyrics that are obviously gender specific. But other songs work equally well being sung by either a male or a female artist. In these instances, one option is to record two separate demos.

Recording the same song in two different keys, and hiring both a male and a female singer, is less expensive than producing demos of two separate songs. If you are using a live band, once the first version has been recorded it should only take your musicians another ten or fifteen minutes to duplicate their parts in another key. For a synthesizer programmer the process is often as simple as pressing the "transpose" button. Of course, you still incur the added expense of an additional singer, as well as the time to mix another version.

If your budget does not allow for both a male and a female version of your song, the conventional wisdom has always been to use a male vocalist. Female artists frequently record songs that have male vocalists on the demo, but men are far less likely to do the reverse. Several female rock stars are reputed to actually prefer demos with male vocals, but I've rarely heard of a male artist actively seeking out demos that have female vocalists. That's not to say that a male artist will never record a song that has been sung by a woman. Country star Collin Raye has recorded several songs from demos that Karen Taylor-Good sang. But this is more the exception than the rule.

Generally, I use a male vocalist for those songs that could go either way. But for the songs that are my personal favorites, I usually invest the extra time and money to record both male and female demos. You'll have a similar decision to make if your song lends itself to more than one style of music (for example, country and pop). In several instances—for example, "Back at One" (Brian McKnight), "I Swear" (Gary Baker and Frank J. Myers), and "Nobody Knows" (Joseph Richards and Don Dubose)—a song has been recorded in one genre and then a producer or record label executive was talented enough to envision that this song could also be successful in another musical style. However, if you can afford to do demos that reflect both styles, that will probably increase your chances for success.

One more important consideration: Remember that the vocalists and musicians you hire are sensitive artists. To elicit the best possible performance from them, be encouraging and supportive. You will likely leave the studio with a much better final product if you try an approach like, "That's really good. It's very close and the tone you're getting sounds great—but I just know you can get it even better if we keep working on it" than if you are highly critical. Comments along the lines of, "That sounds horrible and you're costing me a fortune in studio time—so would you please try being in tune this time?" will demoralize your singer or musician, and that negativity will likely be evident on the finished product.

If all of this seems overwhelming, remember that it's a learning process. When I began songwriting I never imagined that I would ever be able to competently produce a demo session. But each time I recorded a demo, I learned a little bit more and was a little less stressed. Now I do it with great success on a regular basis.

CHAPTER 10

Mixing

*In a mixing situation you can take your song in so many different directions.
Do you want it to be really aggressive sounding track-wise, or more laid back?
What kind of reverbs do you want to use? How hot is the vocal going to be
in the mix? Where are you going to place stuff like the background vocals?*

*Before you mix you need to know which direction you want to take, because
it's like making a cake. You can have all these ingredients but you need to know
ahead of time which type you're making—chocolate, vanilla, or three-layer
cake—or you can waste a lot of time. It's critical to have the correct balance
of all the ingredients.*

LEE GROITZSCH (Recording Engineer)

In Chapter 9 you learned about multitrack recording—recording each instrument and vocal on its own track. Using electronic equipment to improve the quality of those sounds, finding the proper balance between them, and placing those sounds (left, right, or center) within the track defines the art of "mixing." Mixing is the job of your recording engineer, but ultimately, the songwriter producing his or her own demo session oversees the process and has the final say.

Mixes can be accomplished either manually (with the engineer sliding the faders and turning the knobs by hand) or by using automation, which is generally found in more sophisticated studios. When automation is used, the engineer programs each "move" (change in level) into a computer and then the computer automatically executes those moves. The advantage is that you are able to change the volume on any given track for any amount of time (e.g., you may want the piano to be louder during one specific bar), without altering the volume of the other tracks. With automation, it's not necessary to remix your entire song to raise or lower the level of the sounds recorded on any given track. It's easy to adjust the volume of the vocals to make them louder or softer for different lines or words. This process is referred to as "riding" the vocal.

The recording engineer may spend an hour or more just adjusting the sounds of the various drums. Since I have no expertise in this area (and it's incredibly boring to listen to drum sounds) I hire the best engineers I can afford and let them do what they do best. When they have a "rough mix" ready, I listen and make suggestions. I may want the guitar solo to be a tiny bit louder, or I might want to raise or lower the level of several lines of the vocals.

Unless you are a skilled engineer, the recording console probably resembles the cockpit of an alien spacecraft—and it is about as easy to operate. You don't need to know how to operate "the board," as it is frequently called. If something sounds too loud or too soft, or the vocal sounds "muddy" or "tinny," ask the engineer to adjust the equalization ("eq," pronounced "EE-CUE") levels. The eq refers to the high end (treble), low end (bass), and midrange sound waves. Once again, it helps to use your verbal skills to describe what you want, or don't want, your demo to sound like.

It's helpful to listen to your mix on a stereo you're accustomed to (e.g., your car stereo or a boombox) during the mixing process. It can also help to listen to your mix while standing outside the studio control room or down the hall to be sure you can hear the vocals clearly. If you're unsure whether you've captured the best mix for your song, have your engineer run several "alternate mixes." For example, depending on the song, you may want to record a version with the lead vocal a bit louder, another with additional (or less) bass, and a third mix that places the guitars at a higher volume. Having done this, if you don't like one of the mixes when you listen to them away from the incredible studio sound system (where everything sounds great), you'll have several options.

RECORDING FORMATS

There are quite a few recording formats you may encounter in the process of recording a demo. The technology is continuously evolving and in the span of only a few years recording systems may come into vogue and then find their way to extinction. The formats discussed below are those most commonly used to record song and artist demos at the time of this book's publication.

Hard Drive

Hard drive recording refers to recording directly onto the hard drive of a computer. When using this recording format, a computer serves as a multitrack recorder. The digitized musical information on each separate track is recorded directly into the computer and is stored on a hard drive, as any other data might be. This recording format has become the most prevalent mode of recording albums and professional-sounding demos, almost completely eliminating the use of digital multitrack tape-based recorders.

The most popular hard drive systems for demo recording are ProTools, Logic, Digital Performer, and Nuendo. Radar, Fairlight, and Euphonics are hard drive systems that are more typically found in professional, as opposed to demo, studios. These systems are also used for pitch correction and for altering placement within the vocal and instrumental tracks. Each individual track can be expressed visually on the computer monitor, allowing the recording engineer to alter the shape of the wave, thereby correcting notes that are sharp or flat. These and similar systems also allow the engineer to shift the location of the instrument or vocal, either subtly, to improve the timing, or by actually moving lines from one location within a song to another.

Hard drive formats provide amazing capability to manipulate recorded information. Using these formats it's easy for a competent engineer to move and alter any of the recorded data. During one recent recording session (using the Radar system) there was a place within my song where the singer didn't clearly enunciate the "T" sound at the end of a word, so my engineer copied a "T" from another word and inserted it. On that same song, in the final measure the drums were a bit sloppy, so my engineer copied that same drum pattern from a spot where it had been better executed.

The advantages of hard drive formats are: since no tape is used, any tape noise, or "hiss," is eliminated; there's no time required to rewind or fast forward—you can go instantly to any location within the song; there's an "undo" command if you make a mistake; it's easier to edit and manipulate data without losing any sound quality with this format; and you can splice without the risks inherent in putting razor to tape.

CD

Compact discs, or CDs, have become the industry standard for the presentation of song and artist demos. Machines referred to as "CD burners" provide songwriters with an inexpensive way to record their material onto CDs at home. A CD burner is often included as standard equipment with a computer, or may be purchased as a separate, external unit. The advantages of the CD format include the "clean" digital sound and the fact that there is no "fidelity degradation," meaning that you are able to make copies onto additional CDs and other digital sources without sacrificing the quality of the sound. The other benefit of this format is the ease with which you can locate any given song on a CD.

MP3

Moving Picture Experts Group Layer Three (MP3) is a technology for file compression. It reduces normal audio files to approximately one-tenth their original size, allowing them to be easily downloaded and sent across the Internet in minutes rather than hours. The advantages are that music in an MP3 (or other file compression) format can be readily shared via the Internet. You can send a song to a long-distance collaborator, or pitch it (for example, to a publisher or a recording artist) as easily as sending a text attachment to an e-mail. Since there is no physical product required (only data), artists have the potential to share their music with millions of listeners without incurring manufacturing or mailing costs. However, this also became a huge liability to the music industry when millions of listeners shared MP3s of their favorite songs for free—instead of buying the albums.

In addition to being downloaded into computers, music stored as digital files can be loaded into portable players (for example, iPods), allowing listeners to carry hundreds of songs in a machine that can fit in the palm of their hand. The disadvantage of this format is that in order to compress the file size some of the highest and lowest frequencies of the audio spectrum are eliminated. Therefore some of the sound quality is sacrificed. Audiophiles with discerning ears can tell the difference, but to the average listener, the sound will seem indistinguishable from CD quality.

It is both cost-effective and time saving to pitch your songs by sending MP3 versions via the Internet; there are no costs for CDs, envelopes, labels, or postage, and no cover letters to type or trips to the post office. However, many publishers and record label executives prefer receiving a CD to downloading an MP3. I strongly suspect that during the time this book is in print, it will become the norm to pitch songs via the Internet using MP3 or another, newer audio file format. But in the interim, to play it safe, inquire what format the recipient would prefer to receive.

Cassette

Until recently, when you played a song for a publisher or pitched it to a recording artist, label executive, or record producer, it was expected that your song would be presented on an audiocassette. However, for these purposes, cassettes have now gone the way of 8-track tapes, vinyl records, and dinosaurs. Professional songwriters present their songs on CDs or in audio files; using a cassette will signify that your demo has been submitted by an amateur.

Portable cassette recorders are still often used by songwriters, during the writing process, in order to record their ideas. It is acceptable to play a rough work tape in cassette format to acquire feedback from a publisher with whom you already have a business relationship, but this is not to be confused with a demo—which would be presented on a CD or as an audio file.

Reel-to-Reel

As the name implies, this format consists of two separate reels of tape—the "supply" reel and the "take-up" reel. Reel-to-reel formats may still be found in inexpensive, older studios, but in major music centers, they have largely been replaced by hard drive systems. Different multitrack formats use reel-to-reel tape in a variety of widths: 24-track analog recorders use 2-inch reel-to-reel tape; 16-track analog recorders use 1/2-inch, 1-inch, or 2-inch reel-to-reel tape, depending on the machine; 32-track digital recorders use 1-inch digital tape; and 1/4-inch reel-to-reel tape is generally used only for 2-track or 4-track recording.

Most reel-to-reel tape recorders offer the option of recording at "low" or "high" speeds. (Recording speed is measured in inches per second, or "ips.") Faster speeds result in better recording quality. But, the difference in sound quality between songs recorded at high speed versus low speed is so subtle that most listeners are unable to differentiate them. Therefore, when recording a demo, many writers opt for using the slower speed, which uses less tape and results in a lower cost.

Until the late 1980s, it was standard practice to mix multitrack recordings onto a 1/2-inch reel-to-reel format. This became the "master" recording, from which all other recordings were produced. Reel-to-reel masters have since become obsolete. The current industry standard requires mixing your multitrack recordings onto either a CD, a DAT master, or an audio file.

DAT

An acronym for "digital audio tape," a DAT is about two-thirds the size of a regular audiocassette and contains digital recording tape. DATs are manufactured in varying lengths that can record from just a few minutes to up to two hours. Prior to the advent of the CD, the DAT was the standard format for a master. Now it is used only occasionally. When your demo is mixed, it may be recorded onto a DAT. This becomes the master from which your first CD is recorded. Alternately, the first CD may be burned directly from the information stored on a hard drive; this CD becomes the master. Since, like a CD, the music on a DAT is digital information, there is virtually no loss of quality when a copy is made from one DAT to another. If a publisher decides to publish your song he or she may request a DAT copy in addition to a CD.

ADAT

"ADAT" is an acronym for Alesis Digital Audio Technology. Alesis is the name of the company that manufactures this 8-track digital tape recording format. Until quite recently, the ADAT was the most prevalent recording format found in home studios. It is still occasionally used; however, computer hard drive systems have become much more prevalent. When it initially appeared on the market, one advantage of ADAT recording was that it was relatively inexpensive. Also, several of these 8-track machines could be linked up to each other to allow 16, 24, 32, 48, or more tracks to be recorded. The primary disadvantage of this format is that when two or more machines are linked together, there is sometimes a delay of several seconds before the recorders "sync up," or are ready to record. The recording machine itself and the high-resolution (S-VHS) tape used in this format are both referred to as "ADATs."

Analog Versus Digital

The analog recording process records the actual wave forms of the sounds onto magnetic particles on a tape. The digital recording process records sound waves by converting them to digital numbers (ones and zeros). During playback, the digital numbers are converted back to sound waves. This is all far too complicated for me to comprehend. I can barely program my VCR, so I leave the technical matters to my engineer. But you should be aware of some differences between analog and digital recording.

Analog recording is done onto reel-to-reel tape or audiocassettes. Digital recordings may be recorded onto DATs, CDs, digital 1-inch reel-to-reel tape (for 32-track digital machines), ADATs, or directly onto the hard drive of a computer. Producers with very discerning ears sometimes prefer the sound that can be achieved via analog recording, as opposed to digital— or vice versa. Analog recording is reputed to have additional warmth. Digital recordings are said to be cleaner, more accurate sound reproductions. Some professional producers and engineers prefer to record particular instruments (typically, bass and drums) onto an analog multitrack recorder that is synchronized to a hard disk system in order to capture the sounds they prefer. However, advances in the sound quality of disk-based recording systems have improved them dramatically, and most recording engineers and producers now record entire projects digitally.

One of the big advantages of the digital format is its capability to record from one digital source to another digital source (e.g., DAT to DAT, DAT to CD, or CD to CD) without sacrificing the sound quality. The sound remains virtually the same, no matter how many generations removed you are from the original master DAT or CD. On the other hand, when copies are made from one analog source to another (e.g., cassette to cassette), each successive recording has less clarity and more unwanted tape hiss than the previous one.

LEARNING ABOUT TRACK MIXES

A "track mix" is a recording of the final mix of your song without any vocals. A "TV mix" includes all the music and the background vocals—but no lead vocal. Although the TV mix has other uses, it was so named because it allows a performer to sing live on television to pre-recorded music tracks that include the background vocals.

There are several reasons why it is crucial to always record a track mix and a TV mix, in addition to a complete mix. Let's say you decide to rewrite your lyric after your demo has been recorded. If you have a track mix on a CD, a DAT, or an audio file, all you need to do is "dump" (transfer) your track mix onto a multitrack recorder. Then, when you record your new vocal, your music tracks are already mixed. All the engineer needs to do is mix the vocals (with the new lyric) into the premixed musical tracks. You save the considerable expense of having to start from scratch to mix your song again. When you record a track mix (or a TV mix), do not fade the track so that your engineer can initiate a fade at the spot that sounds best with your new vocal. Having a track mix also allows you the flexibility to put a different vocalist on your song and to alter the melody (as long as it works with the existing chords) without incurring the expense of an additional full mix.

There are instances when an artist may request a track mix so that he or she can practice singing your song and determine whether it is something he or she wants to record. In 1998 I received a call from Eric Beall, who at the time was one of the publishers at Zomba's New York office. I was a staff writer for Zomba at the time, and during a recent visit to New York City I had played Eric a song, "I'll Never Stop Loving You," that I had cowritten with Steve Diamond. The publisher thought the song might work well for a fifteen-year-old singer the company was developing, and he asked if I could provide a track mix so that the A&R executives could assess how she sounded singing the song.

The good news was that I had a track mix; the bad news was that it was in a male key. I learned that technology existed that could transpose the track to a higher (or lower) key—

without altering the tempo. Zomba's studio owned the equipment necessary to change the key. The engineer explained that the sound quality of a track that had been altered with this technology would be good enough to be used for a demo, or for an artist to practice with. However, the sounds would be very slightly changed and a trained ear would be able to hear that the track had been altered. We would be able to raise or lower the key by a maximum of one-and-a-half steps; going beyond that would cause the sound to distort significantly. The engineer raised the key a half step, a whole step, and a step-and-a-half so the singer would have several different options. To my ear, the tracks sounded almost perfect.

Several months went by before I learned that the record label executives liked how the teenager had sounded singing with my track mix and had decided to have her record my song for her album. I was pleased but not very excited at the time because she was a new artist and I knew that most new artists never become very successful. The kid's name was Britney Spears. Always run a track mix.

MASTERING

Mastering is the process by which a mixed sound recording is improved by an engineer who performs final sonic tweaks. During the mastering process, a specialist called a "mastering engineer" might typically add additional compression, raise the overall volume level, and alter the overall equalization. Mastering does not involve altering individual tracks. It is a process that affects the sound of the finished, mixed recording. While virtually all albums are mastered, many professional songwriters, and artists who are hoping to secure recording contracts, have their demos mastered to improve the sound quality. Many demo studios have equipment that can approximate the results achieved by professional mastering. The cost of having a recording professionally mastered at a studio that specializes in this ranges from $35 to $250 per song.

STEP 4: CONCLUSION

Probably the most important skill to acquire as a demo producer is the ability to surround yourself with the most talented musicians, vocalists, and recording engineers you can afford. Like most of the other elements of songwriting, learning to produce demos that successfully communicate and demonstrate the potential of your songs is a skill that takes patience and practice to develop. It's not realistic to expect the first several demos you produce to be perfect. It's a learning process and there will be successes and failures along the way. But as you learn new ways to express your vision for your songs, and find those professionals who can help you achieve it, you'll find that you can produce demos that make your songs sound as good as you'd imagined—and sometimes even better!

DEMO CHECKLIST

Photocopy this checklist and refer to it when planning for and evaluating each of your song demos.

Prior to Recording—Preparing for Your Session

❑ Song has been critiqued and deemed ready

❑ A work tape has been recorded

❑ Lyric sheets have been typed and copied

❑ Chord charts have been prepared

❑ An arrangement has been created

❑ A demo singer who is appropriate for this particular song has been selected

❑ A work tape, lyric sheet, and directions to the session have been sent to the singer

❑ The proper key has been determined

❑ Signature licks have been written (or planned for)

❑ Blank tape has been purchased or arranged for (if applicable)

❑ Musicians, studio, and vocalist have been confirmed

After Recording—Evaluating Your Demo's Effectiveness

❑ The quality of your musicians measures up to the professional standard

❑ The recording is clear (no discernible hiss or distortion)

❑ The vocalist's pitch is accurate

❑ The vocal is easy to hear and you can understand the words

❑ A track mix and TV mix have been recorded

Taking Care of Business

The most successful writers I've seen are the ones who really get out there. It's imperative to do the business.

FRANNE GOLDE (Hit songwriter with cuts by artists including Whitney Houston, Celine Dion, and Faith Hill)

CHAPTER 11

Learning Where the Money Comes From

One of the things songwriters can do to help themselves is literally to sit down and go through the Songwriters Guild of America (song publishing) contract paragraph by paragraph, with a large yellow pad nearby. Any words or concepts they don't understand should be written down—even if they fill up ten pages. This list will give them all the questions they'll need to ask from industry people. I think it's unfortunate when songwriters spend too much time on the craft and neglect the business side and then get taken advantage of.

AARON MEZA (Western Regional Director,
The Songwriters Guild of America)

Many developing songwriters resent having to be businesspeople. I've heard them lament, "I've written the song—now let somebody else take care of the business." But the reality is that this is the music *business*. The greatest song in the world will not become a hit if it's neither demoed nor brought to the attention of music business professionals. Although it's perfectly acceptable to write solely for your own pleasure, if your goal is to be successful in the music business, you have to pay as much attention to the *business* as you do to the *music*.

Before continuing further, it will be helpful to understand the difference between a music publishing company and a record label. A publishing company (also referred to as a music publisher or a song publisher) has many functions (see Chapter 12). However, its primary function is to generate and collect income from songwriters' songs. This income typically results from getting these songs recorded by recording artists, or included in television shows or films. The term "publisher" is often used interchangeably to refer to an individual who's employed by a publishing company to pitch songs and to the company itself.

A record label (or record company) is a company that's in the business of producing, distributing, and selling albums and singles (e.g., CDs, cassettes, and music available online). A record label signs recording artists (e.g., singers, bands, and instrumental performers). If these artists do not write their own songs, members of the record label's A&R department will typically meet with publishers with the hope of finding hit songs for their artists.

Record labels pay separate royalties to the recording artist (for their performance), to the producer (for the production), and to the songwriter and publisher (for use of the song). If the recording artist is also the songwriter, he or she will receive two different royalties from the record label—one as the artist and one as the songwriter. Since this book is focused on songwriters, this chapter will explain the sources from which songwriters' incomes are derived. But it is important to remember that if the songwriter is also the recording artist, he or she will receive a totally separate royalty, paid by the record label to the artist, in addition to the monies this artist will receive as the writer of his or her songs.

Songwriters earn money primarily from mechanical royalties, performance royalties, print royalties, synchronization licenses, and publishers' advances. When I was beginning to develop my songwriting skills, I attended more workshops and classes than I can count. My teachers tried to explain how songwriters got paid, but the source of that money somehow remained a mystery to me. It was only after I began receiving income from my songs that the pieces of the puzzle started to fit together. Hopefully, before long, your songs will be earning income—and then all this will make perfect "cents"!

MECHANICAL ROYALTIES

"Mechanical royalties" is the name given to royalties paid for the sale of a physical, tangible product containing music; audiocassettes, CDs, record albums, and videocassettes all generate mechanical royalties. In plain English, mechanical royalties are the monies you are paid for the copies of your songs that are sold.

In the US, the mechanical royalty rate is established by Congress and is called the "statutory rate." With one exception (the 3/4 rate, discussed later in this chapter) it is not negotiable and applies equally to all songwriters. Therefore, Madonna, Diane Warren, Garth Brooks, and you all receive the same mechanical royalty for each album or single sold.

Payment is made per unit. A "unit" refers to one recording of a song on an audiocassette, CD, or other format, whether it's an album or a single. Each song included on an album is considered one unit. If you are lucky enough to have written ten songs on an album, you will be paid for ten units for each album sold. Occasionally, more than one version of a song may be included on an album or a single (e.g., the radio mix and a dance mix, acoustic mix, or urban mix). In these instances, the writer is paid for each version of the song, just as if it were a separate song.

For single releases, mechanical royalties (sometimes referred to as "mechanicals") are paid equally for the "A" side (the song that is sent to radio stations and marketed as the probable hit) and the "B" side (a song that the buyer is probably not familiar with). Although we no longer have vinyl singles, and all songs are included on one side of a CD, the hit song on a commercially released CD single is still sometimes referred to as the "A" side. Therefore, the writer of the hit song and the writer of the unknown song receive the same amount of money for the sale of each single. This may not seem fair, but don't worry. As you'll learn later in this chapter, the writer of the hit will earn the bulk of his or her income from performance royalties.

The mechanical royalty rate for the US has been negotiated to allow for increases in songwriters' incomes through January 1, 2006. The rate structure is as follows:

- January 1, 2004 to December 31, 2005: 8.50 cents or 1.65 cents per minute (whichever is greater)
- January 1, 2006: 9.10 cents or 1.75 cents per minute (whichever is greater)

Some quick math shows that, using the rate in effect January 1, 2004 through December 31, 2005, a song (less than five minutes long) that is included on an album or a single earns the following mechanical royalties:

```
        1,000 units: . . . . . . . . . . . . . . . . . . . . . . . . . . . . . . . $85.00
       10,000 units: . . . . . . . . . . . . . . . . . . . . . . . . . . . . . . $850.00
      100,000 units: . . . . . . . . . . . . . . . . . . . . . . . . . . . . $ 8,500.00
      500,000 units (designated "Gold" in the US): . . . . . . . . . $42,250.00
    1,000,000 units (designated "Platinum" in the US): . . . . . . $85,000.00
   10,000,000 units (designated "Diamond" in the US): . . . . . $850,000.00
```

(An explanation of how this money is divided between writers and publishers appears in Chapter 12.)

Mechanical royalties are paid from the record label to the publisher approximately six months after the sale of the product (for sales within the US). The publisher distributes the writers' share of this income to the writers either quarterly or biannually, depending on their contractual agreement. It sometimes takes eighteen months or longer for publishers to receive mechanical royalties generated outside the US. Keeping track of and collecting the money is not always an easy job for music publishers. Therefore, the majority of publishers contract with an outside firm (e.g., The Harry Fox Agency, Inc. or Copyright Management, Inc.) to handle the paperwork involved in the collection of their mechanical royalties (see Appendix).

The Harry Fox Agency, Inc. (HFA) is the main organization for the administration of mechanical rights in the US. (This function is served in Canada by the Canadian Mechanical Rights Reproduction Agency, or CMRRA.) HFA represents more than 19,000 music publishers, licensing the use of music on tapes and CDs. They distribute more than $400,000,000 per year in royalties.

Although the mechanical royalty rate is set by Congress, there are instances in which a record label contacts a publishing company and requests that it (acting on a songwriter's behalf) accept only three-quarters of the regular (statutory) mechanical royalty rate. This is referred to as the "3/4 rate," or "controlled composition clause," and most commonly occurs when the record label anticipates that the recording artist or record producer will be writing, or cowriting, his or her own songs. If you collaborate with a recording artist or producer, some of the record labels insist that the artist, producer, and his or her cowriters agree to accept a 3/4 rate.

Other instances in which a record label might feel justified paying a 3/4 rate or even a 50-percent rate include the re-release of a product as part of a lower-priced "catalog" series, sales to record clubs, inclusion in a compilation, or inclusion in a box set that will be sold at a reduced price. When these situations occur, the songwriter may be consulted by the publisher, but it is the publisher's decision as to whether to accept a reduced mechanical royalty rate.

DOMESTIC AND FOREIGN ROYALTIES

Royalties generated within the US are referred to as "domestic royalties." As you have already learned, mechanical royalties in the US are determined by legislative process. They are a fixed amount regardless of the selling price of the recording. In Canada there is also a fixed mechanical royalty rate, but this rate is determined by a contractual agreement between major music publishers and the Canadian Record Company Association.

"Foreign royalties" are those that come from sales outside the US. The mechanical royalty rate varies from country to country and is often considerably higher than in the US. In the vast majority of countries outside the US and Canada, the mechanical royalty rate is a percentage of the selling price of the recording. A sample of international mechanical royalty rates at the time of this book's publication follows:

Europe: 9.504 percent of the wholesale selling price

Latin America: 6.75 percent of the retail price

Japan: 5.6 percent of the retail price

Note that these amounts refer to the total mechanical royalty paid for the sum of all songs on the project and are periodically adjusted for inflation. This royalty is divided among all the copyright owners whose songs are included on a given album.

Foreign mechanical royalties are typically collected by "subpublishers." A subpublisher is a publishing company that acts on another publisher's behalf to represent their catalog and collect royalties in other countries ("territories"). Publishers may contract with a different subpublisher in each of the countries where their catalog is generating income, or they may choose to work with one major company that has offices throughout the world. For a percentage of the mechanical royalties they collect, subpublishers eliminate the administrative responsibilities, some of the expense, and the hassle (e.g., language barriers) of collecting income from foreign countries.

PERFORMANCE ROYALTIES AND PERFORMING RIGHTS ORGANIZATIONS

"Performance royalties" are monies paid for performances of a song. However, the definition of performance in this instance encompasses far more than live concerts. Performances include radio airplay, television broadcasts, and the use of live or recorded music in a variety of establishments that use music in an effort to enhance their business. Music played on jukeboxes or airplanes; at sporting events; and in restaurants (with some exceptions), bowling alleys, roller rinks, nightclubs, retail stores, and many other establishments constitutes performances that generate performance royalties.

Songs fall under the category of intellectual (nontangible) property. Under the US Copyright Act, they cannot be performed for commercial profit without paying the copyright owner. Therefore, businesses and individuals that use songs for commercial profit are required to pay the writer and publisher of those songs.

When a song becomes a major hit, it is often broadcast on the radio more than ten thousand times per week—and in some instances, up to one hundred thousand times per week. It is not uncommon for a hit song to be played more than one million times on the radio. It's impossible for songwriters and publishers to keep track of all of the performances of their songs, and to collect royalties for those performances. Performing rights organizations (PROs) have been established for these purposes. These organizations acquire the rights to collect performance royalties on behalf of the writers and publishers they represent. In the US, the PROs are ASCAP (American Society of Composers, Authors, and Publishers), BMI (Broadcast Music International), and SESAC (formerly known as Society of European Stage Authors and Composers).

Songwriters and publishers must join a PRO in order to receive performance royalties. A songwriter may be a member of only one PRO at any given time. However, a publisher must be a member of each organization that collects performance royalties for copyrights he or she controls. For instance, if a publisher represents a song written by an ASCAP-affiliated songwriter, the publisher must be ASCAP affiliated. It's necessary for most major publishers to be ASCAP, BMI, and SESAC affiliated since their various writers may belong to any one of these organizations.

It's perfectly acceptable and quite common for members of the three different PROs to write with one another. When that collaboration results in a recorded song, each organization distributes the share of the performance royalties earned by its respective affiliated writers and publishers. For songs performed outside the US, there are reciprocal agreements that allow the PROs to collect from their international counterparts and distribute those monies accordingly.

For a fee, ASCAP, BMI, and SESAC issue "blanket licenses" to radio stations, broadcast and cable television stations, and hundreds of thousands of other establishments. A blanket license grants the recipient the right to play any music that is licensed by the PRO. The amount of money it costs an establishment to secure a blanket license is determined by a number of factors, including the amount of revenue earned by the establishment and its size. While a small coffeehouse or nightclub might pay as little as $200 a year, a major television network pays millions of dollars annually to obtain a blanket license. After operating expenses are deducted, ASCAP, BMI, and SESAC distribute the money collected as licensing fees to their affiliated writers and publishers.

Each of the PROs has its own system for keeping track of how many times a song has been played. ASCAP hires a firm to tape record hundreds of hours of broadcasts on various television and radio stations on an unannounced basis. From this sample, statistical projections are made to estimate the total number of times a given song is being played. BMI chooses a statistically representative cross section of radio stations each quarter, logging approximately 500,000 hours of commercial radio programming each year. The stations being sampled supply BMI with logs that list all music performed during the period being evaluated. From the information collected they extrapolate to estimate the total number of performances a song receives during any given quarter. SESAC, the smallest of the US PROs, uses technologies that encode audio signals, allowing them to track every broadcast performance.

Performance royalties are not paid by PROs for dramatic usage of songs (e.g., musical theater, ballet, and opera). The rights to use songs in theatrical settings are called "grand rights," and for those uses payment is negotiated and paid directly to the copyright holder. The right to use music in nontheatrical venues (e.g., radio, nightclubs, and television) is called "small rights."

In the US, songs that are included in movies do not receive performance royalties when the films are in theatrical release. A "synchronization license" (discussed later in this chapter), which grants the right to include music in a film or television show, is negotiated for that purpose. With this license, songwriters and publishers are paid directly by the film production company. However, after its theatrical run, if a movie is broadcast on network, local, or cable television, the music included in that film does earn performance royalties. Performance royalties are also paid for songs that are in movies screened outside the US. These fees are typically a percentage of the film's box office receipts and vary by country. A song included in a film that has great international success (for example, *Moulin Rouge, Titanic,* or *Chicago*) might earn hundreds of thousands of dollars in foreign performance royalties. However, some Hollywood films receive limited distribution outside the US; a song included in one of these films might earn only a few hundred dollars in international theatrical performance royalties. Through reciprocal agreements with the foreign PROs, ASCAP, BMI, and SESAC collect and distribute these royalties.

When marketing a successful album, the record label will likely select three or four songs that it believes will have the greatest success of garnering radio airplay. These songs are released, one at a time, as "singles" and are sent and promoted to the radio stations. Many, but not all, of these singles will also be available for purchase, typically along with one or two additional songs from the album, and are referred to as "commercially released singles." Songs that are released as singles receive the vast majority of radio airplay. The songs that are not chosen as singles are referred to as "album cuts" and rarely receive significant radio airplay.

Worldwide, more than three billion dollars in performance royalties are generated annually, with approximately one-third of this amount being collected and distributed to writers and publishers in the US. A hit single typically earns its writer much more money from performance royalties than from mechanical royalties. The amount of money a hit song earns from performances varies considerably because different songs receive different amounts of airplay. For instance, a song that has a slow climb up the charts, taking twenty-six weeks to reach Number One, accumulates much more airplay than a song that zooms to the top of the charts in just eight weeks. The ranges that follow are estimates of the performance royalties typically earned by a Top Ten single in the following genres. (As you'll learn in the next chapter, these amounts are divided between the song's cowriters and publishers.)

Country. . . . . $300,000–$800,000

Top 40/Pop . . . . $300,000–$800,000

Adult Contemporary . . . . $150,000–$400,000

Urban/R&B . . . . $150,000–$400,000

Christian . . . . $10,000–$40,000

Songs that reach the Number One chart position and those that climb the chart slowly and remain high on the chart for many weeks will fall into the highest end of this range. Performance royalties for a "Song of the Year" will likely exceed one million dollars.

The amount of radio airplay a song receives largely determines the amount of performance royalties it earns. If a song crosses over and becomes a hit on more than one chart (e.g., pop and urban, or pop, adult contemporary, and country), it may get double or even triple the amount of airplay that a hit song in only one genre typically receives. For a song to reach the Top Ten on the charts, it must receive the maximum amount of radio play ("heavy rotation") at almost every radio station whose format it fits. Income from performance royalties significantly increases each week that a song remains in the Top Ten. In exceptional instances, a song has remained in the Number One position for several months, generating performance royalties in excess of $4,000,000! However, this occurrence is extremely rare.

The writer's portion (approximately 50 percent) of the performance royalties earned by a song is paid by the PROs directly to the songwriter. The publisher's share is paid by the PROs to the publisher. These monies are paid quarterly, approximately nine months to one year following the performances. Monies from foreign territories typically take an additional one to two years to be distributed.

In addition to collecting and distributing performance royalties, the PROs offer workshops, seminars, and panel discussions in major music centers and throughout the country. They also provide writing rooms for their affiliated writers to use. Representatives may be willing to meet with you, evaluate your songs, and make career recommendations. Before deciding which PRO is right for you, meet with membership representatives at each of the organizations. (See the Appendix for a listing of PROs within the US.)

PRINT SALES

"Print sales" refer to the sale of sheet music, which represents an additional source of revenue for songwriters. Four companies—Warner Bros. Publications, Hal Leonard Corporation, Cherry Lane Music Publishing, and Columbia Pictures Publications—publish virtually all of the secular sheet music in the US. These companies typically pay song publishers 20 percent of the retail price of sheet music, which amounts to approximately 70 cents per song. The amount a songwriter is paid by his or her publisher for each unit of sheet music sold is negotiable and is an important point in the song publishing contract negotiation. It may be represented as either a percentage of the retail price or a flat fee.

In most instances, any income generated by a song is divided equally between the writers and publishers, but this is not the case with sheet music royalties. Publishers typically pay their writers in the range of 5 to 12 cents for each copy of sheet music sold, with the high end being reserved for only those with the most clout. It is preferable to receive a percentage of all royalties received by your publisher for print sales. In the event that you have a huge hit, your publisher may have the leverage to renegotiate and increase the fee he or she earns from the sheet music publisher. In this example, if you are earning a percentage of the money your publisher collects for sheet music royalties, you reap the benefits rather than being locked into a set fee per unit sold.

Of course, if few people have heard your song, there will be little demand for its sheet music. Therefore, only songs that are major hits generate significant sheet music sales. Songwriters can earn quite a bit of money from print sales—but usually only if they've already made far more money from performance royalties. The kind of songs that are performed by bands at weddings and by lounge singers create the biggest demand for sheet music. However, choral and band arrangements of songs that are not well known, and songs that are sung in churches, can also earn significant income from the educational and Christian markets.

Sheet music may be sold individually, or in a book called a "folio." Folios are compilations of sheet music of various songs that have been grouped together because they have a common bond. A folio may contain songs that have all been recorded by the same artist on various albums; songs that were initially included on one album; or, in the case of a "mixed folio," songs that have been popularized by a variety of artists (e.g., *The Greatest Rock Hits of 1999*). When a song is included in a folio, the income is prorated among the various songs.

Publishers and songwriters may receive additional income from lyrics reprinted in books (like this one) or magazines. Permission and a license must be obtained from a song's publisher to reprint song lyrics. This type of income typically represents a tiny fraction of a songwriter's income.

SYNCHRONIZATION LICENSES

"Synchronization licenses," often referred to as sync licenses, are another source of income for songwriters. A sync license is required to synchronize music to visual images in an audiovisual work. A sync license grants the right to include music in a film or television show. The income it generates is in addition to any performance royalties earned as a result of network or cable broadcasts. Like virtually all songwriter income (with the exception of sheet music royalties), income derived from sync licenses is split equally between the writers' and the publishers' shares. Synchronization licenses are issued for cable or broadcast television, motion pictures, commercials, DVDs, and videotapes. However, when a singer sings his or her latest hit on a show such as the *Tonight Show,* a sync license is not required because the song is neither part of the story nor being synchronized to an existing picture—but, the songwriter and publisher do receive performance royalties when the show is broadcast.

When negotiating the fee for a sync license for a television show, it's important to take into account the additional performance royalties your song is likely to earn as a result of its inclusion in this particular show or film. The amount a production company will pay is determined by a number of factors, including how the music is used in the film or television show. For example, if your song is being sung by a character on camera, it will generate a significantly larger sync fee than if twelve seconds of it can barely be heard coming out of a car radio in a film. If a song has previously been a major hit and its inclusion is crucial to the film in order to evoke a time period or a specific feeling, it can, of course, command a much higher fee than an unknown song. The amount budgeted for music, the timing of the song, whether there are multiple uses, and whether a song will be included on a soundtrack album or promoted as a single will all affect the sync fee a publisher is likely to receive.

The amount of the sync fee is also determined by the specific rights being granted, as well as by the length of time covered by the agreement. For example, if you are licensing the right to include your song in all formats and all future uses (e.g., video release, video compilations, and CD-ROM), throughout the world, and in perpetuity, it's likely your publisher will be able to negotiate a higher fee than for a one-time usage. Sync fees to include a song in a major film typically range from $15,000 to $50,000 per song. "Main title" usages (songs that play during the opening credits of a film) pay in the range of $35,000 to $150,000. Songs that play while the end credits are scrolling across the screen are referred to as "end title" or "end credit" songs and a sync license for their usage typically earns $20,000 to $150,000. For low-budget, independent films the amounts may be only a fraction of these fees.

For a major television series, the sync fee per song typically ranges from $1,500 to $5,000 for a five-year worldwide television license. For a life-of-copyright license this fee typically ranges from $6,000 to more than $10,000 per song. The right to sell the program on video and DVD might be negotiated for an additional fee. If the song is to be used as the "theme song" (played at the opening of each episode), the sync license is typically in the range of $4,000 to $10,000 per episode. When performance royalties are added in, a theme song used in a very successful television series may generate more than $1.5 million over a ten-year period.

Having a song included on a video or DVD is another way that songwriters (and publishers) earn money. The sync license to include a song in a home video or DVD is typically handled in one of three ways:

- As a royalty paid for each video sold (usually 8 to 15 cents per song)
- As a one-time buyout fee (for example, $20,000 regardless of how many units are sold)
- As a "roll-over advance" formula (an advance is paid for a specified number of videos with additional fees prenegotiated for situations where certain sales plateaus are achieved)

If an existing recording of a song is being used, a fee, in addition to the sync license paid to the writer and publisher, is negotiated with the owner of the master recording (typically, the record label). This separate license, known as a "Master Use License," provides payment to the artist, producer, and record label. In instances where a television or film producer is not able to secure the rights to use the master recording with the original artist, sometimes a new version that sounds very much like the original is produced. This is called a "sound-alike," and when it is used, the user must secure a sync license from the publisher for the use of the song, but there is no need for a master use license—because the original recording is not being used.

The sync fees that result from placing songs in television shows and films can be a significant source of income for songwriters and publishers. They can also lead to additional royalties if a soundtrack album is produced, or if a film receives television airings or theatrical release in foreign territories. On top of that, it's really exciting to hear your song in a hit movie or TV series! *The Film & Television Music Guide*, published by the Music Business Registry, is an excellent resource for writers and publishers who hope to place their music in these media.

WRITING JINGLES AND PLACING SONGS IN COMMERCIALS

Placing songs in television commercials and writing jingles can be an extremely lucrative outlet for songwriters and publishers. A jingle is essentially a very short (fifteen- to sixty-second) "song" that is designed to be exceptionally memorable—and to be associated with a product.

When composing an original jingle, the writer must take into account the style of music most likely to appeal to the product's target audience. For example, while a hip-hop, rock, pop, or dance track might be effective for the teenaged demographic likely to be targeted by a jeans or sneaker commercial, these styles would probably not be appropriate for the mature audience to which an advertiser of dentures would hope to appeal. Hoping to break through as a jingle writer is analogous to hoping to write and market songs that top the charts; the competition is fierce and your work and ability to network must be exceptional. The first step in pursuing work writing jingles is to compile a sample of your work onto a CD. Your demo should include a variety of the styles of music you write. For example, one five-minute demo might include thirty-second snippets of instrumental new age, jazz, rock, and funk, as well as vocal jingles that you have written and produced in various styles for both existing and imaginary products. In addition to being able to compose catchy music on a deadline, production skills are also important for jingle writers because they are expected to produce finished "masters"—pieces of music that will actually be used in the commercial.

Some writers get their initial breaks by composing a "spot" on spec, with the knowledge that there may be a dozen or more composers vying for that one slot. "Spec" is a shortened form of the word speculation, and I sometimes joke that working on spec usually means that you do the work—and 'spec nothing in return. Most successful composers of music for commercials own their own recording studios, allowing them to work on spec without incurring studio costs.

In addition to the primary US music centers (New York, Los Angeles, and Nashville), many successful advertising agencies and jingle composers are located in Chicago and Dallas. *The Standard Directory of Advertising Agencies* (sometimes referred to as "The Red Book") is a terrific resource that lists contact information and a client list for all major ad agencies. It's an incredibly expensive book—more than $900—but it is available in the reference section of most libraries.

If an advertiser believes that including a specific, well-known song in a commercial has the potential to generate millions of dollars in increased sales for his or her client, a sync license might generate hundreds of thousands of dollars for the songwriter and publisher. A song that has previously been a hit and is now widely used in a successful advertising campaign typically earns $150,000 to $350,000. However, there are instances where the publishers of a huge hit have earned more than a million dollars by granting the rights to include the song in a major ad campaign.

MUSIC LIBRARIES

Music libraries, sometimes called music production libraries, are companies that acquire songs and instrumental music from songwriters and make this music readily available to television and film producers. For a fee, the TV and film producers can access and use any of thousands of works in the libraries' catalogs. This music is typically used as background in films and television shows and can include the full spectrum of musical styles. There are many music libraries in the US; among the most successful are FirstCom (a division of BMG), Network Music, and KPM (licensed by APM Hollywood).

These companies publish the works and attempt to place them in films and television shows. Writers are sometimes paid a one-time fee when their song is accepted to become part of the library's catalog. When their music is broadcast on television, the writers receive the writers' share of the performance royalties generated.

Like other publishers, the top music libraries do not accept unsolicited demos and typically find new writers and music through referrals and networking. However, if you send a well-written letter with a bio including any credits you may have, you may be given permission to submit a demo. Placing your songs with music libraries can be a lucrative outlet for writers who are able to produce master-quality tracks, especially instrumental pieces. Taxi has been very successful in connecting writers with music libraries. (For additional information about Taxi, see Chapter 14.)

CHURCH COPYRIGHT LICENSE ROYALTIES

A source of income unique to writers and publishers of Christian music is derived from the Church Copyright License. Established in 1988, Christian Copyright Licensing International

(CCLI; see www.ccli.com) collects and distributes royalties for the use of songs in churches. This provides an important source of income for writers whose Christian songs may be widely sung in churches—but are not necessarily garnering airplay or sales that would generate mechanical or performance royalties.

Churches affiliated with CCLI pay an annual licensing fee determined by the size of their congregation. These fees range from $46 to $3,791 per year. Procuring this license provides a church with the right to choose from more than 150,000 songs represented by CCLI for use by the congregation, to be reproduced (for example, photocopies of lyric sheets) and projected onto a screen. After an administrative fee is deducted, royalties derived from these licensing fees are distributed to the writers and publishers of the songs. The amount of royalty that each writer and publisher receives is based upon the amount of usage their material is getting. This is determined by a survey, conducted in the US every two-and-a-half years, of the churches that procure the Church Copyright License. CCLI issues licenses in ten territories outside the US. In international territories, the survey is conducted at various intervals. Each song reproduction reported on the survey receives credits, dependent on the number and type of reproductions made, and on the size of the church. The credits from all the song reproductions are totaled. This total number of credits is used to determine what proportion of the funds collected should be paid for each song. Royalties are distributed semiannually. A song reproduced by only one small church might earn only pennies, while an extremely popular song used in many churches might earn thousands of dollars.

WORKS FOR HIRE

We've all heard horror stories about writers of enormously successful songs who sold their songs and their rights to any royalties—in exchange for a few hundred dollars. Writers virtually never sell their songs; instead, we assign the right to publish our songs. The only legitimate exceptions to this might happen when writers are hired to compose music for television, films, commercials, music production libraries, theme parks, or video games. While the ownership and royalties for most of the music composed for these outlets are handled through sync licenses and standard royalty payments, in some instances a writer may be hired to produce music that is considered a "work for hire." This means that the company is contracting the writer to compose specific music in exchange for a flat fee. In these instances, the songwriter acts essentially as an employee, retaining no rights to future royalties, unless otherwise specified.

While composing a work for hire may seem unfair to the songwriter, there may be benefits that outweigh the disadvantages. For instance, the writer may gain access to scripts, as well as the chance to discuss what the music supervisor is looking for, giving him or her a far better shot at getting a song included in the project. In addition, the writer may be paid a substantial fee as soon as the work is completed, instead of having to wait a year or more for royalties to be paid.

USING SAMPLES

Sampling refers to using a portion of another artist's recording in your own recording, as is frequently done in rap music. Among the most famous examples of sampling are MC Hammer's "U Can't Touch This," which was built upon Rick James' "Super Freak," and Eminem's "Sing for the Moment," which uses the chorus of Aerosmith's "Dream On."

Prior to an album's release, record labels require publishers to submit clearances for all samples incorporated into any song within the album. If you use a sample of another artist's music you must obtain two licenses—one from the owner of the master (typically a record label) permitting the use of the original sound recording, and an additional license from the publisher for the use of a portion of the song itself. If you substitute a sound-alike (sometimes called a "replay") for the master recording, you still need to secure the right to use the song—but not the master recording.

There is no standard licensing fee to use a sample, nor are the owners of the copyright and master obligated to grant this permission. On rare occasions, licenses will be issued for a one-time flat fee; this is called a "buyout." These fees range from $5,000 to more than $50,000 for the record label and for the publisher. However, it is much more typical for publishers of the work being sampled to demand a percentage of ownership of the new work that includes their song. Depending on factors including the success of the song and artist being sampled, the amount of the recording being used, and the clout of the artist who hopes to use the sampled material, the publisher might demand from 10 to 50 percent of the copyright (ownership) of the new work.

Fees for sampling can generate significant income for the writers and publishers of the works being sampled. However, unless your song is already a recognizable hit, it is unlikely that it will be sampled.

FUTURE SOURCES OF REVENUE

I strongly suspect that in the very near future the primary way to distribute music will be via electronic transmission, for example, downloading music from the Internet for a fee (which has already begun). The advent of each successive new technology has presented fresh challenges for our lawmakers and music industry executives. However, in each instance, they have found ways to compensate copyright owners for the use of their works—and I trust that this will continue to be the case.

CHAPTER 12

Understanding What Music Publishing Really Means

The writer's job is to write the songs. The publisher's job is to exploit those songs, turn those songs into money, and protect them when they need protecting.

JOHN VAN METER (Chief Creative Officer,
New Sheriff Music Publishing)

Before Thomas Edison invented the phonograph, songs became hits when large numbers of people purchased the sheet music after hearing the songs performed in concerts and in musical theater productions. The sheet music would likely provide the basis for a sing-along in the parlor as the family gathered around the piano. Back then, having a song published literally meant generating sheet music for sale.

In the current market, securing the manufacture of sheet music is a very small part of a publisher's job. Today's music publishers' primary responsibilities are the "exploitation" of the copyrights they've acquired, and collecting the money those songs generate. ("Exploitation" in this instance means to facilitate the uses that will generate the maximum income.) Publishers are also responsible for the acquisition of songs for their company's catalog. They may acquire songs one at a time, by signing staff-writers, or by purchasing existing catalogs.

For many beginning songwriters, getting a song published seems like the ultimate success. But in reality, it's only one more important step along the journey. As you learned in Chapter 11, the bulk of a song's income comes from mechanical royalties, performance royalties, and sync licenses. In order to generate this income, your song must first be recorded and commercially released by an artist who garners sales and/or airplay, or must be included in a film or television show. From the songwriter's point of view, securing these recordings and placements is a publisher's most important job. Before continuing to explain a publisher's functions it's important that you understand the nature of a publisher's income.

All income generated by a song (with the exception of royalties paid for sheet music) is divided equally between the "writer's share" and the "publisher's share." For each dollar earned by a song, 50 cents represents 100 percent of the writer's share, and the remaining 50 cents equals 100 percent of the publisher's share. When songwriters say they have "published" a song, this means that they have assigned the publishing rights (representing 50 percent of any income the song generates) to an individual or company whose function includes generating and collecting income from that copyright. If you have not published a particular song, you own both the writer's and the publisher's share of any income this song generates.

> *(Many people) believe that a published song is going to make them tons of money, and that all they have to do is write one published song and poof— they are millionaires! If only that were true. What counts now is being recorded and released. Even being recorded isn't enough, since a significant percentage of songs that are cut are never released for various reasons.*
>
> GLORIA SKLEROV (Hit songwriter and two-time Emmy Award winner whose songs have been recorded by artists including Cher, Frank Sinatra, Anne Murray, and Kenny Rogers)

The writer's share (50 percent of the song's income) is divided among all of the song's cowriters. If there are three cowriters, barring any other agreement between them, each owns one-third of the writer's share (one-sixth of the total) of any income the song generates. In addition, each writer also owns a percentage of the publisher's share, equal to the percentage owned as a writer—unless the writer signs an agreement assigning the publishing rights to another individual or publishing company. If twenty songwriters contribute to the same song, this song may have twenty publishers.

In theory, just as there's no limit to how many writers may collaborate on any given song, there's no maximum number of publishers who can divide the publisher's portion of the pie. A writer could assign half of his share of the publishing to one publisher, one-quarter to another publisher, and the remaining quarter of the publishers' share to yet another publisher. However, in reality it is extremely unlikely that any legitimate publishers would agree to this arrangement.

HOW TO GET A PUBLISHER—AND WHY

> *For a new songwriter to get a meeting with a publisher, the best first step is to be referred by someone who already knows the publisher. Then, bring them up-tempo songs!!! You should start your CD with a few up-tempo songs in a row. I would guess that we, as publishers, hear ballads seven out of ten times. You can separate yourself from the pack from the beginning.*
>
> TOM LUTERAN (Director of Creative, EMI Music Publishing)

As you just learned, publishing a song is analogous to giving away 50 percent of your income. For a big hit, that could amount to hundreds of thousands of dollars. Why would anyone want to do such a crazy thing? There are several good reasons, but probably the best reason to assign your publishing rights and income to a music publisher is because 50 percent of an enormous amount of money is better than 100 percent of nothing.

Successful publishers maintain a high level of credibility by representing excellent songs, and by recognizing which songs might best suit a particular recording artist. They have the connections to get your songs heard by the industry professionals who have the power to get them recorded. A substantial part of a music publisher's job is developing the relationships with artists, managers, record label executives, and producers that lead to getting songs recorded.

> *Often, the most valuable thing a publisher does is provide constructive feedback and an atmosphere where a new writer can make contacts, as well as be exposed to the work of other professional writers. A good publisher will be able to see your strengths and arrange collaborations with other writers that will complement your talents and help you improve your craft.*
>
> TERI MUENCH-DIAMOND (President, Diamond Cuts/Diamond
> Mine Music, publisher of hits including "Not a Day
> Goes By," "I Can Love You Like That," and "Let Me Let Go")

At various times, I've seen superstar recording artists, including Reba McEntire, Wynonna, and members of Lonestar, at my publisher's Nashville Music Row offices, looking for songs. I was at the office when Garth Brooks telephoned for this same purpose. While no publisher has direct access to every recording artist, the best publishers have good business relationships with the A&R executives, artists' managers, and producers who look for hit songs for virtually every major artist. Effective publishers also make it their business to know which artists are looking for material at any given time, and what type of songs those artists are looking for.

Another important part of a publisher's job is setting up collaborations between the songwriters they represent and other writers and artists. These collaborations are often ones that the writer might never have been able to establish on his or her own. Many of my most successful songs are the result of cowrites initiated by my publisher.

Ideally, a publisher helps a writer to achieve his or her highest creative potential by offering constructive critiques of the writer's songs. Good publishers have their fingers on the pulse of the current market and can help their writers craft songs that have the best chance of being recorded. They can also guide the writers by pointing out the strengths and weaknesses in their songs, and encouraging rewrites.

In addition to the creative benefits, there are financial incentives to working with a publisher. It's unlikely you'll receive an advance to publish a single song, unless that song has already been recorded by a major artist. However, a publisher may pay to record a professionally produced demo of your song, or reimburse you for your demo costs. It is a good idea to take advantage of a publisher's demo-producing expertise if offered. When a publisher provides creative input into the writing and/or production of a song and its demo, he or she may be more apt to pitch it. (The financial and other benefits of a staff-writing deal are extensive and are discussed in Chapter 13.)

It very seldom works to call and say, "I'm new in town and I want to have a meeting." That's like us accepting an unsolicited tape—usually we don't. With the increased litigation possibilities, I prefer someone who has been referred by someone I know, or from one of the performing rights societies. That's where I've found the majority of staff-writers without track records that I've signed. Going through the songwriters' organizations and showcases to find other songwriters who have publishing deals is a good, creative way to make inroads and have more impact. Turn those contacts into introductions to publishers.

MICHAEL HOLLANDSWORTH
(President, Full Circle Music Publishing)

An additional financial benefit of working with a publisher is that publishers absorb many of the expenses of doing business—for instance, the costs of long-distance phone calls, office supplies, making CD copies, envelopes, and postage. (Depending on your contract, some of these costs may be recoupable from future royalties.) Many publishers, especially in Nashville, provide writing rooms where their writers can work. In these rooms, the publisher may also furnish a guitar, keyboard, and recording equipment. Office equipment (e.g., fax machines and computers) and access to recording studios may be available, too.

You can see that there are many advantages to working with a music publisher. However, it's impossible to place a price tag on one of the most important benefits a publisher offers. The credibility that accompanies being associated with a respected publishing company opens up doors (to record labels, producers, managers, artists, and successful cowriters) that might otherwise remain permanently locked. The importance of this built-in credibility should not be underestimated.

So, now you know why to get a publisher. But how do you get one?

When I first moved to Nashville, I was hired to teach songwriting at Watkins Institute, one of the nation's oldest establishments for education in the arts. In preparation for my classes, I called at least a dozen music publishers and asked for permission to include them on a list of publishers who were willing to review unsolicited songs. (The term "unsolicited" is commonly used to refer to material that is neither requested nor represented by a reputable music publisher, artist manager, or entertainment attorney.) In every instance the answer was a resounding "No." When I asked these publishers where they typically found new material and writers, I heard the same answer over and over again—referrals.

Referrals may come from a variety of sources, including other songwriters, PROs, and songwriters' organizations. However, your work needs to be strong to induce industry professionals to put their own credibility on the line by referring you to their associates.

One way to attract the attention of a publisher is by attending an event (e.g., a songwriter's expo, workshop, or camp) where publishers will be reviewing songs. It will take an exceptional song to grab their ear, but if a publisher hears your song and loves it, you should be able to parlay that into a meeting, or an invitation to send additional material.

Here's a "guaranteed" four-step formula for getting a foot in the door with any music publisher:

1. Write an incredible song with a songwriter who has already established a relationship with a publisher. (Note: I did not say a "pretty good" song.)

2. Have your collaborator present the song to the publisher he or she works with.

3. Call to introduce yourself as the cowriter of the song and thank the publisher for his or her praise, enthusiasm, and excellent constructive feedback.

4. Request a meeting to discuss plans for the song, and to play several others.

If your portion of the publishing rights is available, the publisher will be eager to acquire it, since he or she will be pitching your song anyway, on your collaborator's behalf. Obtaining your publishing rights will be a feather in his or her cap because it will double his or her company's share of any income your song generates—all for the same amount of work. Besides, if your song is exceptional, any publisher will be excited to hear additional songs you've written.

While "cold calling" is not typically an effective way to find a publisher, occasionally it can work. Another way to find a publisher is by responding to ads in songwriter publications. However, before conducting business with companies found in this manner, it's important to check that they are legitimate publishers. (See "Avoiding the Scams," page 231, for additional information.) Major companies don't actively pursue songwriters. However, several of my students have published songs and begun good working relationships with small publishing companies they found this way. *American Songwriter Magazine* (see Appendix) includes a comprehensive listing of music publishers (including many small, independent companies) in one of its issues each year. The *Songwriter's Market* and the *Publisher Registry* are excellent resources for writers seeking publishers (see Appendix).

Many songwriters explore the pros and cons of signing with small, independent publishing companies versus affiliating with larger publishers. Independent publishers operate "independently" from large music business conglomerates. They may be owned and operated by one individual, or may have significant financial backing and a staff of employees. Some independent publishing companies have a small stable of staff-writers, while others acquire songs individually. The "independents" are smaller companies and have fewer songs in their catalogs.

Major publishing companies are either subsidiaries of large corporations or are companies that have grown from independent status to attaining a significant market share. It's not unusual for a major publishing company to have anywhere from 30 to 100 staff-writers. If, as an unsigned writer, you are hoping to publish a song with a company that has numerous staff-writers and a catalog of thousands of songs, it's unlikely that this company will have a need for your song.

I remember a particularly frustrating meeting I had with a publisher at Jobete Music, a division of Motown. After listening to one of my songs, he said it was a "staff-writer song." When I asked what he meant, he explained that this song was of equal quality to those songs that any of his staff-writers were capable of turning in on any given day. If I was writing songs that were as good as his staff-writers' songs, why couldn't I get a publishing deal? At the time l didn't understand that for a major publisher with a large staff of exclusive writers to sign one of my songs, my song had to be different, or *better*—not just as good as—anything he had in his catalog.

> *If you compare your songs to those on the radio and think, "My song is just as good as that, that has a bunch of clichés, it's not really that good," that is not going to help you as a writer. There are reasons why that song got cut—many political reasons behind the scenes. There's the producer and the producer's wife and the producer's staff-writers who are being paid to come up with songs, so the quality of songs on the radio isn't always the measure of what you've got to surpass. They can always come up with those "average" songs. You have to be better than that in order to get your songs cut.*

> STEVE DIAMOND (Hit songwriter/producer)

Most developing songwriters find it easier to place songs, at least initially, with smaller independent publishers. Independent companies are more likely to have a genuine need for your song to fill a particular slot in their smaller catalog than a company representing 100,000 songs. But there are other advantages to working with a smaller publisher as well. Smaller companies can often provide additional attention to developing writers. They may be better able to nurture and devote more time to developing a fledgling writer's career by helping to produce demos, suggesting ways to improve the songs, and recommending collaborators. An independent company may also be "hungrier," more aggressive, and more determined to place your song. There are plenty of legitimate small, independent publishing companies that have great success placing songs with recording artists, as well as in films and television. However, there are also many independent companies that, despite the best intentions, lack the resources and means to promote songs effectively.

Many beginning songwriters are so anxious to publish a song that they jump at any offer. It's important to remember that a song with potential to become a major hit is a tremendous resource. Before assigning publishing rights to any company, explore your options. If your song is special enough to attract the attention of one publisher, it's likely that others will also recognize its merits. Before signing any song publishing contract (but especially one with a small, independent firm), take the time to develop relationships with key individuals at the company. Get feedback about the company's track record and trustworthiness from other industry professionals, and always have an entertainment industry attorney review your contract.

Whether you decide on a major publishing company or an independent publisher, don't be afraid to ask questions. It's perfectly acceptable to ask a prospective publisher, "Who do you hear recording this song?" (Also, be prepared with your own list of artists appropriate for the song.) If the publisher's answer is, "Garth Brooks," ask how he or she might get your song heard by Garth. Look for answers along the lines of: "I have a good relationship with the president of Capitol Records (Garth's label). I usually get a call back when I drop tapes off for Allen

Reynolds (Garth's producer) at his studio, and I'll also see if I can schedule a lunch with Bob Doyle (Garth's manager)." If the response is vague or unprofessional (e.g., "Uh, I once met his bus driver's wife at the Piggly Wiggly store and she might just show up again some day"), you haven't yet found the right publisher.

> *Ask when you are leaving if it is okay to call from time to time with new songs and if you should drop them off or have a face-to-face meeting with the publisher. If a publisher is really into your songs, he will call you for the most part. After the meeting, follow up—but not too often. Usually no answer is a "no" answer.*
>
> TOM LUTERAN (Director of Creative, EMI Music Publishing)

WORKING WITH YOUR PUBLISHER TO ACHIEVE YOUR GOALS

Let's assume you've written a wonderful song and it's been published by a music publisher who loves it. Now what do you do? If you assume your work is over and that it's the publisher's job to get your song recorded, it's likely you'll be very disappointed. Publishers have hundreds, if not thousands, of songs in their catalogs. The song that your publisher was so excited about when you turned it in may find itself on a shelf collecting dust several months later.

> *The proper relationship between a publisher and a writer is that the publisher works for the writer—not vice versa. It's a cooperative relationship. Ninety percent of the time, what is in the best interest of the writer is also in the best interest of the company. Maintain contact with your publisher. Try to be aware of the things the publisher is doing. It helps if the writer is involved in the music community, aware of what artists are recording and when. Also, writers can help pitch songs. But, the best thing a writer can do to help me get them cuts is to write great songs.*
>
> JOHN VAN METER (CCO, New Sheriff Music Publishing)

Approach the relationship with your publisher as a partnership. Your song won't generate any income for your publisher if it doesn't earn anything for you, so you're helping if your efforts result in getting your song recorded. Establish a game plan together. Use a "pitch sheet" (discussed in Chapter 14) to identify an initial group of artists to target and be specific about what actions each of you will take. For instance, your publisher may say, "I'll set up a meeting with the artist's producer and A&R person." You may respond with, "I'll drop off a CD at the artist's manager's office." Then, follow up with your publisher two or three weeks later to discuss your progress, as well as any feedback either of you may have received.

"Out of sight—out of mind" definitely applies to your relationship with your publisher. It's important to visit your publisher often. I can't count how many times I've overheard a casual conversation at my publisher's office regarding an artist who was looking for songs. In many of those instances, I was able to suggest a song of mine that my publisher might not have thought of—and my song got pitched.

Although it's important to maintain regular contact with your publisher, remember that there's a fine line between persistence and pestering. Call every few weeks for an update. Following are some tactics for keeping your songs fresh in your publisher's mind:

- Ask if he or she has had opportunities to pitch your song, and if so, what the feedback was.

- Request that your publisher send you a pitch sheet or "casting list" (a listing of artists who are currently looking for songs). Discuss possible pitches for your songs. (Be realistic. No song is appropriate for every artist.)

- Periodically give your publisher a CD of your very strongest songs that are included in his or her catalog.

- Apprise your publisher of any significant positive feedback your song receives from industry professionals.

All of these actions will help your song avoid drifting to a back burner—if it's as strong as you and your publisher initially thought. But, if a publisher receives consistently poor feedback about a particular song, it's likely he or she will not continue pitching it. As you continue to work in the music business, your list of contacts inevitably expands. You may have opportunities to pitch your songs yourself. Talk about those possibilities with your publisher to be certain you're on the same track.

SELF-PUBLISHING

Unless you have entered into a publishing agreement, thereby assigning your publishing rights to someone else (e.g., a publishing company), you own the publishing rights, and the corresponding publishing income, to any song you have written or cowritten. When you write a song by yourself, you own 100 percent of the writer's share, as well as 100 percent of the corresponding publisher's share, of any income that song may generate. If you have one collaborator, you each own 50 percent of the writer's share and 50 percent of the publisher's share.

Therefore, if you've written a song (and haven't published it), you are a song publisher. Maintaining your publishing rights has several big advantages: you earn double the money, you get to make the important decisions regarding your song, and you have leverage to negotiate a lucrative publishing deal in the event your song is recorded by a major artist. Once you have a song to represent (either one of your own compositions or another writer's song whose publishing rights have been assigned to you), it's easy to become a publisher. All you need to do is the following:

- Choose a name for your company;
- Decide which PRO to join;
- "Clear" the name you've selected (by checking with your PRO to be sure no other company is already using it); and
- Print up some letterhead on your computer.

But owning the publishing rights and successfully generating income from your songs are two very different things. Earlier in this chapter you learned the functions of an effective publisher. Before you decide to become your own publisher, you need to assess honestly whether you have the necessary time, personality, resources, and objectivity about your own songs to properly exploit them. A note about objectivity: it is the rare songwriter who can objectively assess whether his or her latest masterpiece is indeed as good as the songs being written by the best professionals in the business. A publisher may be better able to make this determination.

If your time is limited due to the responsibilities of working a "day job," then the work you do as your own publisher is taking valuable time away from your songwriting. To successfully publish your own songs you'll need to: investigate who is looking for songs; develop business relationships; make CD copies (or use the latest technology); mail or deliver your pitches; type cover letters, CD labels, and mailing labels; follow up your pitches with phone calls; handle administrative functions (e.g., applying for copyright registration, registering your songs with your PRO, keeping track of royalties, etc.); issue licenses; and negotiate licensing fees.

In addition to the time investment, publishing your own songs requires a substantial outlay of money. Expenses incurred by song publishers include the costs of producing demos, purchasing duplicating equipment, equipment maintenance, office supplies (including mailing envelopes, letterhead, mailing labels, etc.), blank CDs and labels, postage, photocopying (lyric sheets and correspondence), long-distance telephone charges, and resources such as pitch sheets and music industry directories to help you know which artists are seeking songs—and how to contact them. A computer and fax machine are also tremendously helpful, if not mandatory. While many of these expenses may be tax deductible (see your accountant for details), they still add up to a considerable amount.

Perhaps the most important factor to consider when deciding whether you should represent your own songs is your personality type. Song publishing (like songwriting) requires talent, long-term persistence, and the ability to withstand repeated disappointment and rejection—without losing faith in your songs. Successful publishers have the ability to discern which songs are best suited for particular artists. They also have the tenacity and the ability to forge the relationships necessary to get your songs considered by the professionals who call the shots. Publishers need to have excellent communication skills, both over the telephone and in meetings. If you're shy or nervous about making cold calls or "selling" yourself, self-publishing is probably not for you.

> *Throughout my career I've never had a publisher. I publish my own songs and I've had to shop my own songs. I find the fact that I'm able to pick up a telephone and call people certainly helps. You've got to have the goods first, but it also helps to have the ability to talk to people to sell one's self and one's songs.*
>
> BILLY STEINBERG (Songwriter of hits including "I Drove All Night," "True Colors," "Like a Virgin," and "Eternal Flame")

Many songwriters publish their own material as a temporary measure, while looking for a publisher to represent their songs. Songwriters who love the business side of the music business and fit all of the criteria listed above may enjoy great success publishing their own material. But those who are self-publishing because legitimate publishers are not willing to represent their material would put their time to better use by concentrating on honing their songwriting skills. Remember: 100 percent of nothing equals nothing.

USING SONGPLUGGERS

Since one of a music publisher's primary functions is to "plug" songs (pitch songs to recording artists and industry professionals who screen songs for artists), publishers are often referred to as "songpluggers," or "pluggers." But there are individuals who pitch songs for a fee—without necessarily acquiring ownership of the publishing rights—who are also referred to as songpluggers.

A small but growing percentage of successful, professional songwriters engage the services of a songplugger to augment the efforts of their publisher, or to act in lieu of a publisher. The rewards are high and the competition is fierce in the music business. There may be thousands of songs in a major publishing company's catalog, but when a publisher has a meeting to play songs for a recording artist or his or her representative, there may only be time to play a few songs. Your songs may not be among those your publisher chooses to play—or your publisher may play only one of your songs while you were hoping to have several pitched at the meeting. A good songplugger increases your opportunities to have your song played for industry pros. My career was propelled to a whole new level as a result of the efforts of a Nashville songplugger who secured the John Berry recording of "Change My Mind," my first Top Ten single and Gold record.

There's no standard payment in these situations. It's negotiated between the songwriter and plugger. Many songpluggers command a retainer of $200 to $500 or more per month for their services. In addition to these up-front payments, the agreement with the songwriter may also entitle the plugger to substantial bonuses in the event that he or she is responsible for securing a major recording.

Bonus payments are typically determined by the highest chart position attained and the number of units sold. Depending on the agreement between the writer and plugger, the payment for securing a Number One hit may exceed $10,000. While this may sound like an enormous amount of money, keep in mind that it may amount to only a tiny percentage of the songwriter's income on that song. That's a relatively small price to pay considering that, without the plugger's efforts, there might be no income generated at all.

Some songpluggers work exclusively on a bonus system. They get paid only upon securing a recording for the writer. Obviously, this is an ideal situation for the songwriter because if the plugger fails to get results, it costs the writer nothing. Agreements that do not require up-front payments typically provide higher bonuses, since the plugger is working solely on "commission." There are also songpluggers who receive a percentage of the publishing income if they successfully secure the recording and release of a song.

The best songpluggers are extremely selective about the writers whose catalogs they represent. They have close relationships with the decision makers and set up meetings to play songs for them. When they secure a meeting with a high-level industry professional, they know they must present exceptional songs in order to maintain their credibility and an open door. They usually place a strict limit on the number of writers they'll represent at any given time, so they are able to give attention to each writer's songs.

Beware of unscrupulous songpluggers who will, for a fee, represent any writer's songs—regardless of the quality or commercial potential of those songs. These individuals rely on up-front payments to earn their living, since it's highly unlikely the songs they represent will ever be recorded. Pluggers who fall into this category can be more of a detriment than a benefit, because their reputations precede them. While they may indeed deliver or mail copies of your songs to industry professionals, it's doubtful they will be listened to. It's unlikely these pluggers will be able to secure the important sit-down meetings to play songs. If they do, they certainly won't be invited back.

Effective independent pluggers provide an important service for those writers with top-notch, competitive songs who need some extra help pitching them. It is certainly easier for an aspiring writer to write a check to an independent plugger than it is to partake in the networking required to develop relationships with reputable publishers. However, this rarely achieves the desired results. It's great to believe in your talent and your songs, but for those writers who have tried repeatedly, and have not been able to place their songs with a publisher, it's highly unlikely that an independent plugger will be able to secure legitimate recordings of those songs.

CHAPTER 13

Understanding Publishing Agreements

There is no such thing as a "standard" songwriting contract. PERIOD! My advice to any writer, but particularly the writer looking at his or her first publishing deal, is to find an attorney experienced in entertainment law and surrender the negotiation of your contract to that person. You are dealing with a document that will have an effect on your income and, if you are signing a staff-writing deal, it will govern the business relationship between you and your publisher for three to five years on average. Contracts are a serious professional matter and should be treated as such. And by the way, a legitimate publisher will encourage you to seek independent legal counsel and may refuse to sign you if you do not. If you want to be a pro—act like one.

C. STEPHEN WEAVER, ESQ.
(Entertainment attorney)

A publishing agreement is a contract entered into to assign publishing rights from a songwriter to another individual or firm. Publishing agreements set out the terms that define the amount you will be paid for various uses of your song. They specify the territories (countries) covered and the length of time the agreement will remain in force. They also define the publisher's responsibilities to the songwriter (e.g., how and when royalties are to be distributed).

There are many other points covered in publishing agreements, including:

- The degree to which the songwriter will be consulted regarding any creative changes the publisher may want to implement
- The amount paid for print sales (and whether that amount will be expressed as a dollar figure or a percentage of the publisher's income)
- Monetary advances
- What costs shall be recoupable by the publisher—and what sources of income will be applied toward recoupment
- Whether the publisher pays for a demo
- Each party's responsibilities in the event of a copyright infringement suit or other legal problems
- When royalty statements are to be issued

- The writer's rights to audit the publisher's books
- Maximum percentage to be paid to subpublishers
- How translations to foreign languages will be handled

Some publishing agreements exceed twenty pages in length and appear to be written in a foreign language that only vaguely resembles English. It's crucial to retain an entertainment attorney prior to signing any song publishing agreement. (Your cousin Seymour who's studying to be a divorce lawyer does not have the expertise required.) Depending on the amount of clout you have, and your attorney's expertise, many of the contract points are negotiable. Hiring an attorney who specializes in the music business is expensive. Rates may exceed $300 per hour. Unfortunately, this is a necessary expense if you are to protect your interests. Points that may seem insignificant when you enter into a contract can be monumental if your song becomes a huge hit.

While it's not realistic for you to expect to have an attorney's knowledge of every detail of your publishing agreement, a savvy songwriter will learn what the major contract points mean. When you review your contract, make notes and ask questions prior to signing. The Bar Associations in Beverly Hills, Nashville, and New York City offer referrals to knowledgeable entertainment attorneys, and the *Music Attorney, Legal & Business Affairs Registry* offers extensive listings of attorneys who specialize in this area. *This Business of Music*, by Sidney Shemel and M. William Krasilovsky (Billboard Books), is an excellent resource for additional information about song publishing contracts and other technical aspects of the music business.

SINGLE-SONG AGREEMENTS

If a publisher feels strongly enough about one of your songs to want to publish it, you will be asked to sign a "single-song agreement." As the name implies, a single-song agreement is the contract a writer and publisher sign in order to publish one song. The terms laid out in this type of agreement apply exclusively to that one song.

As you have previously learned, there is no such thing as a "standard agreement," although some publishing agreements may have that phrase printed on top of the page. While a contract may be standard for a given publisher, many of the points may still be negotiable. The terms of the agreements between songwriters and publishers are limited only by the imaginations of the parties involved. A publisher's willingness to negotiate is determined by your track record and clout, your attorney's expertise, and, most importantly, by how badly the publisher wants to acquire a particular song.

The Songwriters Guild of America (SGA) has developed a song publishing agreement designed to represent the songwriter's best interests. While it's unlikely that a publisher will agree to every point in the SGA contract, a copy of it may be obtained from SGA's Web site and can be used as a model for the writer (see Appendix).

REVERSION CLAUSES

A reversion clause is a crucial point in single-song agreements and it's one you need to understand. It's the part of the contract that states that the publisher must achieve certain criteria within a set amount of time—or all rights to the song "revert" back to the songwriter. Typically, this clause requires the publisher to secure a commercially released recording, or inclusion of the song in a film or television show, within a specified amount of time.

It's in the publisher's best interests to ask for a long period before the song reverts back to the writer. Some publishers are hesitant to offer any reversion clause, or ask for a period of three or even five years before the reversion may be invoked. Of course, from the writer's point of view, if the publisher has not secured a commercially released recording, it's advantageous to have a shorter amount of time before the rights revert back. One year, eighteen months, or two years should be sufficient time for a publisher to show what he or she is capable of accomplishing with a given song. Although the publisher may not secure a cut in that amount of time, if he or she is still excited about your song, is continuing to actively pitch it, and is getting some interest, it's likely the songwriter will choose not to invoke the reversion clause, and will extend the agreement for another year or more. A reversion clause is your primary protection against any of the following possibilities:

- Your publisher is not successful in placing your song.
- The publisher who signed your song leaves the company.
- Your publisher loses interest in or excitement about your song.
- The company goes out of business or its catalog is sold.

It's tough to get songs recorded in the current market. There are numerous examples of enormously successful songs that have taken years to be recorded. Most artists record approximately one album every year-and-a-half. If a publisher has the right to represent your song for only one year, there may not be sufficient time for an artist to record your song and have an album commercially released before your song reverts back to you. Songwriters need to be protected, but they also need to be fair to their publishers and not put up unnecessary roadblocks to success.

Many publishers will offer a reversion clause with the stipulation that, in order to reclaim his or her song, the writer must reimburse the publishing company for any demo expenses incurred on the song's behalf. This is a perfectly reasonable request.

STAFF-WRITING DEALS

A staff-writing deal is an *exclusive* publishing deal and is occasionally referred to as a "term songwriter agreement." A staff-writer is not an actual employee of the publishing company, but assigns the publisher the exclusive right to publish everything the staff-writer writes during the term of the contract. Under most circumstances the publisher pays the writer an advance in exchange for that right. The money paid to a staff-writer is typically recoupable from the writer's share of mechanical royalties generated by any of the songs written under the terms of the agreement. Under some circumstances, a publisher may ask that your advance also be recoupable from any performance royalties you might generate. However, this is quite unusual and should be avoided if at all possible. In the event that the songs written during the contract period do not generate sufficient income to allow the publisher to recoup the money advanced to the writer, the writer is not responsible for reimbursing that money.

Staff-writers are required to fulfill a quota—a specified number of songs per year. The number of songs required to meet this quota varies and is an important part of the contract negotiation. Typically, a songwriter is required to turn in ten to fifteen songs per year, provided the writer has written 100 percent of each song. If each of the songs is a 50-50 collaboration, the writer would be required to submit twenty to thirty songs per year to fulfill the same quota. There is almost always a clause that specifies that these songs must be "acceptable" to the publisher. The definition of what constitutes an acceptable song is vague, however. This clause is included to avoid a situation whereby a writer churns out ten songs in a week for the sole purpose of fulfilling the quota. In some extremely rare circumstances a writer's quota may be defined not by the number of songs that are written, but by the number of songs that are recorded and commercially released. This is not typical and should be avoided, as it can keep you contractually bound to a company indefinitely.

Hit songwriter A.J. Masters ("Change My Mind," "An Old Pair of Shoes," "Love Ain't Like That") has said, "My publisher wouldn't care if I only wrote one song per year—if it was 'Song of the Year.'" I suspect that would be true of most publishers. A songwriter who writes a handful of extraordinary songs per year will generate far more income for his or her publisher than the same writer would by turning in fifty mediocre, or even "pretty good," songs.

You may wonder why a publisher would want to incur the financial risk of signing staff-writers. There are several reasons. When a writer signs an exclusive publishing agreement, he or she grants the publisher the right to publish all songs he or she creates during the length of time covered by the agreement. The contract typically encompasses a one-year period, followed by two or three additional one-year options. The decision as to whether to exercise those options belongs solely to the publisher. In the event the publisher exercises the additional options, the amount of the advances to be paid is negotiated when the contract is initially drafted.

A publisher may be able to sign a developing writer (with no major track record) by paying a recoupable advance of as little as $12,000, $15,000, or $20,000 per year. The writer may be contractually locked in for two or three additional one-year option periods at only slightly higher rates. If one, or more, of the writer's songs becomes a hit during that period, the publisher will have earned the right to exclusively publish everything written by a "hit" songwriter—for a fraction of what it would cost the publisher to sign an already established writer.

It's in a publisher's best interests to keep hit songwriters happy. So, in most instances, if you do write a hit, your publisher will be willing to increase the amount of your advances, even though he or she is not contractually bound to do so. If you have royalty income in the pipeline, your publisher is not risking anything by advancing additional money to you; he knows he will recoup it.

Large companies typically have greater financial resources and are able to offer an established writer more money for a staff-writing deal. However, they are often accused of acting as glorified banks for successful songwriters, meaning that they provide little more than money. But being signed to a major publishing company can have many benefits. The advantages include having your songs pitched by top-notch songpluggers, the level of credibility that comes along with the company name, and the increased opportunities for collaborating with other successful artists and writers also signed to that firm. In addition, with a large staff of songpluggers, if one doesn't like a particular song you've written, other pluggers may love it. The biggest disadvantages of working at a large publishing company are the increased competition, the lack of individual attention, and the risk that your material may be overshadowed by songs written by more successful writers.

The majority of successful songwriters are signed to staff-writing deals. During the early stages of a writer's career, the monetary advances may allow the writer to quit his or her day job and focus exclusively on songwriting. Unless a writer has a proven track record, or brings songs that are already generating income to the deal, it's unlikely he or she will get rich from the advance. Depending on where they are located and other factors (e.g., their clout, length of the contract, and their attorney's skill), beginning staff-writers are typically paid between $200 and $500 per week. Advances are typically much higher in Los Angeles and New York than they are in Nashville. Those advances may be paid weekly, monthly, or even annually.

For writers with major track records, the sky's the limit, with advances sometimes exceeding $200,000 per year. But remember: presuming that these writers continue their success, any monies advanced will be deducted from their future royalties. Although it's not commonly done, a writer might sign an exclusive publishing agreement without receiving any monetary advance. These writers decide they need the opportunities they receive as a staff-writer even more than the money.

The benefits of being a staff-writer typically include:

- Receiving an advance so you don't have to work a day job

- Having a staff of songpluggers to pitch your songs

- Access to professional feedback and creative input

- Having demo expenses paid

- The credibility that comes with being associated with a reputable publishing company

- Access to CD-copying equipment

- A room to write in

- Possible access to a recording studio

- Information about who is looking for songs

- The added discipline of having a song "quota" to fulfill

- Opportunities to network and collaborate with other staff-writers at that company

- In the event you receive an advance, your publisher having a vested interest in your success (i.e., he or she wants to recoup the investment)

However, there are also advantages to remaining an independent songwriter:

- In the event you secure a recording of your song, you retain 100 percent of the income.

- When a publisher goes to the effort of signing a single song, you know that publisher is enthusiastic about the song. (As a staff-writer your publisher owns the publishing share of every song you write, including the ones that he or she may not like—and may not pitch.)

- In the event you become very successful, you have more clout if you later decide to pursue an exclusive publishing deal, or assign the publishing rights to one of your songs that has already been recorded.

- You can place different songs with various publishers and see who is most effective in securing cuts.

- There's no risk of being signed exclusively to a publisher who loses interest in your songs or doesn't meet your expectations.

- You have your publishing rights to offer as incentive in the event a producer or artist requests a portion of your publishing in exchange for recording your song.

- You do not have the pressure of a song "quota" to meet.

There are no hard and fast rules regarding how to secure a staff-writing deal. However, there are two scenarios that most commonly lead to deals:

1. The writer publishes a single song with a given publisher. They develop a good working relationship, and over a period of time, the writer consistently presents songs the publisher feels have strong commercial potential. The publisher signs several more of the writer's songs using single-song agreements, and begins to get some "action" (i.e., holds or recordings) or interest in the songs. During this period, the publisher may set up collaborations and evaluate the writer's attitude and progress. Simultaneously, the writer assesses the publisher's ability to secure recordings, provide valuable creative input, and make proper business decisions. If both parties are satisfied with the relationship, it's likely (if the publisher has the budget and an opening for a staff-writer) that the writer will be offered an exclusive songwriting deal.

2. The writer "brings something to the table." The writer has either proven himself by writing songs that have been recorded, or is willing to grant the publishing rights to a song that is already generating income, or has money in the pipeline.

Signing a staff-writer is a major investment as well as a risk for a publisher. Quite often, a publisher does not recoup the advances paid to a writer during the time that writer is signed to the company. (Although songs written during a writer's contract period remain in the publisher's catalog and may generate income for the publisher after the writer has left.)

It's difficult, even for a major publisher, to secure recordings in this highly competitive market. Therefore, publishers are most likely to sign writers who not only write strong songs, but also demonstrate the ability to help generate their own cuts. Writers who are also record producers or recording artists provide built-in outlets for their own songs, as well as for other songs in a publisher's catalog. In addition, many publishers sign aspiring writer/artists and help them to secure record deals.

Particularly in the pop, hip-hop and urban markets, where the vast majority of songs are written or cowritten by the artist or the producer, it's much tougher for a songwriter who "only" writes to secure a staff-writing position. If you are neither a recording artist nor a record producer, you can increase your chances of becoming not only a staff-writer, but also a successful songwriter, by developing business and cowriting relationships with individuals who are pursuing those goals.

In addition to writing great songs, one of the keys to securing a staff-writing position is developing long-term relationships with publishers. One of the ways this can be accomplished is by collaborating with writers who are signed to publishing companies. It's unrealistic to expect to set a meeting with a publisher, play three good songs, and be offered a staff-writing position. Developing a staff-writer represents a major investment of time, energy, and money for a publisher. (In my case, it took more than five years before my publisher began to see a profit from his investment.) It's extremely unlikely that a music publisher will make such a commitment to an "unproven" writer without taking time to allow the relationship to unfold.

COPUBLISHING DEALS

A copublishing deal allows a songwriter to retain a portion of his or her publishing rights and income (often referred to as "the publishing"). By becoming one of the publishers of a song, a writer participates in the publisher's share of the revenues. Copublishing deals may apply to a single-song agreement or an exclusive (staff-writing) deal.

Publishers are understandably reluctant to relinquish a portion of their income and typically do so only when a writer has established a significant level of clout and credibility (e.g., major hit songs, cowriting with a major artist, or being signed to a deal as a recording artist). In some instances a publisher may agree to a deal that grants copublishing in the event that the writer (or an independent plugger acting on his or her behalf) is the one who secures the recording. A copublishing deal may assign any percentage of the publishing rights and income to the various parties. To make the following examples less confusing, assume the writer is the sole writer of a song.

If a writer and his or her publisher split the publishing 50-50, the writer retains 100 percent of the "writer's share" *and* 50 percent of the "publisher's share." For each dollar earned, the writer receives 50 cents (100 percent of the writer's share) and an additional 25 cents (50 percent of the 50 cents allocated to the publishers). If a writer, who is the sole writer of a song, retains 25 percent of his or her publishing, for each dollar generated by a given song the writer receives 50 cents (100 percent of the writer's share) and an additional 12.5 cents (one-quarter ownership of the 50 cents of publishing income).

Under the terms of a copublishing agreement, the writer (as "publisher") may be responsible for a percentage of costs incurred by the publisher (i.e., demo costs, copyright fees, postage, etc.). Typically, this percentage corresponds to the percentage of the writer's share of ownership of the publishing rights.

Retaining a portion of your publishing increases your income and has an added benefit. In the event your songs generate significant long-term revenue, you have the option of selling your own catalog (assigning your publishing rights to another publisher) at some point in the future, for a substantial sum. As in any publishing agreement, when negotiating a copublishing deal, it's important to be represented by a competent entertainment attorney.

CHAPTER 14

Making Connections and Pitching Your Songs

The songwriter who sits and depends on a publisher, publishing company, producer, or friend is in denial.

FRANNE GOLDE (Hit songwriter)

Successful songwriters, including those signed to exclusive publishing deals, frequently secure many of their own recordings. This doesn't mean that working with a publisher isn't valuable for these writers. A publisher may provide many other services that contribute directly or indirectly to a writer securing recordings of his or her songs, including setting up collaborations and providing introductions to music industry decision makers.

It's a safe bet that since the first time a caveman grunted out a melody, there's never been a songwriter who felt his or her publisher was providing the attention the writer's songs deserved. Publishers may have hundreds, if not thousands, of good songs in their catalogs, so it's unlikely that every one of your songs will be among your publisher's top priorities. The reality of the music business is such that songwriters need to take an active role in networking in the industry, developing connections, and pitching their own songs.

NETWORKING

More so than ever now, it takes a detective to succeed in this business, since there are so few slots for songwriters. It's even more important to somehow find a way into a camp or a project, because so many of the cuts are "in-house."

ALLAN RICH (Hit songwriter with cuts by artists including 'NSync, Whitney Houston, Barbra Streisand, Barry Manilow, and Patti LaBelle)

Networking is the act of interacting and sharing information with others who share a common interest. We've all heard it said that success in the music business is based on who you know and what connections you have. There's a lot of truth to that statement. But, while very few songwriters are born with those connections, somehow, the successful ones manage to develop them.

> *Developing songwriters should find a way to connect with the industry in some way to network and expand their horizons. Take advantage of seminars and showcases. Even if you are not performing, go to meet other writers and industry people. Relationships are essential to evolving in this industry, and those seeds need to be planted and nurtured over what are sometimes long periods of time. But, they do pay off. Everyone needs help and feedback.*

BRENDAN OKRENT
(Senior Director of Repertory, ASCAP)

It's easier to establish relationships with people who are working toward success than with those who have already achieved it. Today's record label receptionist may well be tomorrow's A&R executive. The songwriter sitting next to you in a workshop may become a Grammy winner five years from now. The vocalist who's singing your demo for $85 may be signed to a major record label tomorrow. That's the nature of the business.

Networking with those who are on their way up is important for success in any business, but it's crucial in the songwriting business. One of the best ways for developing writers to hone their skills, learn about the music business, and begin networking is through membership in a local songwriting organization. These organizations provide an opportunity for songwriters to share information and resources, receive feedback and support, and, most importantly, connect to the songwriting community. Most of these organizations meet monthly and some periodically sponsor educational seminars featuring guest speakers who are successful music industry professionals.

Nashville Songwriters Association International (NSAI), the world's largest not-for-profit songwriter's trade association, has more than one hundred chapters throughout the US and the world—and despite the association between Nashville and country music, NSAI's members include writers of many different styles of music. At monthly meetings, members have an opportunity to receive peer critiques and to work on exercises to hone their songwriting skills. Membership benefits include a free song evaluation service (by mail), pitch opportunities, an in-house bookstore, a newsletter, writing rooms, and more.

NSAI also offers three-day educational retreats called "Song Camps," as well as the Tin Pan South Songwriters' Festival and Spring Symposium (a two-day educational symposium). These events all offer excellent opportunities to interact with music industry professionals, as well as with aspiring songwriters. For information about contacting NSAI, or to find the local chapter nearest your home, see the Appendix.

The Songwriters Guild of America (SGA) provides services for its members that include the free review of contracts, collection of mechanical royalties (for a fee), and review of royalty statements and publisher audits. Educational activities include Ask-A-Pro (an opportunity to ask questions of music industry professionals), song critiques, and periodic songwriter showcases. With offices in New York, Los Angeles, and Nashville, SGA sponsors educational workshops, song critiques, and an opportunity to pitch songs to industry professionals (also available through the mail for out-of-towners), song evaluation (by mail), a Collaborators Network (a bimonthly listing of members looking for collaborators), and reduced fees for legal services. (See Appendix for contact information.)

Just Plain Folks (JPF) is an organization of more than 25,000 songwriters, recording artists, music publishers, producers, and other music business professionals, as well as those who aspire to work or perform in the music business. JPF has local chapters throughout the US and sponsors showcases and competitions. They offer excellent networking and educational opportunities, a message board, and an online newsletter featuring articles by the organization's mentors, top music industry professionals. (See Appendix for contact information.)

The Taxi Road Rally, held in Los Angeles each November, provides one of the industry's best networking opportunities. The four-day event is free but is open only to Taxi members. The Road Rally offers showcase and performance opportunities; excellent educational workshops and clinics; chances to meet with, and pitch to, publishers, producers, and record label executives; and a place to hang out with more than 1,500 other musicians and songwriters from around the world. For additional information about Taxi, see "Using Pitch Sheets Effectively" later in this chapter (page 213).

Classes and workshops offered by ASCAP and BMI also provide terrific opportunities to network with both well-established and up-and-coming songwriters, publishers, and record label executives. Songwriting and music business classes, offered at many local colleges, also provide networking opportunities. Another way to expand your network of music industry contacts is through collaboration. The bottom line is that writing songs in the privacy of your own home—and keeping them there—won't accomplish your goals.

COLLABORATING

Collaboration is the act of cowriting a song with one or more writers. Some of the best-loved songs in popular music have been written by teams, including Lieber and Stoller ("Hound Dog," "Heartbreak Hotel"), Rodgers and Hammerstein ("The Sound of Music," "Oklahoma!"), George and Ira Gershwin ("I Got Rhythm," "Someone to Watch over Me"), Burt Bacharach and Hal David ("Do You Know the Way to San Jose," "Walk on By"), Holland-Dozier-Holland, ("Heat Wave," "You Keep Me Hangin' On"), and, of course, Lennon and McCartney ("Yesterday," "I Want to Hold Your Hand"). More recently, countless hit songs were the result of collaborations between artists and songwriting/production teams including the Matrix (Avril Lavigne, Britney Spears, Jason Mraz), Jimmy Jam and Terry Lewis (Janet Jackson, Toni Braxton), and the Neptunes (Justin Timberlake, No Doubt, P. Diddy).

Cowriting is a great way to step outside yourself to expand your creative horizons; to expand your craft, and gain some perspective. Cowriting is often like playing tennis ... you want to find someone better than yourself so you can improve. Not all people make good matches, but like all personal relationships there should be at least a few people out there who will work well with you. Even if you eventually wind up writing by yourself, it can be an excellent experience and exercise. You may do things you might never have done by yourself.

BRENDAN OKRENT (Senior Director of Repertory, ASCAP)

Some songwriters collaborate because they write only words or only music. However, many writers who are adept at writing both lyrics and melody choose to collaborate to take advantage of some of the additional benefits cowriting can offer. The vast majority of hit songs are indeed cowritten. Naturally, the main reason to collaborate is to write a song that's different, and hopefully better, than one you would have written on your own. Here are some of the other reasons to collaborate:

- "Writing up": The best way to push yourself and expand your songwriting skills is to cowrite with someone who's a step ahead of you on the ladder. (Note. I said *one* step ahead on the ladder. It's not realistic for an unpublished writer to expect to write with a Grammy-winning songwriter.)

- Political considerations: Success in the music business can definitely be influenced by who you know. Your cowriter's publishing company may have access to an artist you want to write songs for, or may have successful producers and recording artists on staff. Or, you may want to establish relationships with the publishers themselves.

- Writing with an artist or producer: There's no better route to getting a song cut than cowriting it with an artist or producer. While this doesn't guarantee a cut, there will be no question that your song will be heard by the right people. All other things being equal, the artist or producer will have a vested interest in recording your song—but you will still need to write a very strong song.

- Increased pitches: By writing with another writer, you double your staff of songpluggers. You may both have publishers pitching your song, and hopefully, you'll both also be actively pitching your song.

- Someone to inspire you: A good collaborator encourages you not to settle for mediocrity. You can push each other to do the best work you're capable of.

- Expanding your network: Cowriting expands your network of connections and contacts. If your collaborator is a published writer, you'll likely gain an open door at his or her publishing company. You may also be introduced to your cowriter's demo musicians and vocalists, as well as the studios he or she works in, and may meet some additional cowriters.

- Promoting discipline: Having a cowriting appointment that is scheduled in advance causes many songwriters to write on days when they might not feel creative. Your responsibility to another writer may lead you to work a little bit harder at developing an idea, or to work on yet another rewrite.
- Instant feedback: Your collaborator will let you know if he or she feels you are hitting the mark—or missing the target.
- Emotional support: The art and business of songwriting can be wonderfully rewarding, but it can also be frustrating and disappointing. Cowriters can provide much-needed emotional support and encouragement.

If you're going to collaborate, write with writers who are as good as or better than you so that you're always learning. I think a lot of writers who are shy and withdrawn have a harder time unless they write with someone. In a lot of teams, one person is more aggressive and the other one is more laid back. It's a great dynamic when the one that's the aggressor is out there pumpin' and doing the biz.

FRANNE GOLDE (Hit songwriter)

The best collaborations are the result of a hard-to-define chemistry between cowriters. I've written mediocre songs with tremendously successful writers for whom I have great respect and admiration. I've also written some very good songs with writers who have not yet established track records. Although I've written with more than a hundred different collaborators, my best songs have been written with only a handful of them. For a reason I may never understand, when I write with these particular cowriters, something more comes out of me because they're in the room—and they report the same phenomenon. To find that connection, you may have to work with many different collaborators, and bear in mind that the chemistry may not be apparent the first time you work together.

When collaborating, it's important to define your business arrangement prior to beginning the creative process. Establish what the "split" will be (i.e., if there are two writers, will each writer own 50 percent of the song?). It's unlikely that each writer will contribute exactly 50 percent, but typically that is the split between two collaborators. It's not productive to count who wrote which words and notes in order to determine the percentages of ownership; it may be one specific word or melodic phrase that's responsible for the song's success. In a long-term collaboration, inevitably there will be some songs that include more of one writer's contribution and others that have more input from the other writer in the team.

It's also important to establish how the publishing portions of the song will be divided. Unless otherwise specified, each writer owns the publishing portion of a song equal to his or her writer's share. (For instance, if there are two writers, each owns 50 percent of the writer's share and 50 percent of the publisher's share.) Clarify these arrangements before you begin working.

It's important to discuss how your cowritten song will be demoed. One of the writers may assume there will be a full-band demo with a $1,000 budget, while the other may expect to sing and play on an inexpensive guitar/vocal demo, or may not have the money to do any demo at all. It's impossible to determine what kind of demo will best serve a given song before you've written it. But you can discuss the issue by stating, for example, that if the song that results from this collaboration is an up-tempo or dance song, the demo will be approached in a specified manner.

Collaboration can be a delicate process. It sometimes requires baring your soul and risking criticism. It's important in any successful collaboration for all of the writers to feel respected and safe. There needs to be a level of comfort that allows you to share whatever pops into your head without fear of being harshly criticized. By blurting out a line that you think is "stupid," you may spark something in your cowriter that leads to his or her coming up with the great line you've been looking for.

Many successful collaborations take place with the cowriters in the same room, feeding off each other's creative energy. However, it's also possible to collaborate long distance. I cowrote two songs with Grammy winner Todd Cerney and had one of them recorded before ever meeting him. In one of those instances, I mailed finished lyrics to Todd, who set them to music. The other time, Todd mailed me a finished melody to which I wrote the lyrics. Co-writing via mail can be a viable option for songwriters who live in an area with limited access to many potential collaborators. Fax machines, MP3s, and e-mail make the process even more immediate, allowing almost-instant feedback.

> *Hang out with people who are smarter, more creative, and more talented than you are and aspire to their level. I think that's what mentoring is all about and that's what the songwriting community is all about. You should hear and be exposed to as many people who are better than you are as you possibly can and hope that through osmosis it sinks in.*
>
> ROBERT K. OERMANN
> (Music journalist; judge, *Nashville Star*)

Following are some common problems with collaborations—and how to solve them:

- *You simply can't agree on a specific line of melody or lyric.* Collaboration should be a positive experience, bringing out the best in all parties involved. Ideally, you and your cowriter(s) will share a common vision for your song. However, as in most relationships, there may be times when you and your collaborator disagree. When this happens, it can help to have each writer express why he or she feels so strongly about the particular line of lyric, melody, or chord. If you express a legitimate reason why this line is not working for you, your cowriter may come to agree with your point of view, or vice versa. If, however, you reach an impasse, you might record rough versions reflecting each of your suggestions and get some objective feedback from a professional song critique service, a critique group, a publisher, or others whose opinions you both trust. Hopefully, based on the input you receive, a compromise will be reached. For example, if you are not able to agree on either of your lines, you might decide to continue to work on the song until you come up with something that pleases both of you.

- *One of the writers doesn't like the resulting song.* In this case:

    1. Suggest revisiting and rewriting the song until both writers are pleased.

    2. Accept that this will not be one of his or her favorite songs, but will still allow the other writer(s) to demo and pitch it; or

    3. Say "I want my contribution back—and I don't want my name on this song."

    When writing for the first time with a new collaborator, it's a good idea to suggest that if you're not both happy with the song you cowrite, you can each take back your respective contributions. For example, if one writer brought in an existing lyric or melody, he or she may choose to give that lyric or melody to a different cowriter. This way you eliminate the risk inherent in bringing a great lyric idea or melody you've been saving to the collaboration.

- *Your collaborator doesn't seem to want to finish a song you've started together; your repeated phone messages and e-mails go unanswered.* Leave a telephone message and/or send one more e-mail stating that if you are not able to schedule a writing session within a reasonable amount of time (for example, within the next thirty days) you will either finish the song on your own or bring in an additional collaborator. You might add that if your collaborator does not choose to be a part of the song that he or she is welcome to take back his or her contribution, or to leave it and be credited. If you still do not receive a response, finish the song on your own (or with an additional collaborator), credit your initial collaborator, and mail him or her a copy of the finished song.

- *Your collaborator doesn't want to rewrite—but you do.* Express the reasons why you feel the song might benefit from a rewrite. For example: "The opening lines are not special enough to grab a listener's attention and I believe we can make them stronger." Or, "I received a professional song critique and I agree with the evaluator, who suggested that we could improve the chorus melody."

    If your collaborator is adamant about leaving the song "as is," offer to work on the rewrite alone. Hopefully, he or she will recognize that you have improved the song and will thank you. But if this is not the case and you are not able to reach an agreement, a last resort is to have two different versions of the song—and see which one receives the best professional feedback. An individual who is not open to rewriting is one whom I would probably not choose to work with in the future.

- *One of the cowriters does not want to contribute money or input to record a demo.* As stated previously, this issue should have been addressed prior to writing the song. But, if your collaborator has decided not to demo your song after the song is finished, you have several options. Your decision will be based upon the reason why your collaborator does not want to demo the song—and your own financial circumstances.

If your cowriter would like to make a demo of the song, but cannot afford to pay for it, you have to decide if you feel sufficiently strong about the song to warrant absorbing 100 percent of the demo expense. You might ask if your cowriter would be willing to reimburse his or her share of the demo expense if his or her financial circumstances improve—or out of any future income the song might generate.

If your cowriter does not choose to invest in a demo because he or she does not feel the song warrants it, your options are paying for the demo yourself or choosing not to demo the song.

- *One of the writers wants to grant an artist a recording license or wants to commercially release the song on his or her own independent album—but the other writer does not want this artist to record the song.* Hopefully, you will reach an agreement, but from a legal standpoint any of the copyright owners has the right to grant nonexclusive licenses (to record companies, film companies, etc.) as long as all copyright owners are paid. However, it is unlikely that a film or television production company will be willing to use a song unless all copyright owners agree to the terms and sign licenses.

  In the eyes of the copyright law, once a work has been jointly created it cannot be separated any more so than an egg could be unscrambled. If one writer contributes 100 percent of the lyric, while the other writer composes 100 percent of the melody, in the eyes of the law each collaborator owns 50 percent of the entire song. Therefore, if a lyric is translated and the title and concept of the original lyric are completely abandoned, the lyricist still owns 50 percent of the resulting song (after a percentage of ownership has been assigned to the translator). Likewise, if the copyright owners are found guilty of plagiarizing another song's melody, the lyricist and composer, as joint owners of the song, are equally liable.

As in any relationship, open communication is the key to successfully resolving problems with your collaborators. However, you may learn that a given collaborator is simply not a good match for you. Sometimes you have to kiss a lot of frogs....

HOW TO FIND A COLLABORATOR

As in so many areas of the music business, networking is typically the key to finding that special cowriter who brings out the best in you. There are many ways to find writers whose work you respect, and with whom you feel at ease. However, your odds will improve if you place yourself in a setting where there are many songwriters. If you don't live in or near a city with a thriving music scene, you may be able to spend your vacation at a song camp or attending a songwriter's event in a major music center. Music industry publications advertise these events. You can also find out about them from songwriter organizations.

Writers' nights, classes, and workshops where songs are critiqued present an opportunity to hear, and essentially audition, other writers' work. Approach writers whose songs appeal to you, and whose writing style and personality seem compatible with yours. As mentioned previously, writing up is important. Your skills will increase as you work with collaborators who share their knowledge and contacts.

When approaching a potential collaborator, remember that he or she also wants to write up. You need to bring something to the table to make the other writer want to write with you. This may be a great title or idea, a draft of a strong lyric, a beautiful melody, great music business connections, or your attitude and enthusiasm. It's a good idea to exchange copies of your songs (or samples of your lyrics, if you are primarily a lyricist) prior to committing to a cowriting session.

"I really respect your work. I have a great idea for a song. Would you be interested in discussing it and possibly collaborating?" is an ideal way to approach a potential cowriter. If your ideas are indeed exceptional, you may be able to attract writers who are further along in their careers. Some professional songwriters have a policy of never writing with unsigned writers. Some are just too busy, and others might not be looking to begin any new collaborations. Don't take these rejections personally. As in any relationship, you may have to approach many different writers before you find your perfect match.

Songwriters who are unable to find collaborators via networking might run an advertisement seeking collaborators (or answer one) in a music industry publication. *Music Connection* magazine (see Appendix) includes the world's largest listing of musicians' classified ads. The Internet offers terrific opportunities to "meet" potential collaborators. Visiting songwriting Web sites and chatrooms, such as those listed in the Appendix, is one way many writers, especially those who do not have access to music centers, may find cowriters.

HOW AND WHEN TO COPYRIGHT YOUR SONGS

"Copyright" means the legal protection of original works a writer creates. Songs, jingles, underscores to films and television shows, symphonic pieces, or any other original music, lyric, or both may be copyrighted. However, you cannot copyright a title or an idea for a song—only the actual melody and lyrics. If another writer hears your brilliant idea and writes another song that expresses your exact same idea, but with different words and music, it does not constitute copyright infringement.

Copyright law grants the copyright owner (the writer, or in the event that the work is published, the publisher) some exclusive rights for a specified number of years. These include the right to produce and distribute copies of a work, the right to prepare derivative works, the right to perform the work, the right to display the work, and the right to have the work performed via digital transmission.

The moment that you write and record a song (even a rough version sung a cappella into a handheld recorder), you own it—whether you've registered your song with the Copyright Office or not. However, there must be a *tangible* version (i.e., a recording or a piece of sheet music) generated to constitute a copyright; it is not enough to simply write the song in your head. In the event that its ownership is contested, a copyright is the best evidence of your claim to have created the song on the date specified.

Many major music publishers do not copyright the songs in their catalogs until they've been recorded and commercially released. However, some songwriters choose to copyright their songs before playing them in public or distributing demos. While it is not mandatory to register your songs with the Copyright Office to pitch them or perform them in public, it is important that the works be registered when they are recorded for commercial release or included in a film, television show, or commercial. Failure to do so takes away your legal right to collect compulsory mechanical royalties, file an infringement suit, stop others from using your song, and recover attorney's fees and statutory damages.

Registering your songs with the Copyright Office is certainly the safest way to protect them, but it can get expensive if you're a prolific writer. The fee to copyright a song is $30. However, there are less expensive alternatives. One popular option is to compile a collection of songs you've written or cowritten, and copyright them together under one name. For instance: "The Best Songs of Jamie Goldberg: Volume One." Your compilation may include as many unpublished songs as you can fit on one audiocassette or CD. Formerly, to register a song with the Copyright Office, you had to send a lead sheet. Now, it's acceptable to submit either a lead sheet or a recorded version of your song on cassette or CD. The form used to register music and/or lyrics (as well as other works of performing arts) is called Form PA.

If you register a collection of songs under one name by submitting a cassette or CD, state the title of each individual song prior to recording it. In the event that one of the songs in your collection is published, or recorded and commercially released, it will become necessary to copyright the song individually. (In the space provided for that purpose on the PA form, specify that the song has previously been copyrighted as part of a collection of songs that were collectively registered under one name—and provide that name.)

Another alternative to copyrighting your song is to send it to yourself via registered mail and keep the envelope sealed. The postmark will serve as evidence that you claimed ownership of the song on that particular date. This is sometimes referred to as the "poor man's copyright." Although this method is better than no protection, it does not guarantee all the rights that come with legitimate copyright registration.

In 1998, Congress passed the Sonny Bono Copyright Term Extension Act that, for songs written on or after January 1, 1978, provides copyright protection for seventy years after the death of the work's creator. In the event that the work is owned by a corporation (for example, a major publisher), the length of copyright protection is a total of ninety-five years. The US Copyright Office Web site (see Appendix) provides extensive information, including registration procedures and copyright laws. Copyright forms and instructions may be downloaded at no charge from the Web site.

Whether you decide to invest $30 for copyright registration, copyright multiple songs as part of a collection, choose the poor man's copyright, or use an alternative song registration service, it's safest to have some form of protection for your song before pitching it or playing it in public.

FINDING OUT WHO'S LOOKING FOR SONGS AND WHAT THEY'RE LOOKING FOR

Art and commerce are an interesting mix. My notion is that you should create art from a pure place and when you can call it art, then it's time to try to sell it. Don't let commerce poison the art or dictate what it should contain.

STEVE SESKIN (Publisher/hit songwriter with Number One cuts by artists including Tim McGraw, Mark Wills, John Michael Montgomery, Neal McCoy, and Collin Raye)

Timing is crucial in pitching your songs successfully. You may have written the quintessential Whitney Houston song, but if Ms. Houston's album has just been finished, the best you can hope for is that she and her record label's executives will still be enthusiastic about your song a year from now. While there are instances of artists holding onto songs for a year or more prior to recording them, those are rare. It's far more common for artists to tire of songs after several months. Songs that have been pitched too early are frequently replaced during the recording process when an exciting, new song comes along.

Artists, and those who screen songs for them, typically begin actively looking for songs three or four months prior to recording. Producers and A&R executives tend to focus on finding hits for their "next" project. So, how can you know who's currently looking for songs?

One way to know which artists are looking for songs is by networking with other writers who are actively pitching their songs. At events held by songwriter organizations, guest speakers from publishing companies or record labels may provide valuable information. Another way to gather information regarding who is looking for songs (and what they're looking for) is by contacting the record labels directly. Some of the labels maintain "Hotlines," prerecorded messages that tell the listener what type of songs the A&R department is looking for. (The A&R department at a record label is responsible for song selection for those artists signed to the label, as well as signing new artists).

It's important to do your research. Prior to calling the record label, find out the name of an A&R executive at the label and ask to speak with his or her assistant. The easiest way to get this information is by reading trade magazines and pitch sheets. (More about pitch sheets later in this chapter). You can also learn this information by reading publications such as *The A&R Registry* (see Appendix).

In Chapter 12, you learned that if you are not affiliated with a publishing company, you are essentially acting as your own publisher. Labels tend to give more credibility to publishers than songwriters. So, when you call, introduce yourself as Janice Cook, with "Empress Music Publishing" (of course, insert the actual name you've chosen for your company), and be very professional and confident. By the way, it's probably a good idea to choose a name for your publishing company that does not sound as if it is a tiny firm, simply representing your own songs. For example, to garner additional respect, instead of naming your company "Adam Goldberg Music," or "Serinsky Songs," you might garner more credibility with a bigger-sounding name like "Hitz Incorporated" or "The Entertainment Group."

There's no need to be intimidated by the person on the other end of the telephone. You're simply doing your job, and besides, he or she does not hold the key to the success or failure of your entire career. Let the A&R assistant know that you represent a small catalog of songs you feel strongly about and ask who on their roster is currently looking for songs. When you get that information, ask what *direction* each of these artists is going in, and if they're looking for something specific (e.g., up-tempo songs versus ballads). The answer you'll most often hear is, "We're looking for hits." Occasionally you may be told, "We need a positive love ballad with a mature lyric," or something just as specific and helpful.

Sometimes you may encounter an assistant with an attitude. I once had one tell me, "If you were a legitimate publisher, you'd already know who's looking for songs." There was nothing I knew to say or do to break through that particular wall, so I went around it and pursued the information from other sources. More often, you'll get the information you need.

If the thought of being a salesman and making cold calls makes you nervous, try rehearsing what you'll say. Role-play with another songwriter and take turns being the caller and the A&R assistant (or publisher). This is the music *business*, after all, and you have to conduct business, in addition to writing hit songs, if you want to achieve success.

Music industry publications, such as *Billboard's Talent and Touring Directory*, *The A&R Registry*, and *The Billboard Sourcebook*, as well as trade magazines (e.g., *Billboard*, *Music Connection*, *American Songwriter Magazine*, and *Music Row*) provide a wealth of information (see Appendix). By reading the music charts, you can learn who the producer, publishers, and writers of any given song are. Music industry magazines often include interviews and articles about recording artists, producers, and music industry executives. There is often valuable information in these articles regarding the recording projects these individuals are working on.

USING PITCH SHEETS EFFECTIVELY

"Pitch sheets" (also referred to as "tip sheets" or "casting lists") are publications that list artists who are looking for songs. They also typically describe the types of songs these artists are seeking, and, sometimes, the name and address of the individual reviewing songs for the project. By subscribing to a pitch sheet, essentially you are paying to have someone else do some of your investigative legwork. The publisher of the pitch sheet has his or her staff contact record labels, producers, and artists' managers on a regular basis to determine the songs they need. This information is passed along to subscribers.

Some of the pitch sheets also include interviews with industry professionals, articles, and information about songwriting contests. *New on the Charts*, one of the most popular pitch sheets, includes a roster of current pop, country, and urban hits listed in the *Billboard* charts. It provides the names, addresses, e-mail addresses, and telephone and fax numbers of the publishers, producers, record labels, managers, and booking agents for every song and artist on the charts, as well as an extensive listing of new and established artists who are looking for songs—and how to contact their representatives. See the Appendix for a listing of the most popular pitch sheets.

Taxi is an organization that publishes a pitch sheet with a twist. Twice per month, members receive listings (typically, via e-mail) of music publishers, record labels, artists' managers, and film and television music supervisors who are looking for songs and for recording artists. Many top producers and record labels do not want to be deluged with songs from amateurs. Taxi addresses this issue by prescreening material and sending on only the best. Submissions are sent directly to Taxi, where they are reviewed by a staff of industry professionals, including former A&R executives, producers, and publishers. The best and most appropriate submissions (approximately the top 6 percent) are forwarded to the publishers, producers, record label executives, music libraries, and others who requested material. This certainly does not guarantee that these songs will be published or recorded, but they will be listened to by those who make the decisions.

Taxi membership costs $299.95 for the first year and $199 for subsequent years. There is also a $5.00 fee for each song submitted for each project. Of course, if your songs are not competitive in the current marketplace they will not be forwarded to the industry professionals in *Taxi's* listings. However, if your song is not forwarded, a critique is provided. This is a legitimate firm that provides an important service for writers who have excellent songs but limited industry connections. As you read in the section about networking, Taxi also hosts an excellent annual educational and networking event, the Taxi Road Rally. See the Appendix for information about how to contact Taxi.

When I worked as a production coordinator and an A&R assistant, one of my responsibilities was screening songs. When pitch sheets available to the general public listed that my company was looking for songs, we received some of the worst material imaginable—unintelligible, a cappella versions of songs that were not even in the ballpark of the industry standard. I wanted to give unpublished writers a chance and kept hoping to find that undiscovered gem. But after spending far too many hours reviewing substandard songs, when I would receive queries from certain pitch sheets asking who we were looking for songs for, I learned to say, "No one." My time was better spent listening to songs submitted by publishers and writers with track records. Many producers and record labels choose not to list their projects in pitch sheets that are available to the general public. That's why it's not smart to rely solely on them for your information.

Some of these publications are available only to publishers and professional writers, or require an audition CD. In addition to information regarding major labels and producers who choose to be included, pitch sheets are often a valuable source of information regarding artists who are looking for material to release on small, independent record labels. While these recordings typically do not generate significant income, they may help connect you to artists and producers on their way up the ladder. Some of these pitch sheets (particularly, the excellent *SongLink International*) include tips, as well as articles relating to the international, as well as US, markets. This information can be expensive and difficult to find on your own.

Most music publishers use commercially available pitch sheets, and in addition, often compile their own. When you publish a song, ask the publisher if he or she will provide you with a copy of a "casting list" (pitch sheet) on a monthly basis, so you can make pitch suggestions, and augment his or her efforts with your own.

It's always best to call or e-mail first before sending your songs to anyone listed on a pitch sheet. Although most of the publications do a good job, there are instances when the information listed is not accurate. Artists' recording plans may change, or projects may already be finished by the time you receive your pitch sheet. It's also a good idea to confirm that the recipient is willing to review your submission, and to confirm the spelling of his or her name, as well as the address. Use this call as an opportunity to present yourself professionally and confidently. It can be as simple as: "Hello. This is Jason Blume calling from Moondream Music. I want to confirm that you're still looking for songs for Faith Hill." Presuming you get an affirmative answer, you might add, "I'm an independent publisher and have a song I feel strongly about for the project. I wanted to let you know to expect the package within the next few days." Confirm the address and the spelling of the recipient's name—and get your package ready!

PITCHING YOUR SONGS TO THE RIGHT PEOPLE

Presuming you've got a fantastic demo of a potential hit song, to whom should you pitch it? The first step in successfully placing your song is deciding which artists the song is appropriate for. That's called "casting" and it's a talent in itself. When matching a song to an artist, some of the factors to consider include:

- The vocal range required.
- The lyrical content—is it appropriate for the artist's image? (For instance, Tina Turner is known for her tough "survivor" persona and would be unlikely to record a song with a lyric that presented her as weak, vulnerable, or a victim.)
- The musical style—is it consistent with other songs this artist has had success with?
- Whether the artist ever records outside songs. (There's not much point in pitching songs to bands or singer-songwriters who write all their own songs.)

Many developing writers make the mistake of thinking their new song is so wonderful, any artist would surely want to record it. They indiscriminately spend their time and money sending out fifty or more copies of their latest demo with little regard for whether the song is right for the artists they are targeting. No matter how well written, any one song is probably not appropriate for pop-rockers Aerosmith, R&B diva Beyoncé, and Christian/pop star Amy Grant. Even within the same genre, there are songs that are a good fit for certain artists, but not for others. It can help to seek out casting suggestions from other songwriters.

A common pitfall is pitching a song to a given artist because it's similar to another song that artist has previously recorded. The last thing Bette Midler would record is a song with the same message as "From a Distance." She's already been there and done that. While it's true that certain artists have consistent success with specific types of songs (for example, Celine Dion is best known for her soaring, rangy ballads), artists do not want to repeat themselves. Once you've decided which artists your song is genuinely appropriate for, how do you get it to them? The best answer is, "Any and every way you can."

> When I am looking for a song for a particular artist, there are factors
> I take into consideration. In addition to looking for a great song or a
> "hit" song, I have to take the artist's needs into consideration. This may
> include range, lyrical content, or even the artist's personality. There are
> a lot of variables.
>
> FRANK LIDDELL (Hit Producer;
> Carnival Music Publishing)

When pitching songs, there are many routes to take and it's best to pursue more than one of them. Here are the most direct avenues to pursue to get your song listened to and considered for recording projects.

Pitching to A&R Staff

One of the major functions of the A&R (Artists and Repertoires) staff at a record label is to oversee song selection for artists' albums. A&R executives and their assistants are deluged with song submissions—and most of those songs come from publishers and professional songwriters with track records. Therefore, many of the record labels have a "No Unsolicited Submissions" policy. While "unsolicited" literally means material sent without being requested, it typically refers to songs from sources other than legitimate music publishers, artists' managers, or entertainment attorneys. One of the reasons so many professionals are unwilling to review unsolicited material is the concern that they might be sued in a frivolous copyright infringement case. They feel that if they listen only to songs submitted by industry professionals, they can reduce their chance of having to defend an expensive lawsuit. In addition, A&R executives (as well as publishers and producers) have a limited amount of time to listen to the enormous number of songs and artists that are submitted. Most of them feel they have a better chance of finding that elusive hit if they listen exclusively to material from writers with a track record.

Few things are more frustrating than having your CD returned unopened, stamped "Unsolicited Material: Return to Sender." To avoid this, prior to sending any songs, call to ascertain the company's submission policy (as well as to confirm that they are looking for songs for the project you're targeting). You may need to obtain a permission code—a specific word, phrase, or number to include on the outside of your package signifying that you've secured permission to submit your material.

Take the time to research to whose attention your submission should go. Addressing a package to "Attn: A&R Department" is the kiss of death. Various A&R executives at the same label may be responsible for different acts. Ask the A&R assistant to whom you should direct your songs for a particular artist. *The A&R Registry* is a listing of the A&R staffs at major and independent record labels in the US, Canada, and the UK. It does your research for you, providing the names and titles of the entire A&R staff, their assistants' names, direct phone and fax numbers, e-mail and mailing addresses, and company Web sites. This information is updated every two months and a one-year subscription (six issues) costs $354.50, with single issues available for $69.50 (see Appendix).

An A&R executive represents the first level in a series of hoops your song has to jump through. In the event that an A&R person feels strongly about your song, he or she will play it for the artist and the producer. Members of the A&R staff can be important allies and generate excitement about your song, but are rarely able to secure a recording of your song unless the artist and record producer share their enthusiasm.

Pitching to Producers/Production Coordinators

One of the record producer's most important responsibilities is finding hit songs for his or her artist to record. (If the artist writes his or her own songs, one of the producer's functions is choosing which of the artist's songs should be recorded and included on the album.) Circumventing the A&R department by getting your song directly to the producer eliminates one hurdle. But it is often difficult to locate record producers and to get them to listen to your songs, particularly if you don't have a proven track record.

If you have well-established relationships with publishers and A&R executives, they may be willing to provide you with a producer's address and telephone number. Otherwise, you might have to do some investigating to locate this information, but it's usually possible. If you're unable to find it, here's a hot tip: many producers are also songwriters. If the producer you're looking for is a songwriter, his or her publishing information will be listed on recordings he or she produced, as well as on the charts. It's likely that the producer picks up correspondence and CDs at the publishing company he or she is signed to. Some producers maintain offices at their publishing companies, or regularly work out of certain recording studios that are likely to be listed as part of an album's credits. Most producers hire a production coordinator to handle administrative tasks as well as screen song submissions. There's no guarantee that they will listen to unsolicited material from an unknown source, but by sending it to a producer's publishing company or recording studio, it will likely get directly into the producer's or production coordinator's hands.

Pitching to Artists

A local band was opening a show for country star Sammy Kershaw. I had somebody in the band give him a tape with a song of mine—and he cut it!

WADE KIRBY (Hit songwriter)

Getting your song directly to an artist is the best route to take whenever possible. Typically, an artist with considerable success has the clout to insist on recording certain songs he or she loves. In these instances, getting your song to that individual eliminates the necessity of having it approved by a committee of record label executives and the record producer, any one of whom may nix it along the way.

Very few songwriters have personal access to many recording artists, but there are ways to get to artists—if you are creative. I once met a songwriter at a party who told me a great story. He had written a song that he was convinced would be a hit for Jimmy Buffett and took a copy of it with him to one of Buffett's concerts. He struck up a conversation with the sound engineer and told him that when his band played this song at local clubs he'd been told repeatedly it was a perfect Jimmy Buffett song. The engineer agreed to listen to the song. Several months later, the songwriter (who was previously unpublished and unrecorded) received a phone call congratulating him on his Jimmy Buffett cut!

There's also a legendary story about a writer who slipped Garth Brooks a song under a toilet stall, and another about a determined songplugger who gave Faith Hill a song at a shopping mall. The song, "Love Ain't Like That," became a hit single for Faith and was included on a multiplatinum-selling album. Randy Travis' "An Old Pair of Shoes" was delivered to the country star by his bus driver. While it's not always possible to get your song directly to an artist, when you are able to accomplish this, it's often the most direct route to getting your song recorded.

Pitching to Artists' Managers

It may not be easy to get your song directly to an artist, but it's not difficult to get songs to artists' managers. Some managers screen songs and decide which songs to play for their artists. Others simply forward all songs and correspondence they receive to the artists they represent. I once dropped off a song for Randy Travis' manager and soon afterwards received a call notifying me that the song had gone "on hold." When I inquired as to who had placed the song on hold, I was told Randy Travis had been at the office and popped the song into a stereo. He liked the song and asked his record label to request the hold. It didn't wind up being included on his album, but I knew I had done my job by getting it listened to.

There are several ways to find out the name of an artist's manager. The manager is almost always listed as part of the album credits. There are also publications that list artists, as well as addresses, telephone, and fax numbers for their managers, booking agencies, publicists, and record labels. For example, *Billboard's Talent and Touring Directory* is updated annually and includes this information (see Appendix). The *Country Music Association Directory* is a terrific source for information about country music artists' managers—and it's free to members.

Some managers do not accept submissions, preferring songs to go to the A&R department at the record label. Others may only accept songs from publishers and professional song-writers. It's advisable to call first to confirm submission policies, as well as the address.

The art of pitching songs can be as creative as writing them. When you believe you've got that one extraordinary song that's ideal for a specific artist (and you are receiving objective professional feedback confirming your belief) make every effort to be sure your song gets listened to by someone with the power to say "yes."

Frequently, you don't receive any acknowledgment that your song has been received or reviewed unless the recipient is excited about your song. Companies that receive box loads of CDs don't usually take the enormous amount of time required to return them, or to write rejection letters. So, there's no way to know what percentage of the songs you send are ever actually listened to. If you feel very strongly about a specific pitch, cover all your bases. Send copies of your song to each member of the A&R staff; the artist's producer, manager, publicist, booking agent, attorney, hairstylist, video director, and makeup artist; and anyone else you can think of. The "right" person to pitch to is all of them.

Pitching to New Artists and Independent Labels

It's easier to get songs recorded by an artist who is recording his or her first album than it is to secure a recording with an established superstar. Once an artist achieves chart success, your competition will get even tougher; the top songwriters and publishers will be pitching their very best material to this act. While it may not be quite as difficult to get a song recorded by a new artist, the downside is that, according to the Recording Industry Association of America (RIAA), approximately 90 percent of all new artists signed to major labels do not become successful. In 2002, of 30,000 CDs released in the US, 25,000 of these CDs (five out of six) sold fewer than 1,000 copies apiece; only 404 sold more than 100,000 copies. As you learned in Chapter 11, if an artist does not generate sales or airplay, the writers and publishers receive no income.

There are many successful independent labels that generate significant album sales and radio airplay for their artists. These labels typically affiliate with a major label or acquire a national distributor. However, there are also countless tiny, independent labels, many of which are owned by the sole artist who is on the label. These labels typically generate very little sales or airplay. I've had dozens of songs recorded by talented artists who sell their CDs at their gigs and on their Web sites. While I'm pleased to have my songs included on these albums and exposed to an audience who might not otherwise hear them, most of these acts sell less than a few thousand copies, barely recouping their investment. With few exceptions, they rarely go through the expense and hassle of acquiring a recording license, accounting for, and distributing royalties. Since the royalties generated by these projects are so small, it's not typically worth the effort that would be required to collect them. (For example, a song written by two writers and included on an album that sells 1,000 copies would earn each writer approximately $21 if they do not own their publishing or double that if the writers were also their own publishers.)

Although a recording on a small independent label, or one by a new artist, might earn its writer(s) very little income, or none at all, there are instances in which these cuts pave the way to great success. One of my former students, Joyce Harrison, had a song recorded by an eleven-year-old girl with a voice as big as her home state of Texas. The song was included on an independently released album that the girl's father produced. A couple of years later, when that kid signed to Curb Records, Joyce's song, "Good Lookin' Man" was included on the major-label release. The album? LeAnn Rimes' multimillion-selling *Blue*.

My first cut, "I Had a Heart" (recorded by Darlene Austin) was released in 1987 on a tiny independent label called Magi Records. Although the song was released as a single and did exceptionally well by independent standards (rising to #63 on the *Billboard* Country Singles chart), my performance royalties totaled $87. Sales were insignificant because the label had no national distribution, and I never did receive any mechanical royalties. However, in retrospect it's clear to see that this cut began a chain of events that included my first major release, a cut with the Oak Ridge Boys, and it put me on the road to success.

If a new artist on a major label, or an act on an independent label, records one of your songs and fails to get any recognition, the only thing you've lost is time. You can continue to pitch your song and, hopefully, you will find another artist who has success with it. The risk in this situation is that your recording by a new act or one signed to an indie label might achieve a little bit of success. For example, it may be released as a single and only rise to #45 on the chart, or a video of your song may be produced and receive occasional airplay. This may deter a more successful artist from recording your song since it has already received a certain degree of exposure.

Aim high. If you believe your song is a hit, pitch it first to the top artists for whom you feel it is appropriate. However, if you fail to get your song recorded by an established act, you may find that a recording by a new artist or one on a small independent label might provide your ticket to success—or one more step in the right direction. Collaborating with talented artists before they achieve superstar status can also be a terrific way to get your songs recorded. Remember, every established superstar was an unknown artist when he or she started out.

DEVELOPING YOUR PITCH PRESENTATION

I can't overemphasize the importance of making a good first impression with your songs and your pitch presentation. Be sure to receive strong, positive feedback from objective professionals (e.g., songwriting teachers and professional critiquing services) before allowing your song to represent you to publishers, A&R executives, artists, producers, or other music business contacts.

It's always preferable to get a sit-down meeting, as opposed to dropping off a CD. However, it's very difficult to get meetings with high-level industry professionals unless you have an established track record. It's much easier for them to listen to CDs in their car or alone at home—without having to take the time to provide feedback. When you are able to meet face-to-face you'll be better able to begin developing a working relationship. You may also get specific feedback that will help you craft stronger songs. In addition, you might get a better sense of the type of songs the person you're meeting with responds to. You may have to settle for dropping off or mailing your songs initially, but when an industry pro feels strongly about your songs, he or she will be more likely to schedule a meeting with you.

> *A songwriter doesn't need pictures or bios. That's not important. Any publisher who's worth his salt will be signing you because of the songs, not because of what high school you went to or your slick package. Try to make the presentation as professional as possible. Try to get in and get out without taking too much time. Do follow-up calls, but not excessively. Too many calls can do more harm than good. If you don't get called back after two or three times, take the hint because a lot of people have trouble telling writers "no." The standard line is "It's really good, but it's not what we're looking for at this time." I'd rather say, "You need to change this or that."*

> MICHAEL HOLLANDSWORTH
> (President, Full Circle Music Publishing)

Pitching to Publishers

Many publishers maintain a "No Unsolicited Submissions" policy. But there are several tactics that can help you break through that invisible wall:

- Attend music industry events where publishers screen songs, for example, the BMI Nashville Songwriters' Workshops, Taxi's Road Rally, the West Coast Songwriters' Association's Creation:Craft:Connection, and NSAI's Spring Symposium.
- Enroll in workshops and songwriting classes to network with published writers—and with those who may someday become published writers.
- Perform at "Writers' Nights."
- Seek referrals from PROs.
- Collaborate with writers who have relationships with publishers.

When pitching your songs to a publisher, ascertain that the publisher you are targeting indeed publishes the style of music that you are pitching. All publishers do not publish all genres. A quick phone call should provide the information you need.

Music publishers and other industry professionals review only complete songs—words and music. It's never appropriate to send a lyric (or a melody) to a publisher or an artist unless you have specifically been requested to do so. If you write only words or only music, you need to find a collaborator.

Ideally, you will have received a referral prior to contacting a given publisher. If that is not the case, call or write to request permission to submit your songs before sending them. When sending songs to a publisher, do not target a specific artist. If a publisher feels strongly enough about your songs to make a commitment to represent them, he or she will presumably pitch them to many artists. It is not unusual for a publisher to pitch the same song to more than fifty acts before securing a cut. Therefore, when sending your song to a publisher it is not appropriate to specify that you are sending it for a particular artist. However, it's not wrong to make a suggestion (e.g., "I think this song would be great for Barbra Streisand") in your cover letter.

When pitching your songs to a publisher, it is not appropriate to include a biography or a photo unless you are also pursuing a recording deal as an artist. If this is the case, include a professional 8-by-10-inch photo. Let's discuss the components of the submission package.

The Cover Letter Your cover letter represents you in your absence and tells the recipient a great deal about you. Be sure it's up to the same professional standards as your songs. When designing your letterhead, choose a logo that's eye-catching, yet businesslike. Stationery adorned with fancy musical notes screams "AMATEUR." Save the bulk of your creativity for your songs and your pitching.

When composing your cover letter, keep it brief and to the point. Do not include extraneous information (i.e., how many songs you've written, where you work, or information about your personal life). Your cover letter, mailing label, CD label, and CD insert (explained later in this chapter) must be typed, and error-free.

It is never appropriate to include lead sheets or chord charts unless requested. No publisher will take the time to learn your song and plunk it out at a piano. (In fact, chances are that no one at the publishing company will even be able to read your lead sheet.)

Never apologize for your song or demo. Nor should you explain what the song *really* means. A songwriting teacher once told me, "If your song requires an explanation, you'll have to write out thousands, if not millions, of notes to attach one to each copy sold." Also, do not describe your song; doing so will identify you as an amateur. Besides, if the listener can't tell that it's a love ballad or a positive up-tempo song when he or she hears it, you're in big trouble anyway.

If you have major songwriting credits or other information pertinent to your songwriting (e.g., "My songs have been recorded by artists including Dolly Parton and Busta Rhymes," or "The enclosed song was awarded first place in the *Billboard* Songwriting Competition"), include that information to establish your credibility. However, a publisher will not be impressed by information like, "I once sang a song I wrote that got fourth place in my high school talent pageant." Also, do not include information about where the song was recorded or who the demo vocalists and musicians are.

On page 223 is an example of a well-crafted cover letter to a publisher.

Sample Cover Letter to a Publisher

WILL B. AHITRITER

#1 Wannabee Lane, Hometown, PA 56789 (123) 456-7890

Date

Publisher's Name
Company Name
Address
City, State Zip Code

Dear (Publisher's first name):

As we discussed, I was referred to your company by my collaborator,
Anita Hitnow. As promised, I've enclosed two songs I've written.
I feel strongly about these songs and appreciate your reviewing them.
I look forward to speaking with you when you've had a chance to listen.

Sincerely,

Will B. Ahitriter

Encl.
CD

Your song must be professionally recorded and presented on a CD. You may only need a guitar or a keyboard and a vocal, but the recording must match the industry standards, as discussed in Chapter 9. If you're sending more than one song, all of the songs should be included on the same CD, unless you've been specifically instructed otherwise.

Your CD should have nothing recorded on it but your professionally recorded song(s). It is never appropriate to speak on the CD, or to announce the title of your songs (except when sending your songs to the US Copyright Office). On your CD label (see below), type the name of the individual to whom you are pitching the song; the name of the artist the song is for (unless you are pitching to a publisher); the title of the song(s); and your name, address, and telephone number. If you have a fax number and e-mail address, these should also be included.

TO: DANN HUFF
FOR: LONESTAR

FROM: JASON BLUME

"A SIMPLE
COUNTRY SONG"

(Jason Blume)

Moondream Music

9 Music Square South, PMB 352
Nashville, TN 37203
615-665-2381; fax: 615-665-2589
JBSongdoc1@aol.com

When pitching songs, it is not common practice to include an insert with your CD unless you are pitching an artist's album project with photos. Therefore, it's a good idea to make an additional copy of your label and attach it to the inside of your CD case. This allows the listener to view a track listing (the song titles) after he or she has put the CD into a player.

One last note: be sure to use a high-quality CD that is intended for music reproduction (as opposed to data storage), and before mailing your CD or playing it at a pitch meeting, listen to it to be sure that your songs are properly recorded, finalized, and without any skips or scratches.

Lyric Sheet Include a lyric sheet for each song on your CD. It's also a good idea to bring lyric sheets to your pitch meetings; many publishers and industry professionals will not want to follow along—but some will. Type your lyric sheet as shown in the example on page 145 in Chapter 9. As discussed in Chapter 9, the only pieces of information that should be included on your lyric sheet are the words to your song, the writers' names, contact information (e.g., address, telephone number, fax number, and e-mail address), the copyright symbol, and the year of copyright registration.

By the way, if you've ever wondered how it is determined which writer's name goes first on the lyric sheet (and the album credits) it's simple; each publisher lists his own writer first. So if your publisher has secured the cut and provides the lyric sheet and label copy (writer and publisher information included on the album), your name will appear first.

Pitching to A&R, Producers, Artists, and Managers

Publishers look for great songs. A&R executives, record producers, artists, and managers look for great songs *that are suited to their particular recording projects*. When pitching to any of these professionals, be specific regarding which artist you are asking them to consider your song for. For example: "I've enclosed a song I feel strongly about for Ruben Studdard." Otherwise, the guidelines are essentially the same as those described in the previous section. But remember that while a publisher may be willing to listen to a rough or sparsely produced demo, you typically need a professional-sounding demo for these pitches.

> *We get eight songs on a cassette for Lorrie Morgan and they're all rock and roll songs, or just out of whack. That's so far off that people aren't stopping to think.*
>
> THOM SCHUYLER (Hit songwriter;
> formerly Senior A&R Vice President, RCA Records)

Do your homework. When you target a specific artist, do your best to be objective about whether your song is truly a good match for this artist. The overwhelming majority of the songs that you pitch will not be recorded on the projects you pitch them for. That's reality. Therefore, a primary goal for the pitch should be to maintain credibility and an open door. You won't accomplish this if you send a demo of a song that's not up to industry standards, or is completely inappropriate for this particular artist.

I admit that early in my career I was guilty of drop-offs that were more memorable than my songs. Once, after overhearing a producer at a songwriting workshop mention that he loved cookies, I delivered a song to the studio where he was producing an album for a legendary singer. The song was in a bag of chocolate chip cookies. Unfortunately, in retrospect it's clear that the cookies were fresher and tastier than my songs. If your songs are exceptional, and you take care of business, you probably won't need a lot of hoopla to attract attention. If your songs are not exceptional, a creative delivery may get them listened to quicker—but it won't get them recorded.

Many A&R executives, record producers, and artists' managers will not accept material unless it comes from a reputable publisher, entertainment attorney, or professional songwriter or is specifically requested. Consequently, it's always important to check an individual's submission policy before sending your material. Presuming you secure permission to send your songs, your package should essentially be the same as if you were sending it to a music publisher. A sample cover letter follows on page 227. Note that when contacting record labels, producers, managers, and artists, you may want to use your publishing company letterhead to gain added credibility. If you are acting as your own publisher, also include your publishing company's name and address on your CD label.

Knowing How Many Songs to Include

Unless instructed otherwise, send no more than three songs at a time. Less is definitely more. You'll have greater success sending one incredible song than five mediocre ones. No industry professional wants to take the time to weed through a dozen songs. It's the writer's job to determine which songs are his or her strongest, or the most appropriate for a specific project, and send only those.

When I screened songs for artists, I always listened first to those packages containing one song. There were two reasons for this choice: If the writer sent only one song, he or she must have thought it's very special and just right for the project; and, I could get through more packages by listening only to those with one song. (When I had a huge box of submissions to review, it felt good to see that number dwindle.)

Limiting the number of songs that you submit can be difficult. Early in my career I thought all my songs were terrific (they weren't) and I was afraid to leave one off—what if it was the one that would have been a hit? As I wrote more songs, I realized that they can't all be the "best." Now, I send one or two songs at a time—and always put the strongest song first.

When you send songs, it's quality—not quantity. How many great songs are there? Not a lot. The best thing is to play your best shot. How about one? Or two? Sometimes I'll call a publisher or a writer and say I'm recording "so and so" and they send six or eight things. It's like they're sort of asking you to edit through them.

TOMMY LiPUMA (Chairman, GRP Recording;
Coproducer, Natalie Cole's *Unforgettable* LP; Producer
of Anita Baker, George Benson, and Al Jarreau)

J'SONGS MUSIC

#1 Wannabee Lane, Hometown, PA 56789 (123) 456-7890

Date

A&R Executive/Producer/Manager's Name and Title
Company Name
Address
City, State Zip Code

Dear (first name):

As discussed with your assistant, I've enclosed a song I feel very strongly about for Bonnie Raitt's upcoming album. I appreciate your listening and look forward to speaking with you when you've had a chance to review the song.

Sincerely,

Will B. Ahitriter

UNDERSTANDING HOLDS

A hold is a verbal agreement whereby a writer or publisher agrees to reserve, or "hold," a given song for an artist. This agreement is typically between a writer or publisher and an A&R person, producer, artist manager, or recording artist. A hold is requested when a person reviewing songs feels there's a strong possibility of your song being recorded for a specific project. This allows the individual who requests it time to play your song for the other decision makers involved in the recording process. If they concur, your song may remain on hold until the artist records his or her album. By granting a hold, the publisher and writer promise that they will not allow anyone else to record this song prior to its commercial release by the artist they've granted the hold for.

Holds are more common in Nashville than in New York and Los Angeles, because country artists generally record using live musicians and, therefore, typically record their albums all at once (during a given week) or in two or three installments, several songs at a time. A country artist may not be scheduled to record for six months or more from the time he or she expresses interest in recording your song. If you want your song considered for the artist's album, you have no choice but to grant the hold and keep your fingers crossed that he or she doesn't tire of your song, or find another he or she likes better. Many pop and urban artists record songs one at a time, using synthesizers and drum programmers (as opposed to a full band of live musicians). Therefore, although a pop or R&B artist may be scheduled to complete an album at a given time, such artists are better able to record an individual song at any time.

Many songwriters resent the hold process. To honor a hold you may have to refrain from pitching your songs for several months (or even longer). You may miss the opportunity to have your song reviewed and recorded by other artists in the interim—only to find that your song has been "bumped" at the last minute. The person requesting the hold has all the power in this situation. He or she may hold your song for a year or more without generating a cut. There is no penalty or inducement for industry professionals to limit the number of songs they hold, or the length of time they hold them. The only leverage songwriters or publishers have is to refuse to grant a hold to a given individual in the future if they have been burned too many times.

So, why honor a hold? The music business is a small one and it's built upon trust and relationships. Artists need great songs to sustain their careers and may be very excited about having found one that they believe will be a big hit for them. If you grant a hold and then revoke it because another opportunity to have your song recorded comes along, the artist, A&R rep, manager, or producer to whom you granted the hold may be very angry and might not be willing to work with you again. Some writers and publishers adopt an attitude of "whoever cuts the song first, gets it." There are many stories of writers and publishers who have not honored holds with varying results. In some instances they've burned bridges. At other times, they've had sufficient clout to call the shots.

There always seems to be discussion among writers, publishers, and songwriter organizations about changing the way holds work. One suggestion proposed is to pay the writer and publisher in exchange for granting a hold beyond a reasonable amount of time. For instance, after holding a song for thirty days, if the artist, A&R person, producer, or manager wants to retain the hold, the record label would be required to pay a fee each month that the song remains on hold.

This would certainly encourage those who place songs on hold to be selective about which songs they tie up. Also, once a song was placed on hold, the person requesting the hold would have an incentive to play the song and get an answer quickly from the other key players in the decision-making process. This would also encourage songwriters and publishers to honor holds. While there's been lots of talk, there is still no standard policy regarding holds and there are still many instances of songs being held for six months or more—without the artist even hearing the song. One of the reasons the system remains unchanged is that if a multimillion-selling artist asked for a hold—but was unwilling to pay for it—few writers or publishers would refuse. Granting and honoring holds is a decision you and your publisher have to make on a situation-by-situation basis.

Many developing writers get excited when an A&R person, producer, or other industry professional asks to "hold on to" a copy of a song. That individual is saying he or she likes your song enough to want to listen again before making a decision as to whether it might suit a particular project. This is important encouragement—but it is not to be confused with having a song on hold. A hold constitutes an *exclusive* agreement not to let any other artist record that song for a limited amount of time.

One reason that holds are important for the writer and publisher is the "compulsory license." This is the license that must be obtained from a song's publisher before the song may be recorded and commercially released. The copyright owner (the publisher—or the songwriter, if the publishing rights have not been assigned to a publisher) has the right to decide to whom a compulsory license (sometimes called a "mechanical license") will be granted, *only the first time a song is recorded*. Once a song has been commercially released, presuming the copyright owner has authorized this release, anyone has the legal right to record it, provided they obtain a license and pay the mechanical rate mandated by Congress (the statutory rate) or a lower rate negotiated with the copyright owner. Therefore, by choosing to grant a hold (or not) to a given artist, a publisher maintains control over who releases the first recording of a given song.

Technically, a hold is meaningless if a song has previously been released. Although a publisher may agree to refrain from actively pursuing other recordings while a given artist waits to record your song, you cannot legally prevent any artist from recording a song subsequent to its first commercial release. Why wouldn't you want an artist to record your song? The reason is because if the first release is by a new artist, or by an artist with a track record of selling very few records, you run the risk of your song being exposed to the public, earning very little, and not being recorded again by a more successful artist. There's no harm done if your song is recorded but never receives significant airplay, sales, or video broadcasts. But, if a song is released as a single (especially if there is a corresponding video to increase its visibility) and performs poorly on the charts, it'll probably lose its potential to be recorded by another artist for several years or more.

After countless disappointments, I've learned to view a hold as wonderful validation that others think my song is as strong as I'd hoped—but not as an indication that I'm about to get this song recorded. Only a small percentage of songs that go on hold for a given album actually get recorded and released on that album. My song "Change My Mind" (written with A.J. Masters) was on hold twelve times for artists including Natalie Cole, Clay Walker, and Reba McEntire before being recorded by the Oak Ridge Boys and, years later, becoming a hit single for John Berry. I have a song that's been on hold seventeen times. It's been recorded three times—but has never been released. I trust that if that many professionals have felt so strongly about this song it'll find a good home some day. When the same song goes on hold repeatedly, it's usually a good indication that it may eventually be recorded.

ENTERING CONTESTS

Songwriting and lyric-writing competitions offer an alternative way for songwriters to have their material reviewed by industry professionals. The rules and regulations to enter these competitions vary. Some contests are open to all songwriters, regardless of professional status, while others are specifically for individuals who do not earn the bulk of their income from song royalties, or have not earned more than a specified amount as a songwriter. The fee to enter songwriting competitions is typically from $10 to $30 per song. Songs may be entered in various categories (i.e., pop, country, R&B, gospel, etc.). Additional fees are typically required to enter the same song in more than one category. Prizes may include a publishing contract, an opportunity to have your song recorded, a live performance opportunity at a major music festival, cash, or merchandise.

There are essentially two types of songwriting contests. In the first type, the song itself is judged, based solely on a recorded demo. The other type of contest requires a live performance by the songwriter or his or her representative. In the latter type of competition, the winners tend to be professional performers chosen as much for their vocal ability as for the quality of their songs.

One thing's for sure—if you don't send out your songs, nothing will happen. Don't wait for the record label to come to you.

IRA GREENFIELD, ESQ. (Assistant Director,
USA Songwriting Competition)

I learned a great deal about songwriting competitions when my song "Wraparound Memory" (written with Bryan Cumming) was selected as a finalist to represent the US in the Castlebar, Ireland, International Song Festival (now defunct). At the point I entered this contest, I had published two or three songs, but had never had any of my material recorded. I figured I had almost no chance of winning, but something told me to go through the effort of procuring an Irish bank draft and sending off my tape.

I could hardly believe it when the telegram arrived notifying me that my song had been selected as a finalist. I received an all-expenses-paid trip to Ireland and an opportunity to compete for the $10,000 grand prize. At the competition, I appeared on a live television broadcast where I performed my song in front of the panel of judges—and a television audience estimated at 30 million.

I was not a seasoned performer and had never been on television. To say that I learned the meaning of sheer terror would be an understatement! Those who competed against me were either professional singers (who also wrote songs) or songwriters who hired top-notch singers to perform their songs for them. While the contest was supposed to judge the quality of the songs themselves, there was no way for the judges (who were celebrities—not music industry professionals) to separate the merit of the songs from the performances. I did not win the $10,000, but I had a great vacation, an incredible learning experience, and an opportunity to network with songwriters and industry professionals from different countries.

Some of the largest competitions receive 30,000 or more entries. Most of these contests have a multitiered screening process to narrow down the contestants, with the finalists being judged by major music industry professionals. Therefore, if your song progresses to the final stages of the competition, it will be listened to by individuals who may be music publishers, A&R reps, record producers, artists' managers, or recording artists themselves. An added benefit of entering songwriting contests is that even if your song doesn't win, judges have the opportunity to contact you if they are interested in your song. (See the Appendix for a listing of major songwriting competitions.)

AVOIDING THE SCAMS

While the majority of music publishers are legitimate, there are unscrupulous individuals and companies that prey upon unsuspecting songwriters. These scam artists are frequently referred to as "song sharks." When you register a song through the US Copyright Office, your name and address become part of the public record and are available to anyone who requests them. Your name may also be sold as part of a mailing list if you subscribe to songwriter-oriented publications. Through these channels, unethical companies find aspiring songwriters to victimize. Some of these companies also advertise in songwriter publications.

Typically the scam works like this: You receive an official-looking letter from a "Publishing Company" or a "Record Label" stating that they are seeking new songs (or lyrics, or song-poems) for publication and for recording by major artists. They offer to review your songs or lyrics at no cost to you. Shortly after your songs or lyrics have been submitted, you receive a notification congratulating you and notifying you that your material has been "selected" to be published. All you need to do is to send a specified amount of money to cover "administrative costs" (or fees to record a professional demo) and your song (or lyric) will be published. Many hopeful songwriters are ecstatic and flattered that their song has been "chosen"; they don't realize that the only criterion for publication is the songwriter's willingness to shell out exorbitant fees.

Some of these so-called publishers are essentially outrageously overpriced demo services in disguise. They promise to produce "master-quality" demo recordings so that they can shop your songs to superstar artists. These companies will "publish" any song or lyric that the writer will pay to demo and will gladly set your lyric to music for free. They have no intention of placing the songs that they publish; they earn their living by charging ridiculously expensive fees—sometimes more than $3,000 per song—to record demos that could be produced by a legitimate demo service for a fraction of that amount.

Another similar scam involves including your song on an album that will be sent to major record labels, as well as to an impressive list of other companies that may include radio stations, artists, producers, and artists' managers. The writer is promised a royalty for every album sold. The only thing the writer needs to do is to reimburse "recording and administrative fees," which may range from several hundred dollars up to thousands of dollars. The song sharks technically live up to their contractual obligation by indeed recording your song and sending it out to the places they've promised to send it to. When these albums arrive at the record labels, radio stations, and their other destinations, they are instantly recognized for the scams that they are, and are either thrown away unopened or laughed at. The only people who ever purchase these albums are the songwriters whose songs have been included on them.

A cowriter of mine played guitar on a recording session for one of these albums and he gave me the inside story. Forty songs were recorded in one day. (For a legitimate album, three songs per day would be an accomplishment.) The musicians and vocalist rehearsed each song one time and then recorded it. Regardless of the quality of the recording or the inevitable mistakes, the song was "finished" after one take and then included on this dreadful album of songs written by unsuspecting amateurs. Another related scam involves the release of a compilation album comprised of demos received from various songwriters who have paid a fee to be included on the album. Some of these shrewd operators even warn those they prey upon to "avoid scams," thereby lending an air of credibility to their own companies.

Aspiring recording artists are also vulnerable to these unethical individuals and companies. I've heard stories of artists and writers being bilked out of more than $10,000 to have demos recorded that should have cost 10 percent of this amount. Aspiring artists should also be suspicious of "custom deals." In this situation a producer, who has typically amassed major credits in the past, offers to use his expertise and industry contacts to find great songs, produce a master-quality demo, and help the artist secure a recording contract—in exchange for a hefty fee. While this seems like an acceptable agreement on the surface, these individuals now earn their livings by producing overpriced demos for aspiring artists—*regardless of whether they believe these artists have talent or any realistic hope of being offered a record deal*. What separates custom deals from legitimate artist demos is the producer's implied promise that his track record and connections will open doors and help the artist achieve his or her goals. The truth is that these producers (who would never identify what they do as "custom deals") and their industry contacts know that these artists have virtually no chance of success.

Remember that the music business is highly competitive and that it's extremely difficult, even for seasoned professionals, to get their songs recorded. Any individual or company that solicits unpublished writers, offering them a publishing deal or a recording contract, is looking to make money from those writers. It's flattering to hear that your song has been "selected" to be published or recorded, but the reality is that legitimate publishing companies and record labels are bombarded with submissions from professional songwriters and recording artists. They have no need to advertise or seek out amateur writers. Keep in mind the old adage "If it seems too good to be true—it probably is."

To protect yourself:

- Never pay to have a song published. Legitimate publishers do not require any payment or administrative fees to publish a song.

- Never pay to have someone compose music to your lyric (unless this is strictly for your own enjoyment). If you do, your lyric will likely get paired with a melody that has been cranked out in five minutes by an individual with no professional songwriting credits. Legitimate cowriters work with you because of your talent, not because of your bank account. Their payment is a percentage of any royalties your cowritten song may generate.

- Be aware that in the event that a fee is required to produce a demo of your song, a legitimate publisher will typically absorb the costs, although these fees may be totally or partially recoupable in the event that your song generates royalties in the future. It's perfectly legitimate (and necessary) to pay to produce demos of your songs in order to pitch them to publishers. However, the fees you pay should be in line with the amounts listed in Chapter 8.

- Do not pay to have your material reviewed unless you are to receive detailed, constructive critiques from a professional songwriting teacher with major credentials. There should never be a fee to determine whether a song is to be published or included on an album.

Request the following information to determine the company's credentials:

- A list of songs they have placed with successful recording artists (if you are dealing with a publisher or songplugger)

- Sales figures from previous albums

- The total amount of mechanical and performance royalties writers received from inclusion on previous albums

- A list of radio stations that have played material from this company's albums

- A copy of previously released albums to determine their quality

- A list of satisfied customers willing to attest to positive experiences with this company

When you submit these requests, if you are dealing with a song shark, it's likely you will never hear from them again. Any of the following phrases should be a red flag: "Sell Your Songs," "Publisher Looking for Songs to Record," "Set Your Lyrics and Song-Poems to Music," and "Free Evaluations of Your Songs/Lyrics/Poems." If you have any question about a company's legitimacy, check them out through songwriters organizations and the local Better Business Bureau.

They don't call this show art—they call it show business. It is a business but at the same time you don't want to lose sight of your craftsmanship and your art. There are too many writers today who are paying way too much attention to what is commercial and what is on the radio and too little to listening to their inner soul, to their inner heart. You have to find a way to bring both of those into your writing to be a great writer.

I have nothing against a commercial, hooky, "instant hit" song, but I think it's really, really important to write from a perspective of innocence of the business. Trying to balance the two is the all-time challenge.

ROBERT K. OERMANN
(Music journalist; judge, *Nashville Star*)

STEP 5: CONCLUSION

Success in the music business is contingent on two factors: creating music that is compelling and taking the necessary steps to deliver your work to the public. Neither one will be sufficient alone. Learn about the business and approach it as you would any other professional endeavor. Be sure that both your music *and* your pitch presentations are up to professional standards and you'll be on the road to success.

BUSINESS CHECKLIST

Photocopy this checklist and keep a copy of it where you write. Refer to this list on ___ basis to evaluate how well you're taking care of the business side of the music busi___

If you are seeking a publisher, are you:

❑ Networking?

❑ Seeking referrals?

❑ Reading music business publications?

❑ Attending music business events?

❑ A member of songwriters' organizations?

❑ Writing "up"?

❑ Phoning before sending songs?

❑ Following up pitches with telephone calls?

❑ Sending typewritten, concise cover letters (on professional-looking letterhead)?

❑ Including typewritten lyric sheets?

❑ Limiting the number of songs per pitch to a maximum of three?

❑ Having an entertainment attorney review contracts before signing?

If you have songs signed with a publisher, are you:

❑ Maintaining regular contact?

❑ Suggesting pitches for your songs?

❑ Actively pitching your own songs?

❑ Aware of which artists are currently looking for songs (either from pitch sheets or your own research)?

❑ Seeking collaborations with other talented writers, aspiring writer/artists, and writer/producers?

Developing Persistence and Realistic Expectations

During my early songwriting period, I fortunately had a delusional idea that I was ready to make it big. Little did I know the years of disappointments and rejections I would have to endure before my first break. Had I known, I don't know that I would have had the perseverance to keep writing song after song.

BILLY STEINBERG (Hit songwriter)

CHAPTER 15

Hanging In There Until the Big Break

I was a waiter for two-and-a-half years at The Source, a health food restaurant. I lived down the block and I chose it because it was convenient. Little did I know that it was a major music business hangout. I still remember the booth number (B-2) of Syreeta Wright ("With You I'm Born Again"), who was married to Stevie Wonder. I told her, "I'm a songwriter" and I thought, "How could she possibly believe me with this apron around my waist? What kind of songwriter could she think I am?"

I sent her some songs and nothing ever happened, but I continued to see her in the restaurant. Then several years later, when Smokey Robinson had his One Heartbeat *album, he did a duet with Syreeta Wright—and it was my song. They invited me down to the recording session. I was so thrilled and so excited, and when I was introduced to Syreeta, I asked her, "Do you remember me?" She said, "You look so familiar, but I can't place the face with the place." When I said, "I was your waiter at The Source," she let out a scream and gave me the biggest hug. She autographed my lyric sheet and wrote, "Dear Allan, music will prevail."*

ALLAN RICH (Hit songwriter with cuts by artists
including Whitney Houston, 'NSync, and Barbra Streisand)

Each of the six steps outlined in this book is necessary for songwriting success. But if I had to choose which one is the most important, I'd say that it's this sixth step. There are hundreds of individual skills that add up to successful songwriting. On the surface, some of these skills appear to be simple and seem as though they ought to be mastered easily. Others can be acquired quickly. However, many of the skills required to transform your ideas and inspiration into songs with the power to touch millions of hearts typically take years of practice. It takes even longer before they're incorporated into your songs with little conscious effort.

An enormous amount of perseverance is required to weather the inevitable frustrations and rejections. Without it, you may not continue your pursuit long enough to master the tools of successful songwriting. I've worked with several cowriters who were far more talented than I am, but who gave up pursuing their dreams of writing hit songs before achieving commercial success. These songwriters had all of the musical talent they needed, but lacked belief in themselves and the determination to stubbornly pursue their goals in a business that offers no guarantees. Choosing a more secure and a less frustrating profession was a valid choice for these writers.

The music business isn't right for everyone, nor can it accommodate every person who wants to be a part of it. The cold, hard reality is that only the best will have success in this competitive field. But, even if you choose not to pursue songwriting as a profession, it can still bring tremendous joy and satisfaction as a hobby.

By learning the rules and acquiring the tools and techniques set out in this book, you can shave years off your journey. However, it's still important to develop persistence and acquire realistic expectations because it's likely that the road to success will be a long one.

For additional insights and anecdotes about how I used the steps in this book to advance my own career, read *Inside Songwriting: Getting to the Heart of Creativity* (Billboard Books).

There's a famous music business joke: "*Oh*, you're a songwriter. What restaurant?" Rod Stewart dug graves, Billy Ray Cyrus sold cars, Randy Travis washed dishes at Nashville's legendary Bluebird Cafe, Macy Gray was a teacher, Garth Brooks sold boots at an outlet mall, several Backstreet Boys worked at DisneyWorld, Buddy Jewell drove a beer truck, and both Shania Twain and Faith Hill sold burgers at McDonald's before achieving international acclaim. Most songwriters have to earn a living by doing something other than writing songs while honing their craft.

There's no doubt that it's tough to have a full time job, maintain relationships, take care of all the responsibilities of life, and still have the time and energy left to write songs. But somehow, some way, virtually every songwriter currently enjoying success has managed to do it. It's not practical to borrow money from friends, put your everyday living expenses on your MasterCard, or deplete your retirement savings account to survive until you become an overnight success, because it's likely that it will take much longer than you're anticipating. Having realistic expectations can help you maintain a healthy perspective and avoid suffering a breakdown while waiting for your big break.

UNDERSTANDING WHAT TO EXPECT

When I began my journey pursuing a career as a songwriter, I was bursting with excitement and belief in my talent. I *knew* that I would have hits on the radio and a Mercedes in my driveway within one year—and there's nothing anyone could have said or done to convince me otherwise. But from the time I said, "I'm going to be a successful songwriter" until I signed a staff-writing deal and earned a meager living writing songs, eleven-and-a-half years had elapsed. From this milestone until I began earning what I considered a "good" living, it was another five years. By 1997, I certainly wasn't a millionaire, but after more than sixteen years of struggling to make ends meet, I felt rich—finally earning enough money as a songwriter to buy a beautiful house and car, and have a "cushion" in the bank. I got some lucky breaks along the way and made some great connections—yet it still took me more than sixteen years to earn a good living doing what I love.

> *It took five years to get "I Swear" cut. In that time it was passed on by everybody, including the biggest stars in the business. Some of them deny it, but others still remember it.*
>
> GARY BAKER (Hit songwriter)

Believing in your talent, setting goals, and developing a positive attitude are important, but when I hear beginning songwriters tell me that they're going to have a hit song on the charts in a year or two, all I can do is smile and tell them I hope that will be the case. The odds of this happening are approximately the same as getting hit by lightning—twice in the same day!

> *One of the biggest mistakes I see beginning songwriters make is that they believe that just because they write a song, something will happen with that particular song. What they don't understand is that in the early stages of writing, each song is really a stepping stone to the next, a learning process that gets you one step closer to the song that might have a chance of being successful. I remember my first songwriting class at UCLA (which I taught 15 years later). Our instructor would remind us to throw away our first hundred songs.*
>
> *The only way to look at this picture and make sense of it is to see "flowers." Consider every song you send out as a seed cast in the wind. It must find a fertile spot where the sun will shine and the rain will fall. Many songs must be cast in the wind to increase the chances of finding that fertile spot for the flower to grow. Most get blown into oblivion. Discouraging? Yes, but it is reality. If your heart and soul tell you that you must be a songwriter, you will eventually grow "flowers," providing you have the courage to face rejection and the perseverance to accept the fact that nothing will happen to most of your songs. But when something does happen, there is no greater feeling— especially if the record turns out well.*
>
> GLORIA SKLEROV (Hit songwriter and two-time Emmy Award winner)

Learning to write effective songs and to market them is a developmental learning process. It's like a baby learning to walk—many individual skills have to be mastered. The baby's muscles need to mature; he or she needs to acquire balance; and he or she must practice the various components that lead up to taking those first wobbly steps. Some of these can't be rushed— they simply take time to develop. It's a similar process for songwriters.

The tools and exercises in this book will help, but unless you're exceptionally lucky, the road to successful songwriting is a long one, filled with twists and turns, disappointments, and frustration. Hopefully, knowing this will help you to be patient with yourself during the learning process. I spent a lengthy phase of my life feeling like a failure, instead of seeing that I was in the midst of a long journey toward success. It often takes many years for writers to achieve commercial success—even after they've written great songs. There are hundreds of stories about extraordinarily successful songs that were rejected repeatedly before being recorded and becoming hits.

"Change My Mind" was pitched for three-and-a-half years and turned down more than a hundred times before being recorded by the Oak Ridge Boys. During that period, a major publisher, whose opinion I respected, told me to change the title. After the Grammy-winning Oak Ridge Boys recorded it, another publisher told me that he didn't like the song—and didn't care who had recorded it. It took five more years, a dozen "holds" that each fell through, and several recordings by various artists before John Berry's version established me as an "overnight success." Stories like this are far more common than stories about songs being recorded quickly.

If you really believe in a song, stick with it, even if it isn't one of your "newer, more exciting" songs. If it is truly great, it will eventually find a home.

MIKE SISTAD (Nashville Director of
Member Relations, ASCAP)

MAKING THE TIME FOR YOURSELF AND YOUR CREATIVITY

As discussed earlier in this chapter, it's not easy to work a full-time job, attend to all of our responsibilities—and still have the time and energy to be creative. It's hard to write when the baby's crying, the kids want supper, the bill collectors are calling, or you're exhausted after a ten-hour workday. But it is possible—if you make it a priority.

At one point along my journey, I worked at a miserable "temp" job at City Hall in Culver City, California, to pay my rent. My boss was the devil's sister, and with the jacket and tie dress code, rigid rules, and time clock, this job was the opposite of everything creative, joyful, and free that I wanted in my life. During one of the fifteen-minute breaks that I lived for, I went for a walk and from a place of the deepest frustration searched for answers. How could I possibly write the songs I was meant to write if I'm trapped behind a desk, being forced to be someone so different from the person I am inside? How could I ever escape this prison when I was so beaten down and exhausted at the end of the day that all I wanted to do was "veg out" in front of the TV?

At that moment it hit me. It *was* too late for me at the end of the day to create from the most genuine part of me. But there was a solution. It occurred to me that I could wake up thirty minutes or even an hour earlier each morning, or even two mornings each week. Before squeezing my soul into a suit and tie, I could lie in bed with my notebook and tape recorder, and write from my heart. I could give myself the gift of thirty minutes of creative time that was just for me—before anyone or anything else got to stake its claims. Before the stress and pressures and bumper-to-bumper traffic, the overdue bills, the "Yes, sirs," and the frustration and exhaustion had a chance to set in, I could write—just like I knew I was meant to. It worked; I found that I could do some of my best work early in the morning. This method worked for me, but it may not be your solution. At other times, it's been effective for me to take a twenty-minute nap and then a shower after a long day of work. I'd wake up refreshed, revitalized, and ready to write.

Some writers find it helpful to schedule a set time and place for their writing. A coffeehouse or the public library can be places to focus on your creative work without interruptions and distractions. Try setting a specific work time in your calendar and honoring that as you would any other appointment—because making time for your creativity and your writing is as important as any other appointment or obligation. While it does not address songwriting specifically, *The Artist's Way* by Julia Cameron, a workbook with a spiritual slant, has been helpful to many of my students. Designed to help creative individuals in all genres discover and recover their creative selves, it includes exercises to help you find time for creative pursuits and to break through to deeper levels of creativity.

When I hear writers complain that they "can't find the time" to write, I suggest they explore where they might have "lost it." How many hours slip by in front of the television? How many additional songs might you have written if you could recapture the hours spent in Internet chat rooms, browsing through catalogs, or playing video games? It's up to us whether we spend our hours productively—or complaining about not having the time to be creative.

CHAPTER 16

Getting Past "No"

Be tenacious and persevere. Find the back door when the front door is shut.

JUDY PHELPS
(Writer/Publisher Relations, BMI)

There are countless songs that have been initially rejected by the same artists who later recorded them and had enormous hits. For example, R&B/pop superstar Chaka Khan had to be convinced to record "I Feel for You," one of her biggest hits, and Lee Ann Womack initially did not want to record "The Fool," which established her as a country star. There are even more examples of songs that went on to become huge hits after being rejected time and time again. Randy Travis' Number One country/Christian crossover hit "Three Wooden Crosses" was turned down by numerous acts including Tim McGraw, Brad Paisley, and Darryl Worley. Lee Ann Womack's multiformat smash "I Hope You Dance" was passed on by Jo Dee Messina and Jessica Andrews before being named the Country Music Association's Song of the Year. Faith Hill's "Let Me Let Go" sat on a shelf for more than seven years and received innumerable rejections before going to the top of the charts. These examples are far more typical than instances of songwriters finding quick success.

There are times when your song may be rejected because it's not as good as those written by your competition, or because it's not appropriate for a particular artist at a given time. But individuals who screen hundreds of songs sometimes make mistakes. Virtually every music industry pro (who's honest) has stories about one or more hit songs that he or she has rejected. It's possible that "no" just means that you have to be creative and find alternate ways to get your song through the doors. The A&R person for a particular artist might not like your song, but the producer and artist may love it—*if they get the chance to hear it.* If you believe strongly in a song for a particular project, keep pitching until it's been heard by the artist and producer.

Similarly, being told "We don't accept unsolicited material" may signify a door that's genuinely locked and bolted shut—or it may mean that a different approach might be required to open that door. For example, you may want to seek a referral to this company, send a fax or an e-mail explaining how strongly you feel about this one song, or try approaching a different individual at this same company. If the professional feedback you've received about your song is that it's exceptional, don't let "no" stop you. You just may not have found the right door.

However, if you are consistently being told that your song does not measure up to professional standards, use this information as an impetus to hone your skills and continue to develop your craft.

OVERCOMING THE OBSTACLES

If the craft and business of writing great songs were easy, everyone would be having hits. There are many obstacles that stand in the way between the developing songwriter and success. However, sometimes the biggest hurdles are those we put up ourselves. They're also often the hardest to see. The thought of acquiring all of the skills necessary to become a successful songwriter can seem overwhelming. You not only need to learn about song structures, effective lyric writing, and melody techniques; you also need to produce demos, find a publisher, learn about the music business, network, and pitch your songs. But the good news is that you don't need to do all of these things today.

It can help to refer back to the list of your strengths and weaknesses (part of the Exercise on page 245) and target one or two specific areas to work on, one at a time. For instance, looking over your list, you may realize that you'd benefit most from spending an additional thirty minutes per day for the next month improving your melody-writing skills. Or you may resolve to seek out additional collaborators. Whatever areas you decide to concentrate your efforts on, remember that it's unrealistic to expect yourself to master all of the skills of successful songwriting immediately.

It's also important to make a game plan that reflects realistic short-term and long-term goals. It's self-defeating to say, "I'll have a Number One song on the radio in three months." This isn't going to happen even if you wrote an extraordinary song yesterday. It takes longer than three months for a song to be recorded, be commercially released, and climb the charts. But it can be very helpful to say, "I'll write thirty minutes, five days per week for the next three months, concentrating specifically on lyrics that are conversational, have universal appeal, and come from my heart." Or, "I'll spend a minimum of one hour per week for the next two months pursuing contacts that have the potential to lead to developing a relationship with a publisher."

> *Life as an aspiring songwriter resembles being in a Twelve-Step program. You constantly have to take a personal inventory of your strengths and weaknesses with hundreds of questions that demand a tremendous amount of honesty. Are you a good lyricist? What kinds of songs do you write—or shy away from writing? What aspects of the business make you uncomfortable? Then, after you start answering those questions and facing the hard realities of the hurdles ahead, the next challenge is to do the necessary work while maintaining your optimism and keeping your dreams alive.*
>
> PHIL GOLDBERG (Member Services Director, NSAI)

It's typically easier to make these plans than it is to stick to them, though. Find support to help you maintain your commitment to your songwriting. Some of my students make a daily commitment to a cowriter, and then call to report that they've fulfilled their commitment for that day.

Look for those obstacles you've built up for yourself, such as failing to develop specific skills, not pursuing your songwriting in a businesslike manner, not giving yourself sufficient

EXERCISE: OVERCOMING THE OBSTACLES TO SUCCESS

This exercise will help you identify and prevail over your obstacles to success.

1. List your strengths as a songwriter, specifically focusing on the craft of writing as opposed to your strengths as a businessperson. (For example, "I write great titles and ideas, and hooky chorus melodies. I incorporate lots of detailed images and action into my lyrics. I fully understand successful song structures.")

2. List those areas in which you need to improve your songwriting skills. (For example, "I tend to write lyrics that are more poetic than conversational. My verse melodies don't seem very fresh. I rarely rewrite my melodies. There's not much rhythmic repetition in my songs.")

3. List your strengths as a businessperson, as they relate to your songwriting. (For example, "I have no fear of approaching music publishers. I've developed a professional pitch presentation. I'm actively networking through membership in a songwriters' organization. I'm producing demos that are up to the professional standard.")

4. List the songwriting business practices you need to improve. (For example, "I've been writing songs but not letting anyone hear them. I haven't recorded any demos. I don't know any other songwriters. I have never had one of my songs professionally critiqued.")

5. Devise a game plan that allows you to focus on those creative areas that need additional attention.

   I will devote _____ hours per week to my songwriting.

   During that time I will concentrate on developing the following skills:

   _____

   _____

   _____

6. Devise a game plan that allows you to focus on those areas of the songwriting business that you need to work on.

   I will devote _____ hours per week to the business of songwriting.

   During that time I will concentrate on developing the following skills:

   _____

   _____

   _____

time for your creativity, or indulging in negative thinking—and break through them one at a time. At the beginning stages of your development as a songwriter, it is best to focus on honing your skills and your craft. However, if you've been writing songs for at least a year, and have completed at least twenty songs, you also need to begin pursuing the business side.

COPING WITH REJECTION

I've been a published, successful songwriter for forty years now, and the one thing I know for sure in business is that you have to follow your own path. When I was fourteen, Elektra Records told me I'd never be a singer, but I should sign with them as a writer. That same day, a very famous manager told me I'd never be a writer, but I should sign with him as a singer. So I learned pretty young that no one knows what they're talking about. At least, if you follow your own path, you'll have no one but yourself to blame.

JANIS IAN (Recording artist/songwriter
and nine-time Grammy nominee)

One of the key skills required for success in the songwriting business is resiliency in the face of inevitable rejection and disappointment. The ability to turn the pain of rejection into even stronger determination to succeed is often what separates the writers who give up from those who realize their dreams.

We don't like their sound, and guitar music is on the way out.

DECCA RECORDS REJECTING THE BEATLES, 1962

Sometimes, the fact that a publisher chooses not to sign your song, or an artist decides not to record it, is not a reflection on the quality of the song itself. The publisher may have similar songs in his or her catalog or may have recently made a commitment to another writer who writes in the same style that you write in. The artist may love your song but feel that it's not right for him, that he can't sing it well, or that it's too similar to, or not consistent with, other songs already recorded for a particular album.

Encouragement kept me in the game. Rejection challenged me, made me dig deeper, and probably made me a better writer in the long run. Maybe my big break was not getting too much too soon.

GEORGE TEREN (Hit songwriter)

There are at least a thousand different reasons why your song may be rejected. If the responses you get imply that you've written a strong song that doesn't fit the needs of this particular company or artist, you may simply have not found the right home for your song yet. But, if you consistently receive feedback that your song is not up to professional standards, or has some specific problems, go back to the drawing board.

It's been estimated that income is generated by only 5 percent of the songs written by professional songwriters. That means that 95 percent of the songs written by professionals never achieve commercial success. It's ironic that in order to be successful, songwriters are frequently called upon to be vulnerable and to bare their souls through their music and lyrics, while simultaneously maintaining a tough exterior, capable of withstanding disappointment that can sometimes be devastating. It helps to develop a healthy sense of detachment from your songs—and remind yourself that your value as a human being is not determined solely by the level of commercial success you achieve as a songwriter.

> *I can think of three instances of songs I produced that became hits that had been turned down by many people. "Steal Away" (Robbie Dupree), "Break My Stride" (Matthew Wilder), and "Just to See Her" (Smokey Robinson) were all rejected as not being "hit"-sounding songs by a number of individuals within the industry, but they all went on to be Top Five songs.*
>
> RICK CHUDACOFF
> (Hit record producer; songwriter)

Rejection is a normal part of the business. In a *SongLink International* magazine interview, superstar producer and record label and publishing company executive Quincy Jones spoke about artists he *didn't* sign:

> WHITNEY HOUSTON: *"When she was 16, Ashford & Simpson told me about her and I couldn't do anything because I was in the middle of the Michael Jackson mania."*

> LUTHER VANDROSS: *"He was on my record and you could hear his talent a mile away, but again, I was too busy to do more with him."*

> BOBBY McFERRIN: *"He was also sent to me when I was busy working with Michael."*

In each of these instances, artists who went on to Grammy-winning successes were "rejected." Although they received what must have been demoralizing rejections, obviously it didn't mean they weren't talented. Nor did it mean they would not achieve their successes at a different point in time, at a different company.

Coping with rejection is very different from not feeling the pain of rejection. Of course it hurts to be told that a publisher has decided not to represent your song, or that it won't be included on an album. It's devastating to learn that the company you've been negotiating with for months has decided to sign someone else as a staff-writer, or that the best song you've ever written has been recorded by a major artist—and is a dismal failure commercially. If you had no emotional response to these disappointments you'd probably lack the sensitivity required to write. But disappointment and rejection are part of the package that is the songwriting business.

Some writers fall prey to substance abuse, or engage in self-defeating behaviors that temporarily numb the fear and pain of rejection. Following are some healthy ways to cope with and grow stronger from rejection:

- *Stay open to constructive criticism.* Learn from each experience; ask yourself if there are good reasons why your song has been rejected. Is there a lesson to be learned—something you might want to change in this song, or in future songs you write, or in the way you conduct business?

- *Increase your determination.* Some of the most successful people in any field are those who use failure as a motivator to work even harder to achieve their goals. An attitude of "I'll show them how good my songs can be. No matter how long it takes, I'll write one that's so powerful they won't be able to resist it" is far more productive than "I guess this proves I'm no good at this. The competition's just too tough. I'll never be successful."

- *Maintain realistic expectations.* You may need to reassess your expectations. It's possible that your sights are set too high for your current stage of development as a writer. If you've only been writing in your spare time during the past year or two, it's unrealistic to expect your songs to be as good as those written by top professional writers who may have been honing their craft for ten years or more.

- *Never give up—as long as you're enjoying the process.* Remember that the fact that you've not yet attained certain manifestations of success does not preclude the possibility of your achieving those goals in the future—but giving up guarantees that you will never attain your goals. You may have already written the song that is destined to change your life—or you may write it tomorrow.

FINDING VALIDATION FROM WITHIN

Write whatever you want to write. I believe that if a writer has talent, and hones and nurtures that talent, he or she will have his or her day in the sun. The great writers of this century are all originals. I bet if you take a look at the most respected writers of the last forty years, you will find that the vast majority of their work was not "commercial" until after it was successful.

FRANK LIDDELL (Hit producer;
Carnival Music Publishing)

Success can be defined in many different ways. For some individuals, songwriting success is synonymous with Number One records, Grammy awards, and a big bank account. Others may define success as the ability to get joy from their writing, to write songs that touch people's hearts, or to effectively communicate their emotions through words and music. Those who find satisfaction in the writing process itself are far more likely to enjoy their journey, persist despite the inevitable rejections, and ultimately find success.

> *I live for my music. I live for the songs I write. That's my responsibility. I have control over how great that song is going to be. No one else is going to be responsible for that except me.*
>
> DIANE WARREN (Four-time ASCAP Writer of the Year whose hits include "Unbreak My Heart," "Because You Loved Me," "How Do I Live," and "I Don't Want to Miss a Thing")

There are countless stories about songwriters whose talents were not recognized for many years. A multitude of factors that contribute to a songwriter's success (or lack thereof)—many of which are completely out of the writer's hands. For instance, you have no control over how well an artist sings your song or how the producer produced it. After your song has been recorded, circumstances, such as the political climate at the artist's record label, the amount of the promotion budget allotted to your song, and whether the artist who recorded your song is a "priority" at the record label, are out of the scope of your control. These, and additional factors, may play a critical role in determining your song's success—yet have nothing to do with the quality of your work.

Allowing your self-esteem to be determined by factors over which you have no control is a recipe for unhappiness. It's far more productive to concentrate on what you *can* control. For example, you can determine the amount of time you devote to developing your songwriting skills, the quality of your work, the care you give to producing your demos, your willingness to rewrite, and the amount of time you spend networking and pursuing the business aspects of your songwriting career.

Successful songwriter Wade Kirby tells a wild story about how one of his songs came to be recorded by country star John Michael Montgomery. The Atlantic Records A&R staff were in the process of making the final determination regarding which songs would be included on Montgomery's next album. When a certain song was played, someone expressed his approval by saying, "That's the ticket." Hearing this phrase reminded another A&R person of the title of one of Wade's songs that was sitting on his desk. He played it for the committee and "You're the Ticket" was included on this hit album—a seemingly random act that had an enormous impact on the songwriter's life.

When I asked Wade how he copes with the unpredictable nature of the business, he answered that he thinks of it like spinning the wheel of fortune. If you're consistently writing excellent, not just "good," songs, it's likely that a certain percentage of times, the wheel will land on you and you'll get your shot. All you can do is write to the very best of your ability—and be ready when opportunity knocks.

> *I don't obsess about what the songs are doing on the charts, because that is not the way to judge yourself. If you attach your self-worth to that crap you will*

be in a rubber room. What makes me feel good is writing the songs and landing the songs. I went so long without getting anywhere that I came to the point where I decided to just write for me.

CRAIG WISEMAN (Hit songwriter with
over 100 cuts and 30 charted singles)

Sometimes, when we're feeling the pain of one of life's disappointments, it's hard to remember that lacking a crystal ball, we may not know what's best for us. Prior to signing my staff-writing deal, there was nothing in the world I wanted more than to earn my living as a songwriter. After more than ten years of honing my skills and learning about the songwriting business it finally seemed as if my most cherished dream was about to come true. The head of a small publishing company expressed interest in signing me to a staff-writing deal. We had several meetings and seemed to be in agreement on the major deal points. This publisher loved the songs that were my personal favorites—the ones that other publishing companies hadn't gotten as excited about. We were clearly on the same wavelength and I knew this was the company I had always been meant to sign to.

I can't begin to express the devastation I felt when this publisher decided that her budget couldn't accommodate an additional staff-writer. As I drove home from the meeting, I heard Garth Brooks singing "Unanswered Prayers" on my car radio. The message of that song (written by Brooks and Kent Blazy), which thanks God for prayers that didn't come true, gave me hope and strength to continue pursuing my goals. Many years went by before I could plainly see that if I had signed to that particular publishing company, I would most likely have never achieved the success I've attained. I couldn't possibly have acknowledged it at the time, but I needed another year or two to develop my songwriting skills—and besides, this particular company would not have provided a good home for my songs.

If I had become a staff-writer at that time, it's probable that I wouldn't have gotten any songs recorded and would have lost my publishing deal within a year or two. I don't know if another deal would have been forthcoming. Instead, I was lucky enough to sign a year later with a company that had the belief in my abilities, as well as the financial resources necessary to nurture and develop my talents for five years before I began generating income for them. Finding a company to stick with you that long is a very rare situation.

Many songwriters and creative artists (myself included) find it difficult to separate their self-worth from their commercial successes. Remind yourself that:

- You've chosen a very difficult, highly competitive field.
- It may take years for your talent to be recognized, and there's a possibility you may never achieve commercial success—regardless of the quality of your work.
- Being told that your song is not right for a given project or publisher is not the same as being told that you are not good enough.
- You can get great satisfaction from writing a wonderful song—even if it doesn't achieve commercial success.

Write from the heart and be persistent. The way that I got "Lifestyles of the Not So Rich and Famous" cut was I approached my cowriter Byron Hill in the hallway at MCA Music and said, "Byron, I've got this great idea for a song, what do you think?" He said, "Let's cancel everything and write that song tomorrow morning." We wrote the song and did a guitar/vocal work tape of it and pitched it to Tracy Byrd's producer. He passed on the song. We played it at a showcase a couple of months later and Larry Willoughby of the A&R Department at MCA Records took a copy. A couple of months went by and we got a call from Tony Brown, President of MCA Records, who said, "I want to get this song cut on this artist and we want it to be the first single." So, the producer who originally passed on it went back in and cut the song on Tracy Byrd. It was the first single and it went to number four on the country chart. It goes to show—never, ever give up.

WAYNE TESTER (Hit songwriter)

DEALING WITH THE BIG CRITIC INSIDE YOUR HEAD

Writers with great attitudes and positive dispositions who crave feedback, and who can take constructive criticism, are usually the ones who make it.

MARK MASON (Director of Writer/
Publisher Relations, BMI)

Most songwriters have been asked questions like "When are you going to give up this crazy dream and get a real job?" by concerned parents, spouses, or friends. When my father asked me that question, I got angry, feeling that it implied a lack of belief in my talent. My sarcastic answer was, "I'm going to give it a hundred years—and if I'm not successful by then, I'll go back to school." Eventually, I came to understand that it was only natural that he was concerned for my happiness. It was hard for him to understand the desire that drove me to continue pursuing my dream in the face of rejection, disappointment, and financial hardship. It's not that my father didn't believe in my talent. He wanted to protect me from struggle and disappointment.

What I sometimes perceived as criticism and a lack of support was painful, but there is frequently no harsher critic than the one within us. "I'll never be good enough." "What makes me think my songs are better than everyone else's?" "There are millions of great songs—why would I think I could ever beat out the competition?" Few of us would tolerate this kind of negative thinking and criticism from others, and yet we so often say things like that to ourselves. Granted, it's hard to maintain a positive attitude without receiving some encouragement—and in the early stages of learning your craft, it's likely that your songs will not measure up to professional standards. Instead of criticizing yourself for what you haven't yet achieved, be proud of yourself for pursuing your goal and for striving to improve your craft. That's an accomplishment in itself.

Look for the milestones and acknowledge them; they may be small at first. For example, maybe you've completed your first song by yourself, recorded a work tape, rewritten a lyric, scheduled an appointment with a publisher, or joined a songwriters' organization. Each is one more important step in the right direction.

Don't wait for your songs to be perfect. This is a common pitfall that can stop your progress. Your songs don't have to be perfect in order to record an inexpensive demo, seek out a collaborator, get professional feedback, or let people hear them. Each of these actions can be a stepping stone to bring your songs to the next level. When that nasty internal critic says you're not good enough, remind yourself that:

- You're in the midst of a learning process.

- Successful songwriting appears deceptively simple, but it takes time and practice.

- It's unrealistic to expect your early songs to be competitive with those written by professionals.

- While it may be true that your latest song lacks Grammy-winning potential, that doesn't mean that you're not talented. Nor does it mean that you won't write an incredible song in the future.

- Every song you write can't be your best.

- Songwriting is a very difficult business and rejection is to be expected.

Few things can immobilize a songwriter more effectively than his or her internal critic. It's impossible to do your best writing with a voice inside you shouting that each line you write isn't good enough, or whispering over your shoulder that you'll never be successful. Being overly self-critical is one of the most common sources of writer's block. The exercise "Ten Magic Minutes," on page 253 can be a powerful remedy both for writer's block and for silencing the critic inside your head.

> *Write, write, write constantly... especially when you're an amateur. There is nothing like practice. There is also nothing like studying and learning. If you play (an instrument), learn the classics—study them, sing them. How did the writer move you? You can't rewrite that song, but there is a lesson to be learned. The radio to me is school and the writing is the student doing his or her lessons. Learn the rules and if you're lucky and smart you can break the rules. The dumb thing would be breaking the rules—and not knowing the rules. That means you're an amateur. Professionals break the rules on purpose.*
>
> HARLAN HOWARD
> (Legendary Nashville songwriter)

EXERCISE: TEN MAGIC MINUTES

Set a timer for ten minutes.

During these ten minutes, write whatever you feel like writing. It doesn't have to be a song. It doesn't have to rhyme. And, it doesn't have to be "good" or geared toward commercial success. You might jot down random thoughts, stream-of-consciousness, images, ideas, or potential titles—or you might simply write about your frustration, your joy, your fears, your dreams, or anything else that's on your mind.

The only rule is that there be no criticism. Tell your internal critic to stay outside the room until your ten minutes are up. As long as you write for ten minutes with no self-criticism or censoring, you have completed this exercise perfectly.

As soon as your timer tells you that ten minutes have elapsed, stop writing. Having the writing period be a specific amount of time helps to remove the anxiety inherent in facing a blank page. If you choose to continue writing, you may do so. However, it's not required, as you have already completed this exercise perfectly.

Repeat this exercise on a daily basis and you may be amazed. Some of my strongest (and most commercially accessible) songs have been started during these safe, "no-critics-allowed" ten-minute writing sessions. Sometimes we just need to feel safe in order to be creative. Other times, we need to clear out some of the baggage and the voices in our heads to allow the best writing we're capable of to emerge.

FINDING A MARKET FOR YOUR TALENT

Many nonperforming songwriters write the kinds of songs that are typically only recorded by artists who compose their own material. Other writers may write songs that do not fit a slot in the current commercial marketplace. If the songs you write don't sound like those that are currently being played on the radio, don't despair. You have several options:

- Write these songs for your own enjoyment—but don't get frustrated by confusing them with the kinds of songs that are better suited to be pitched to publishers and recorded by artists who record outside material. Remember that musical trends change and songs that are not "commercial" today may be the latest rage a year from now.

- Seek out developing artists to collaborate with. The factors that make your songs distinctive may be just what an artist needs to help carve out his or her unique musical identity.

- Research alternative sources of income, such as placing your work with music production libraries for inclusion in television and film.

- Remember that there is a whole world beyond your local and national music scene. Your style of music may be better suited for the international market. You can learn about international pitch opportunities in *SongLink International* (see Appendix).

- *If* your goal is to have your songs published and recorded by artists other than yourself, explore how they might be altered. Expressing your melodies and lyrics in a way that can touch millions of listeners does not have to dilute or alter your message.

STEP 6: CONCLUSION

Every major musical trend began when someone took a chance and was brave enough to write something that sounded fresh and distinctive. Artists such as Norah Jones, Avril Lavigne, the Dixie Chicks, and John Mayer recorded music that was a reflection of their unique artistry. If they had tried to play it safe by emulating those artists who were already successful, it's likely they never would have received their Grammy nods—and phenomenal successes. These artists and their songs found success because of their individuality—not in spite of it. Similarly, songs that top the charts and win accolades rarely are clones of other perfectly crafted songs. The songs that truly move people are those that express the writer's unique voice and perspective, both lyrically and musically. Don't be afraid to be original. For songwriters and recording artists, sometimes, playing it "safe" is the most dangerous thing they can do. Learn your craft. Then use the tools and techniques described in this book to write songs that emanate from a deep, genuine, vulnerable corner of your heart—songs that no one else could write—and you'll be well on the road to success.

PERSISTENCE AND REALISTIC EXPECTATIONS CHECKLIST

Photocopy this list. Keep it where you normally write and answer the following questions on a monthly basis. They'll give you an idea of which areas you still need to work on in order to develop persistence and realistic expectations.

❏ Are you making time for your creativity?

❏ Have you listed your strengths and weaknesses as a songwriter and a businessperson?

❏ Are you targeting specific areas to work on?

❏ Are you finding support for your commitment to songwriting?

❏ Have you devised a game plan? Are you sticking to it?

❏ Are you accepting rejection as a normal part of the songwriting business?

❏ Are you working on developing healthy responses to rejection?

❏ Are your expectations realistic?

❏ Are you finding satisfaction in the writing process itself?

❏ Do you separate your self-worth from your commercial success?

❏ Are you remembering to acknowledge your accomplishments?

It takes time to assimilate some of the ideas presented in this book. They may represent a whole new way of approaching songwriting. Give yourself the gift of writing ten new songs that incorporate the tools you've learned from reading this book. Don't criticize or judge these songs; each one is part of your journey toward success. Be gentle with yourself. Writing songs that successfully communicate (both lyrically and melodically) is not as easy as it seems, but you can acquire the necessary skills with patience and practice.

It is my observation that successful songwriters incorporate what I call "The Three L's of Songwriting Success" into their careers:

LEARN all you can about:

1. *The music business—it is the music business (not just "music").*

2. *The craft of writing—know, understand, and master the tools and techniques of songwriting to help you best express your creativity.*

3. *Yourself—you and your observations are the true source for creative expression.*

LISTEN:

1. *To the wisdom and advice of others so you can learn. Be willing to grow.*

2. *To and also observe the world around you. Remember whom you are writing about and for.*

3. *To your own intuition. Trust yourself.*

LOVE what you are doing as you are doing it, not just when it's done. In other words, love the "process" more than the "prize."

DONNA MICHAEL (Recording artist; composer and songwriter; former
Director of NSAI Regional Workshops and Educational Programs)

Afterword

Reach down in your soul and write a truly great song. Make sure you've gone over it and it doesn't have any weak spots musically or lyrically. Then, if you keep every four-leaf clover you find, always keep change in your pocket in case you pass a fountain, keep your eye out for shooting stars, and watch out for mirrors and ladders—that song has a chance.

WADE KIRBY (Hit songwriter)

It's rare for me to teach a seminar or workshop without having a student raise his or her hand and ask, "Well, what about that song that was such a big hit? It didn't do any of the stuff that you teach. The lyric was stupid and the melody sounded like my dog could've written it." I acknowledge that while most of the hits on the radio are well crafted and original, it's true that there are some songs that indeed become huge hits without being "great" songs. Some of them become hits because of the artist's appeal, others because of an outstanding video, still others for any number of other reasons. But complaining about this isn't likely to bring you any closer to the success you crave. It will be a much better use of your energy to write the very best songs that you can write and do your best to market them. Besides, do you really want to have a hit with a lousy song?

I strongly believe that somewhere deep inside, we each know what it is that we need to do to get past our own personal blocks. I've had several pivotal moments in my career journey, when I asked God/my heart/the universe/my higher power and anything else I thought might help to show me my next step. Each time, an answer came to me that eventually did lead me to the next level. Answer the following questions now and revisit them on the first of each month:

- What is it I need to do to get to the next level?
- What's stopping me from achieving what I want?
- Why aren't I writing at the level I know I'm capable of?
- What do I need to do to achieve the success I deserve?

In some instances, you might identify specific skills that you need to practice. Maybe you'll want to structure additional time for your craft, or record a demo (even though you're afraid it won't be good enough). You might decide to take guitar lessons, give yourself permission to write a dozen songs that aren't commercial hits, say "no" to some social invitations so that you can stay home and write, buy a keyboard, or take a class. Maybe you'll decide you need to find a collaborator, go to a meeting of a local songwriters' organization, rewrite a melody one more time, plan a trip to Nashville, New York, or LA, or buy a handheld tape recorder or a new notebook.

Listen to whatever it is your heart tells you. Instead of focusing on all the obstacles in your way, try looking for the solutions. You just might find them.

> *Songwriters are a rare breed of humans who exhibit incredible patience, spirit, energy, and faith. What they bring to us enriches our lives in every corner of the world. It is a noble and worthy profession. On top of any advice I might give comes my thanks to all songwriters for the gifts they give to each and every one of us.*
>
> BRENDAN OKRENT
> (Senior Director of Repertory, ASCAP)

Every writer who reads this book will not necessarily watch his or her songs climb to the top of the charts. Some will. But, every writer who works hard to learn the craft, while seeking and staying open to constructive criticism, will continue to grow and improve his or her skills. Finding pleasure in the writing process and feeling the sense of accomplishment that comes with knowing that you've communicated your idea in a way that can touch other hearts is success. Enjoy the journey.

Author Information

To receive information about having your songs professionally critiqued (through the mail), instructional recordings by Jason Blume, or scheduling a songwriting seminar in your area, contact:

Moondream Music Group
9 Music Square South, PMB #352
Nashville, TN 37203-3203

Or visit http://www.jasonblume.com

Please do not send songs or lyrics. You will receive a flyer explaining proper submission procedure.

Appendix

PERFORMING RIGHTS ORGANIZATIONS

ASCAP (American Society of Composers, Authors, and Publishers): www.ascap.com
New York: 212-621-6000
Los Angeles: 323-883-1000
Nashville: 615-742-5000
Atlanta: 404-351-1224
Chicago: 773-394-4286
Miami: 305-673-3446
Puerto Rico: 787-281-0782
London: 44-207-439-0909

BMI (Broadcast Music International): www.bmi.com
New York: 212-586-2000
Los Angeles: 310-659-9109
Nashville: 615-401-2000
Miami: 305-266-3636
Atlanta: 404-261-5151
Puerto Rico: 787-754-6490
London: 44-207-486-2036

SESAC: www.sesac.com
New York: 212-586-3450
Los Angeles: 310-393-9671
Nashville: 615-320-0055
London: 44-207-486-9994

SOCAN (Canada): www.socan.ca
Toronto: 416-445-8700
Quebec: 514-844-8377
Vancouver: 604-669-5569
Edmonton: 780-439-9049
Dartmouth: 902-464-7000

COPYRIGHT INFORMATION

US Copyright Office:
www.copyright.gov
To request copyright form PA:
800-366-2998
To request information: 202-707-3000

CISAC (International association of organizations involved in the administration of foreign copyrights): www.cisac.com

MECHANICAL ROYALTY COLLECTION AGENCIES

The Harry Fox Agency, Inc.
www.nmpa.org
711 Third Avenue
New York, NY 10017
telephone: 212-370-5330
fax: 212-953-2384

Bug Music: www.bugmusic.com
323-466-4352

CMRRA (Canadian Mechanical Rights Reproduction Agency): www.cmrra.ca

SGA (Songwriters Guild of America): www.songwriters.org

Links to foreign collection agencies:
www.knopfler.com/Royalty-Link.html

PUBLICATIONS

A&R Music Journal: www.musicjournal.com

American Advertising Federation: www.aaf.org

American Songwriter: www.americansongwriter.com

Billboard magazine: www.billboard.com

> *Talent & Touring Directory*
>
> *Musician's Guide to Touring and Promotion*
>
> *Country Weekly:* www.countryweekly.com

The Music Business Registry: www.musicregistry.com
800-377-7411, 818-995-7458

> *A&R Registry*
>
> *Film & Television Music Guide*
>
> *Music Attorney, Legal & Business Affairs Registry*
>
> *Publisher Registry*

Music Connection magazine: www.musicconnection.com

Music Directory Canada: www.musicdirectorycanada.com

Music Row magazine: www.musicrow.com

Musician's Atlas: www.musiciansatlas.com

Performing Songwriter magazine: www.performingsongwriter.com

Radio and Records: www.rronline.com

Recording Industry Sourcebook: www.artistpro.com

Recording magazine: www.recordingmagazine.com

SongLink International magazine: www.songlink.com

Songwriter's Market www.writersdigest.com

SONGWRITING INSTRUCTORS

Jason Blume: www.jasonblume.com

Danny Arena and Sara Light's online classes: www.songu.com

John and Joann Braheny: www.johnbraheny.com

Kim Copeland and Susan Tucker: www.songwritersconnection.com

Barbara Cloyd: www.barbaracloyd.com

Jai Josefs: www.jaijomusic.com

Pat and Pete Luboff: www.writesongs.com

Pat Pattison: http://members.aol.com/ptpattison/lyricpages

Harriet Schock: www.harrietschock.com

Taxi's Music Industry online classes: www.musicu.com

SONG CAMPS

Alaska Midnight Sun Songwriting Camp: www.songcamp.com/amssc/songcamp.html

Breckenridge Educational and Music Seminars: www.beamsonline.com

Camp SummerSongs/WinterSongs: www.summersongs.com

Durango Songwriter's Expo: www.durangosong.com

NashCamp: www.nashcamp.com

Nashville Songwriters Association International (NSAI) SongCamps: www.nashvillesongwriters.com

Paul Reisler's Songwriting Camp: www.kitheatre.com

Southern Utah Song Camp: www.acousticarts.org

ONLINE RESOURCES

www.jasonblume.com

www.halsguide.com

www.independentsongwriter.com

www.masterwriter.com

www.musesmuse.com

www.musicandmoney.com

www.musicdish.com

www.sethjackson.com

www.singersong.com (links)

www.songsalive.org

www.songu.com

www.songwritersresourchnetwork.com

www.songwriteruniverse.com

www.iwritethesongs.com

www.thesingersworkshop.com (vocal coach/products for singers)

doakt@comcast.net (music events e-update)

RESOURCES/CHILDREN'S SONGS

Best Children's Music:
www.bestchildrensmusic.com

Canadian Children's Songwriters Network:
www.geocities.com/EnchantedForest/
Cottage/5207/ccsn.html

Children's Music Network:
www.cmnonline.org

Children's Music Web:
www.childrensmusic.org

RESOURCES/FOLK MUSIC

Americana Music Association:
www.americanamusic.org

World Music Central:
www.worldmusiccentral.org

Folk Alliance: www.folk.org

Folklinks.com: www.folklinks.com

Northern Journey:
www.northernjourney.com (Canadian links)

RESOURCES/CHRISTIAN SONGS

Songs of Praise:
www.songsofpraise.org (extensive links)

Christian Copyright Licensing International:
www.ccli.com

Contemporary Christian Music:
www.ccmcom.com

Gospel Music Association:
www.gospelmusic.org; 615-242-0303

WorshipMusic.com:
www.christiansongwriters.com

Christian Music Festival listings:
http://christianmusic.about.com/cs/
festivalsevents/ or
http://members.aol.com/clinksgold/
omnmusic.html/festival

PITCH (OR TIP) SHEETS

HitQuarters: www.hitquarters.com
(lists A&R, publishers, producers, etc.)

SongQuarters: www.songquarters.com

New on the Charts (for pros only):
www.notc.com; 914-632-3349

RowFax: www.rowfax.com

SongLink International: wwwSongLink.com
44-207-794-2540

Taxi: www.taxi.com; 800-458-2111
(in US/Canada), 818-888-2111

SONGWRITING COMPETITIONS

www.musesmuse.com/contests.html:
updated listing of current competitions

American Lyric Writers Contest:
www.americanlyric.com

American Songwriter Magazine
Songwriting Contests:
www.americansongwriter.com/contest

Billboard Song Contest:
www.billboard.com/songcontest

CMT/CMT.com NSAI Annual Song Contest:
www.nashvillesongwriters.com
(fall deadline)

Contemporary Christian Songwriting
Contest: http://ccmni.mmgi.org

Eurovision Song Contest:
www.eurosong.net

FIDOF: www.morenofidof.org
(international competitions)

Great American Song Contest:
www.greatamericansong.com

International Songwriting Competition:
www.songwritingcompetition.com

John Lennon Songwriting Contest:
www.jlsc.com

Kerrville New Folk Songwriting
Competition: www.kerrville-music.com

Mid-Atlantic Song Contest: www.saw.org

Nashville Song Search:
www.nashvillesongsearch.com

SIBL Literacy Contest:
www.siblproject.org

Unisong, International:
www.unisong.com

USA Songwriting Competition:
www.songwriting.net

SONG CRITIQUES BY MAIL

www.jasonblume.com

Nashville Songwriters Association
International (for members only):
www.nashvillesongwriters.com

SONGWRITING TOOLS

Nashville Number Systems charts:
diggerlou@soflek.net

www.blanksheetmusic.net

www.drum-tracks.com/
songwriterdrumtracksspecial.htm

www.freesheetmusic.net

www.lyrics.com

www.masterwriter.com

www.musicnotes.com

www.rhymer.com

www.rhymewizard.com

www.rhymezone.com

www.sheetmusicdirect.com

www.songwritersblueprint.com

www.thesaurus.com

NATIONAL SONGWRITER ORGANIZATIONS

Nashville Songwriters Association International (NSAI):
www.nashvillesongwriters.com
800-321-6008, 615-256-3354
(over 100 chapters in the US
and internationally)

Songwriters Guild of America (SGA):
www.songwriters.org

Just Plain Folks: www.jpfolks.com
(chapters in all states and internationally)

Taxi: www.taxi.com

LOCAL SONGWRITING ASSOCIATIONS

Current information on area song-writing groups is maintained by Anne Freeman at www.musicdish.com.
Also, www.songwriteruniverse and www.musesmuse.com are excellent resources.

Alabama

Alabama Songwriters Guild:
P.O. Box 272
Garden City, AL 35070
e-mail: lithics@hiwaay.net

Muscle Shoals Songwriters:
Florence, AL
for meeting details,
call 256-760-0218

Alaska

Alaska Songwriters Association:
P.O. Box 33552
Juneau, AK 99803
e-mail: jdenali@gci.net

Anchorage Songwriter Circle:
907-563-5634

Arizona

Arizona Songwriters Association (ASA):
P.O. Box 678
Phoenix, AZ 85001

Arkansas

Arkansas Songwriters Association:
6817 Gingerbread Lane
Little Rock, AR 72204
e-mail: pvining@aristotle.net

California

West Coast Songwriters Association
(Formerly NCSA):
1724 Laurel Street, Suite #120
San Carlos, CA 94070
650-654-3966 or 800-FOR-SONG
www.westcoastsongwriters.org

Songwriters Guild of America (SGA),
Los Angeles office: 323-462-1108
e-mail: LASGA@aol.com

San Diego Songwriters Guild:
3368 Governor Drive, #F-326
San Diego, CA 92122
www.sdsongwriters.org

San Francisco Folk Music Club:
www.sffmc.org

Southern California Songwriters Association:
www.neonflame.com/scsa

SongNet (The Songwriter's Network):
Los Angeles
www.songnet.org

Songsalive!:
Los Angeles
www.songsalive.org

Colorado

Colorado Music Association:
200 Logan St.
Denver, CO 80203-4028
www.coloradomusic.org

Southern Colorado Songwriters Association:
2023 Vinewood Lane
Pueblo, CO 81005
719-564-0436

DurangoSong.com:
www.durangosong.com/aboutus.html

Colorado Christian Songwriters Association:
Fort Collins, for meeting details,
call 303-778-6182

Rocky Mountain Music Association:
231 Harrison St.
Denver, CO 80206

Pueblo Songwriters & Musicians Association:
P.O. Box 8054
Pueblo, CO 81008
www.pueblosongwriters.com

Connecticut

Connecticut Songwriters Association (CSA):
51 Hillcrest Ave.
Watertown, CT 06795
860-945-1272
www.ctsongs.com

Songshops Co-op:
Westport
203-845-9545
www.songshopscoop.com

Florida

Casements Songwriters Workshop:
859 Riveroak Drive East
Ormond Beach, FL 32174
904-677-8161
e-mail: erstudios@aol.com

Songwriter Association of Jacksonville (SAJ):
P.O. Box 10394
Jacksonville Beach, FL 32207

Treasure Coast Songwriters
Association (TCSA):
Port St. Lucie
407-879-4779

North Florida Christian Music
Writers Association:
Jacksonville
www.christiansongwriter.com

Georgia

Georgia Music Industry Association, Inc.
(GMIA) (formerly Atlanta
Songwriters Association):
P.O. Box 550314
Atlanta, GA 30355
404-266-2666
www.gmia.org/intro.html

Main Street Writers Association:
Cartersville, GA
e-mail: michael@michael-thomas.com

Northeast Georgia Songwriters Association:
770-534-3908

Hawaii

Hawaii Songwriters Association (HSA):
e-mail: HSAsong@aol.com

Idaho

Snake River NSAI Chapter:
www.nashvillesongwriters.com

Idaho Acoustic Arts Association:
9463 N. Swallow Road
Pocatello, ID 83201
208-233-1781
e-mail: picarobe@isu.edu

Illinois

Chicago Songwriters Collective:
203 Chicago Ave.
Oak Park, IL 60302
e-mail: info@chicagosongwriters.com

Indiana

Indianapolis Songwriters Association (ISA):
e-mail: tims@indy.net

Iowa

Osceota NSAI Chapter:
www.nashvillesongwriters.com

Des Moines JPFolks Chapter:
www.jpfolks.com

Kansas

Great Plains Songwriters Association:
706 Massachusetts, Ste. 208
Lawrence, KS 66044

Songwriters Circle of Kansas:
www.SongwritersCircle.org

United Songwriters Association:
6426 Leavenworth Rd.
Kansas City, KS 66104

Wichita Songwriters Group:
2450 Somerset
Wichita, KS

Kentucky

Songwriter Association & Services:
3884 Highway 81 North
Calhoun, KY 42327
502-785-4628

Heartland Songwriters Association
of Kentucky:
for meeting details, contact
Roy Minagawa at 502-769-9933 or
Jerry Williams, President at 502-966-8200

Louisiana

Louisiana Songwriters Association (LSA):
P.O. Box 80425
Baton Rouge, LA 70898-0425
e-mail: info@lasongwriters.org
225-924-0804

Maine

Maine Songwriters Association, Portland:
www.mesongwriters.com

www.mainecountrymusic.com

Maryland

Baltimore Songwriters Association:
P.O. Box 22496
Baltimore, MD 21203
www.electrobus.com/bsa
410-455-3822

Massachusetts

Boston Songwriters Workshop (BSW):
www.bostonsongwriters.org
617-499-6932

Boston Bluegrass Union: www.bbu.org

Michigan

Detroit NSAI Chapter:
www.nashvillesongwriters.com

Battle Creek NSAI Chapter:
www.nashvillesongwriters.com

Minnesota

Minnesota Association of Christian
Songwriters:
www.citilink.com/~foxyfilm/macs

Minnesota Association of Songwriters (MAS):
P.O. Box 333
Chisago City, MN 55013
651-254-9779
www.isc.net.mas

Mississippi

Jackson NSAI Chapter:
www.nashvillesongwriters.com

Missouri

Missouri Society of Songwriters
and Musicians:
Box 157E HCR 1
Eminence, MO 65466

Missouri Songwriters Association:
693 Green Forest Drive
Fenton, MO 63026
636-343-4765

Songwriters Circle of Kansas City:
8646 Chestnut Circle, #2
Kansas City, MO 64131
816-363-1917

Montana

Billings NSAI Chapter:
www.nashvillesongwriters.com

Nebraska

Omaha JPFolks Chapter:
www.jpfolks.com

Nevada

Las Vegas Songwriters Association:
P.O. Box 42683
Las Vegas, NV 89116
702-223-7255

Via The Fantasy Flight
Songwriter Network:
P.O. Box 46015
Las Vegas, NV 89114
702-614-9113

New Hampshire

New Hampshire NSAI Chapter:
www.nashvillesongwriters.com

New Jersey

Composers Guild of NJ:
15 Amboy Rd.
Wayne, NJ 07470
www.cgni.org

The Princeton Songwriters (NSAI):
www.nashvillesongwriters.com

New Jersey Songwriter's Circle:
32 Williamson Ave.
Bloomfield, NJ 07003
973-429-0288
e-mail: daveythek@aol.com

New Jersey & Pennsylvania
Songwriters Association:
226 E. Lawnside Ave.
Westmont, NJ 08108

Garden State Songwriters Association:
Mays Landing, NJ 08330
609-272-7019

NJ Songwriters In the Round:
www.debferrara.com/swrnj/swrnjhome.html

The Folk Project:
www.research.att.com/psa/folkproject

Songwriters Guild of America (SGA),
New Jersey (administration office):
201-867-7603
e-mail: songwritersnj@aol.com

New Mexico

Santa Fe NSAI Chapter:
www.nashvillesongwriters.com

New York

Songwriters Guild of America (SGA):
New York office: 212-768-7902
e-mail: songnews@aol.com

Island Songwriters Showcase:
P.O. Box 430
East Northport, NY 11731
631-462-3300

North Carolina

Central Carolina Songwriters
Association (CCSA):
1144 Amber Acres Lane
Knightdale, NC 27545
919-266-5791

Tri-County Music Coalition,
Box 9459
Hickory, NC 28603

Ohio

Songwriters Workshop at SouthBrook (SWS):
Dayton/Cincinnati area NSAI Chapter

Oklahoma

Southwest Songwriters Association (SWSWA):
2110 Oak St.
Lawton, OK 73501
580-357-8796 or 580-248-9270
e-mail: music@sirinet.net

Oklahoma Songwriters and
Composers Association (OSCA):
P.O. Box 6152
Moore, OK 73153-0152

Songwriters of Oklahoma:
P.O. Box 4121
Edmond, OK 73083-4121
405-348-6534

Tulsa Songwriters Association:
P.O. Box 254
Tulsa, OK 74101-0254
918-492-0366

Oregon

Portland Songwriters Association (PSA):
P.O. Box 16985
Portland, OR 97292
503-727-9072
www.pdxsongwriters.org

Central Oregon Songwriters
Association (COSA):
1811 S.W. Juniper Ave.
Redmond, OR 97756
541-548-3547
e-mail: COSA@teleport.com

Pennsylvania

Philadelphia Songwriters Association (PSA):
e-mail: songwritersphila@aol.com

Philadelphia Songwriters Forum:
332 Eastwood Ave.
Feasterville, PA 19053

Pittsburgh Songwriters Association (PSA):
e-mail: psa@trfn.clpgh.org

Rhode Island

Rhode Island Songwriters
Association (RISA):
159 Elmgrove Ave.
Providence, RI 02906
http://members.apl.com/rhodysong

South Carolina

Carolina Association of Songwriters (CAOS):
P.O. Box 4972
Rock Hill, SC 29732
803-366-0905
(Greenville, SC NSAI Workshop)

South Dakota

Midwestern Songwriters Alliance:
www.midwesternsongwriter.org

Tennessee

Nashville Songwriters Association
International (NSAI):
1701 W. End Ave., 3rd Floor
Nashville, TN 37203
800-321-6008
e-mail: nsai@nashvillesongwriters.com

Songwriters Guild of America (SGA):
Nashville office: 615-329-1782
e-mail: sganash@aol.com

Knoxville Songwriters Association:
P.O. Box 603
Knoxville, TN 37901
865-977-7538
e-mail: greatsongs@yahoo.com

Memphis Songwriters Association:
4500 Summer Ave., Suite 110
Memphis, TN 38122
901-577-0906

Tennessee Songwriters Association:
P.O. Box 2664
Hendersonville, TN 37077-2664
615-969-5967
e-mail: asktsai@aol.com

United Songwriters Association:
P.O. Box 3451
Crossville, TN 38557-3451
e-mail: unitedsongwriters@hotmail.com

Texas

Austin Songwriters Group (ASG):
P.O. Box 2578
Austin, TX 78768
512-422-TUNE
e-mail: asginfo@aol.com

Dallas Songwriters Association (DSA):
www.dallassongwriters.org
214-750-0916

Houston/Fort Bend Songwriters
Association (HFBSA):
P.O. Box 1273
Richmond, TX 77406-1273
e-mail: mailroom@fbsa.org

Fort Worth Songwriters Association (FWSA):
P.O. Box 162443
Fort Worth, TX 76161
817-654-5000
www.fwsa.com

Texas Songwriters Association:
3503 Forrestwood Dr.
Bryan, TX 77801

Utah

Salt Lake City/Provo NSAI Chapter:
www.nashvillesongwriters.com

Logan JPFolks Chapter:
www.jpfolks.com

Vermont

New England Songwriters Association:
P.O. Box 207
Jamaica, VT 05343

Virginia

Southwest Virginia Songwriters
Association (SVSA):
P.O. Box 698
Salem, VA 24153
540-586-5000

Virginia Organization Of Composers
& Lyricists (VOCAL):
P.O. Box 34606
Richmond, VA, 23234
e-mail: VOCAL10@aol.com

Fredericksburg Songwriters Showcase:
122 Laurel Ave.
Fredericksburg, VA 22408
540-898-0611

Washington

Pacific Northwest Songwriters
Association (PNSA):
P.O. Box 98564
Seattle, WA 98198
206-824-1568

Songwriters of the Northwest Guild:
16016 76th Place N.E.
Kenmore, WA 98028
425-487-3100
www.songnw.com

Wisconsin

Songwriters of Wisconsin
International (SOWI):
P.O. Box 1027
Neeneh, WI 54957
920-725-1609
e-mail: sowi@new.rr.com

Washington, D.C.

Songwriters' Association of Washington:
4200 Wisconsin Ave. N.W.
PMB 106-137
Washington, D.C., 20016
301-654-8434
www.saw.org

Washington, D.C. NSAI Chapter:
www.nashvillesongwriters.com

Canada

British Columbia NSAI Chapter:
www.nashvillesongwriters.com

BC Songwriters Showcase Association:
604-581-7999

Songwriters Association of Canada (SAC):
3600 Billings Court, Suite 204
Burlington, Ontario L7N 3N6
905-681-5320
www.songwriters.ca

Ontario Songwriters Association:
905-820-8846
www.noimagerecords.com/osa

Toronto NSAI Chapter:
www.nashvillesongwriters.com

Songwriters Association of
Nova Scotia (SANS):
Box 272
Dartmouth, Nova Scotia B2Y 3Y3
902-465-3174
e-mail: sans2001@hotmail.com

MIANS:
P.O. Box 36119
Halifax, NS B3J 3S9
www.mians.ca

East Coast Music Association:
145 Richmond Street
Charlottetown, PE C1A 1J1
www.ecma.ca

Song Permissions

"Achy Breaky Heart"
By Don Von Tress.
© 1991 Millhouse Music. All Rights Reserved.
Used by Permission.

"As Long As I Believe"
By Jason Blume.
© 2003 Zomba Songs, Inc. All Rights Reserved.
Used by Permission.

"Back to Your Heart"
By Jason Blume, Gary Baker,
and Kevin Richardson.
© 1999 Zomba Songs, Inc., Zomba Enterprises,
Inc., Swear By It Music, and Trek, Inc. All
Rights on behalf of Swear By It Music and Trek,
Inc. administered by Zomba Enterprises, Inc.
All Rights Reserved. Used by Permission.

"Because You Loved Me"
By Diane Warren.
© 1996 Realsongs and Touchstone Song
& Music, Inc. All Rights Reserved. Used
by Permission.

"Better Things to Do"
By Terri Clark, Tom Shapiro, and Chris Waters.
© Sony/ATV Songs LLC. Dba Tree Publishing
Co., Warner-Tamerlane Publishing Corp.,
Hit Haven Music, and Hamstein Cumberland
Music. All Rights on behalf of Hit Haven Music
administered by Warner-Tamerlane Publishing
Corp. All Rights Reserved. Used by Permission.

"Breathe"
Words and Music by Holly Lamar
and Stephanie Bentley.
© 1999 Universal - Songs Of Polygram, Inc.,
Hopechest Music, and Cal IV Songs. All Rights

for Hopechest Music controlled by Universal -
Songs Of Polygram, Inc. All Rights for Cal IV
Songs controlled by Cal IV Entertainment, Inc.
All Rights Reserved. Used by Permission.

"Brokenheartsville"
Words and Music by Donny Kees, Clint Daniels,
Randy Boudreaux, and Blake Mevis.
© 2002 Sony/ATV Songs LLC, Randon Songs,
and Blakebird Music. All Rights on behalf of
Sony/ATV Songs LLC administered by
Sony/ATV Music Publishing, 8 Music Square
West, Nashville, TN 37203. International
Copyright Secured. All Rights Reserved.

"Change My Mind"
By Jason Blume and A.J. Masters.
© 1991 Zomba Enterprises and Bull's Run
Music. All Rights Reserved. Used by
Permission.

"Complicated"
Words and Music by Avril Lavigne, Lauren Christy,
Scott Spock, and Graham Edwards.
© 2002 Almo Music Corp., Avril Lavigne
Publishing Ltd., Warner-Tamerlane Publishing
Corp., Rainbow Fish Publishing, Mr. Spock
Music, WB Music Corp., Hollylodge Music,
Tix Music, and Ferry Hill Songs. All Rights on
behalf of Itself, Mr. Spock Music, Hollylodge
Music, and Rainbow Fish Publishing
administered by Warner-Tamerlane Publishing
Corp. All Rights on behalf of Itself, Tix Music,
and Ferry Hill Songs administered by WB
Music Corp. All Rights for Avril Lavigne
Publishing Ltd. controlled and administered
by Almo Music Corp. All Rights Reserved.
Used by Permission.

"Dear Diary"
By Britney Spears, Jason Blume,
and Eugene Wilde.
© 2000 Zomba Songs Inc., Britney Spears
Music, and Dujuan Publishing. All Rights
administered by Zomba Songs, Inc. All Rights
Reserved. Used by Permission.

"Hit Me with Your Best Shot"
By Eddie Schwartz.
© 1978 Sony/ATV Songs LLC. All Rights
administered by Sony/ATV Music Publishing,
8 Music Square West, Nashville, TN 37203.
All Rights Reserved. Used by Permission.

"How Can I Help You Say Goodbye"
By Karen Taylor-Good and Burton Collins.
© 1993 W.B.M. Music Corp., K.T.Good Music,
Burton B. Collins Publishing, Reynsong
Publishing Corp., and Howe Sound Music.
All Rights on behalf of K.T. Good Music
administered by W.B.M. Music Corp.
All Rights Reserved. Used by Permission.

"I Wanna Dance with Somebody
(Who Loves Me)"
By George Merrill and Shannon Rubicam.
© 1986 Irving Music, Inc. (BMI) and Boy
Meets Girl Music. All Rights Reserved.
Used by Permission.

"I'm Already There"
Words and Music by Gary Baker, Frank J. Myers,
and Richie McDonald.
© 2001 Zomba Enterprises Inc., Zomba Songs
Inc., Swear By It Music, s : Josh/Nick Music,
and Sony/ATV Songs LLC. All Rights on behalf
of Sony/ATV Songs LLC administered by Sony/
ATV Music Publishing, 8 Music Square West,
Nashville, TN 37203. All Rights on behalf of
Swear By It Music and Josh/Nick Music admin-
istered by Zomba Enterprises Inc. International
Copyright Secured. All Rights Reserved.

"If It Hadn't Rained"
By Jason Blume and Claire Ulanoff.
© 2003 Zomba Songs, Inc. and Planet Happy
Publishing/Banner Music. All Rights Reserved.
Used by Permission.

"It Wasn't Me"
By Orville Burrell, Ricardo Ducent, Shaun
Pizzonia, and B. Thompson.
© 2000 WB Music Corp., Livingsting Music,
Warner-Tamerlane Publishing Corp., and Far
Out Music Inc. All Rights on behalf of Itself and
Livingsting Music administered by WB Music
Corp. All Rights Reserved. Used by Permission.

"My Front Porch Looking In"
Words and Music by Richie McDonald,
Frank J. Myers, and Don Pfrimmer.
© 2003 Sony/ATV Songs LLC, Sixteen Stars
Music, Frank Myers Music, Cosmic Muel, and
Don Pfrimmer. All Rights on behalf of Sony/ATV
Songs LLC administered by Sony/ATV Music
Publishing, 8 Music Square West, Nashville, TN
37203. All Rights on behalf of Frank Myers Music
administered by Sixteen Stars Music. International
Copyright Secured. All Rights Reserved.

"One of Us"
By Eric Bazilian.
© 1995 Human Boy Music. All Rights on
behalf of Human Boy Music administered by
WB Music Corp. All Rights Reserved. Used
by Permission.

"Ray of Light"
Words and Music by William Orbit, Madonna,
Clive Muldoon, Dave Curtis, and Christine Leach.
© 1998 Rondor Music (London) Ltd., WB
Music Corp., Webo Girl Publishing, Inc., and
Purple Music Ltd. All Rights for Rondor Music
(London) Ltd. in the USA and Canada
administered by Almo Music Corp. All Rights
on behalf of Webo Girl Publishing, Inc.
administered by WB Music Corp. All Rights
Reserved. Used by Permission.

"Saving All My Love for You"
Words by Gerry Goffin, music by Michael Masser.
© 1978 Screen Gems-EMI Music Inc. and Prince Street Music. All Rights administered jointly. All Rights Reserved. Used by Permission.

"Send in the Clowns"
By Stephen Sondheim.
© 1973 Rilting Music, Inc. (Ascap). All rights administered by WB Music Corp. All Rights Reserved. Used by Permission.

"She's Not the Cheatin' Kind"
By Ronnie Dunn.
© 1994 Sony/ATV Songs LLC. All Rights administered by Sony/ATV Music Publishing, 8 Music Square West, Nashville, TN 37203. All Rights Reserved. Used by Permission.

"Steve McQueen"
By Sheryl Suzanne Crow and John Shanks.
© 2002 Warner-Tamerlane Publishing Corp., Old Crow Music, WB Music Corp., and Dylan Jackson Music. All Rights on behalf of Itself and Old Crow Music administered by Warner-Tamerlane Publishing Corp. All Rights on behalf of Itself and Dylan Jackson Music administered by WB Music Corp. All Rights Reserved. Used by Permission.

"Stuck"
By Kevin Kadish and Stacie Orrico.
© 2003 WB Music Corp., Slowguy Songs, and Star-Struck Music. All Rights on behalf of Itself and Slowguy Songs administered By WB Music Corp. All Rights Reserved. Used by Permission.

"Survivor"
By Anthony Dent, Beyoncé Knowles, and Matthew Knowles.
© 2001 For Chase Muzic Inc., Hitco South, and Mw Publishing. All Rights for Chase Muzic Inc. and Hitco South administered by Music Of Windswept. All Rights Reserved. Used by Permission.

"These Days"
Words and Music by Danny Wells, Steve Robson, and Jeffrey Steele.
© 2002 Sony/ATV Songs LLC, Songs Of Teracel, Rondor Music London Ltd., Songs Of Windswept Pacific, and Gottahaveable Music. All Rights on behalf of Sony/ATV Songs LLC and Songs Of Teracel administered by Sony/ATV Music Publishing, 8 Music Square West, Nashville, TN 37203. All Rights on behalf of Rondor Music London Ltd. in the USA and Canada controlled and administered by Irving Music, Inc. International Copyright Secured. All Rights Reserved.

"Wings"
By Jason Blume.
© 2003 Zomba Songs, Inc. All Rights Reserved. Used by Permission.

Index